ISSUES IN THE ACQUISIT

ISSUES IN THE ACQUISITION AND TEACHING OF HEBREW

edited by

Avital Feuer
Sharon Armon-Lotem
Bernard Dov Cooperman

UNIVERSITY PRESS OF MARYLAND
BETHESDA, MARYLAND
2009

LIBRARY OF CONGRESS CATALOGING-IN-PUBLICATION DATA

Issues in the acquisition and teaching of Hebrew / edited by Avital Feuer, Sharon Armon-Lotem, Bernard Dov Cooperman.
    p. cm. — (Studies and texts in Jewish history and culture)
    ISBN 978-1-934309-21-6
    1. Hebrew language — Study and teaching (Higher) — Congresses. 2. Hebrew language—Study and teaching—Foreign speakers. I. Feuer, Avital. II. Armon-Lotem, Sharon. III. Cooperman, Bernard Dov, 1946-

PJ4536.I87 2009
492.4071'1—dc22

2009020155

ISBN 978-1934309-216

STUDIES AND TEXTS
IN
JEWISH HISTORY AND CULTURE

The Joseph and Rebecca Meyerhoff Center
for Jewish Studies
University of Maryland

XVIII

General Editor: Bernard D. Cooperman

UNIVERSITY PRESS OF MARYLAND

CONTENTS

Hebrew-Yiddish Bilingualism Among Israeli Hasidic Children

Language Policy and the Teaching of Hebrew

PREFACE

IN THE SPRING OF 1883, the Hebrew educator, translator, and anthologist Toviah Pesah Schapiro (1845–1924) was delighted to be bringing out another edition of his textbook of model letters, *Et Ivri* [A Hebrew Pen]. The book was intended, as he tells us on the title page, "for the use of Jewish youths, so that they know and understand how to send letters in language that is clear, clean, and light...as well as appropriate to their age, thoughts, and arguments." Caught up in the excitement of the Hebrew language revival, Schapiro was one of a group of Hebraists then working diligently to provide a new pedagogical infrastructure for the ancient tongue. Schapiro was proud to note that David Gordon, the editor of the Hebrew periodical *Ha-Magid*, had praised his work in particular:

> [Schapiro] has done a wonderful job of teaching the young people of our nation to write clearly in Hebrew about whatever they want. All of the letters in his anthology are composed in a pure Hebrew style, in good taste and in accordance with the understanding and tastes of young people. [The author] has not climbed the high mountains of metaphor that are beyond them.

To his young readers Schapiro acknowledged that there were many other volumes on the market, most more literary than his own. Still "there was still some use in this *Briefsteller* or epistolary." He had limited his examples to practical matters and had omitted letters (such as those to marriage brokers) that his readers wouldn't want.[1]

It seems unlikely that Schapiro, Gordon, or any of the others who contributed to the nascent field of Hebrew-language instruction so long ago

---

1. The quotes are taken from the title page and introduction to Schapiro's *Et Ivri* (Warsaw: Nathan Schriftgisser, 1883), an edition that also contained *Sefer Mikhtavim ha-Shalem* by the even more prolific educator Abraham Morde-chai Piorke, as well as the latter's translation (and bowdlerization) of the unacknowledged Karl Emil Franzos' popular short story, "Baron Schmule" (*Die Juden von Barnow* [4th edition, 1887, pp. 261-278.]).

could have imagined the exploding demand for appropriate Hebrew text-books and skilled Hebrew teachers that characterizes the situation today. Certainly they would have been astonished to learn that thousands of young people, both Jews and non-Jews, study Hebrew in universities and colleges around the world. Of course, the Hebrew we are teaching is quite different from the language of that time. Our pedagogical task would seem also to have changed as well. We now aim primarily for mastery of the spoken language of modern Israel rather than for the kind of writing skills and histor-ical/literary understanding that were the norm a century and a half ago.

And yet, the basic goals enunciated by those writers remain in place. We are still trying for mastery of a clear style, we avoid the overly literary, and we want our students to be able to express themselves effectively in the target language. Whether or not we are more successful at this task than were our predecessors remains a matter for debate.

When I began my graduate studies in Judaica four decades ago, there was an annual required ritual that all of us awaited with, at best, mixed emotions. This was the formal dinner at the home of Professor Isadore Twersky, one of our teachers in the Dept. of Near Eastern Languages and Literatures at Harvard. After drinks in the living-room, we were called to dinner around a huge dining-room table. Conversation was forced and awkward, and there were long uncomfortable pauses—that is, until one of us who had been assigned the task of teaching first-year Hebrew to the undergraduates began to describe the difficulties of his task. Our teacher tried to comfort the young man: "It is impossible," he declared with authority, "to teach anyone enough Hebrew in four years to make them competent at reading the texts we study. What you are doing is just giving students a taste. No one expects you to make them literate."

I remember being stunned by Twersky's *obiter dictum*. "How was it possi-ble," I protested, "that students could master Chinese and Sanskrit but not Hebrew? Surely Hebrew was not more difficult than those languages? Was he arguing that all undergraduate language education was useless?"

As things turned out, it would soon be my turn to take over the first-year Hebrew course and eventually I spent almost twenty years teaching in, and administering, the university's Hebrew-language program. Throughout those years, I was bent on proving that my teacher had been wrong and, in retrospect, I am convinced that I succeeded. By carefully defining my class-room goals, by fine-tuning my methodologies, and above all by setting high standards, I did produce undergraduates who were literate in Hebrew within two academic years and who were capable of doing independent research using a wide range of primary and secondary Hebrew sources.

When I moved from Harvard to the University of Maryland, my academic responsibilities shifted and I have not been able to dedicate very much time to the dynamics and methods of Hebrew language instruction. It was therefore a special delight when an Israeli scholar, Dr. Sharon Armon-Lotem, in the course of a year's fellowship at our Linguistics Department, agreed to organize a conference about Hebrew-language instruction. The conference was a success, but, for various reasons beyond our control, too many of the papers proved unpublishable and the others languished in a drawer for several years. Subsequently, Dr. Avital Feuer joined our Hebrew faculty and, fresh from publishing her own dissertation, enthusiastically took on the task of soliciting further papers and re-shaping the collection into a useful volume of theoretical and applied studies. I am most grateful to both of these scholars for the time and effort that they have devoted to this task, and I see the resulting volume as a credit to their academic vision of a theoretically sophisticated approach to a pressing task.

The publication and distribution of the present volume is part of a broader commitment on the part of the University of Maryland, the Joseph and Rebecca Meyerhoff Center for Jewish Studies, and the Joseph and Alma Gildenhorn Institute for Israel Studies to encourage research and training in Hebrew language. A recent grant from the Morningstar Foundation of Bethesda Md., for example, has enabled us to focus special attention on the training of Hebrew-language instructors at the elementary, secondary, and postsecondary levels. Over the past year I have had the pleasure of working with two of the graduate fellows in this program, developing teaching materials to aid in the incorporation of both documentary and dramatic films into the classroom agenda. The task proved surprisingly complex, requiring fine judgments about the intended audience, the specific cultural information that should or should not be included, and the kinds of language exercises appropriate to this particular format. As part of the experiment, we also sponsored a one-day symposium for area teachers on the general issue of Jewish studies and film. The results of the fellows' work will, we hope, soon be available online so that teachers elsewhere can take advantage of their research. Eventually, I envisage a publication series combining theoretical and practical aspects of this and other aspects of Hebrew-language pedagogy. Sustained and systematic effort can produce substantive results, and it is a personal pleasure for me to be part of this collaborative effort.

Bernard Dov Cooperman
Louis L. Kaplan Assoc. Prof. of Jewish History

INTRODUCTION

Avital Feuer

University of Maryland

THE CHAPTERS OF THIS BOOK examine contemporary issues in Hebrew acquisition, learning, and teaching. Originally born from a 1998 conference on "The Acquisition of Hebrew as a First and Second Language" at the University of Maryland, this volume has developed into a resource on a vast range of issues that affect Hebrew pedagogy. The focus on qualitative and quantitative empirical methodologies (including individual and focus group interviews, textbook and document analysis, large-scale recordings, and participant observation) enables the voices of native and second language students, instructors, and researchers to be heard. This research, together with each scholar's analysis, aims to bridge the gaps and schisms in our language-learning community. The book explores and challenges traditionally held Hebrew teaching philosophies with a new examination of normativism and the authenticity of the target language using today's realities of multilingual-ism, multiculturalism, and multimodalism. We hope our findings will inform future research in the field and will provide theoretical insight and practical ideas for Hebrew instructors in various settings.

There is a paucity of research on the realities of modern Hebrew language teaching and learning in North America. Though academics have previously discussed the state and future of Hebrew learning in North America, the absence of empirical research studies has left the field in a space between disci-plines, perspectives, and definitions. The issues of Diaspora Hebrew acqui-sition and pedagogy are filled with complexities: is Hebrew an academic subject, a foreign language to be studied and dissected linguistically, separate from its religious and ethnic underpinnings? Should the language act primarily as an enhancement or necessary tool for Jewish religious and historical study? Must we view modern Hebrew only through the prism of modern Israel, with its non-normative linguistic features and slang? What is "real" Hebrew and which Hebrew should we teach? Is Hebrew pedagogy a subject that ought to be embedded within the fields of Jewish Education, Linguistics, or Israel Studies?

On the practical level, most educators would agree that the vast majority of modern Hebrew programs in North America are riddled with problems. Many can attest to low college-level enrollment rates in Hebrew programs, lack of standardization, low motivation, restricted time, limited outcomes in supplementary schools, and the inability among day school graduates to communicate fluently in Hebrew. The insufficient training of teachers and lack of a strategic and organized method of standardization or goal system are fundamental problems. Students and parents hold philosophies that conflict with those of instructors and administrators. The deficiency in comprehensible input (that is, sufficient immersion or exposure to comprehensible Hebrew in students' daily lives) poses great challenges for foreign-language study.

The first step in improving the situation is to understand the diversity of both language learners and the target communities whose language they emulate. Educators and researchers must reconsider long-held notions of normative, standard, and authentic Hebrew.

Avital Feuer's chapter sets the scene of the heterogeneous, modern-day Hebrew language class in North America. In a qualitative, ethnographic study, she questioned Canadian Hebrew-learning undergraduates and their professor about their ethnic identity frameworks, the role of Hebrew in their lives, and how perceptions about their identities were manifested in classroom interactions. Though these students (who originated from Canada, the U.S., South Africa, Israel, and the former U.S.S.R.) at times felt united as Jews in solidarity, they more often split into opposing camps of "Israelis" and "Canadians" based on conflicting linguistic features, backgrounds, and cultures as each claimed Hebrew as authentically and rightfully their own. Participants with diverse histories of migration and multilingualism used Hebrew to negotiate an identity and a life in the Diaspora. Elements of these themes are found in language classrooms across the globe.

Equally diverse are perceptions of "standard" Hebrew and whether normative rules are worth teaching to native speakers and second-language learners. The first section of Einat Gonen's large-scale study provides a systematic examination of the times when native speakers abide by the rule of vowel reduction (*ḥituf*). Gonen supplements her findings in the chapter's second section with a textual analysis of several popular course books used in Israel and in North American university Hebrew classes. In these textbooks, authors individually decide when instructors should explicitly teach the rules of the vowel reduction phenomenon. Such decisions seem arbitrary and are made without a large-scale study of authentic, modern-day language use of rules such as vowel reduction. Gonen advocates explicit teaching of such normative rules for the sake of spelling and pronunciation as well as imparting a familiarity with the intellectual strata of the Hebrew language.

Lewis Glinert's chapter provides an alternative approach as he supports a re-examination of Hebrew educators' adherence to traditional grammar rules. He similarly reviews popular course textbooks that teach general grammar rules without a discussion of the reality of modern, spoken, Israeli Hebrew and its non-normative patterns. He encourages instructors to take these factors into account in order to impart a more honest, authentic foundation of Hebrew.

Sharon Armon-Lotem further investigates morphology acquisition among first language (L1) Hebrew learners in Israel, and second language (L2) English learners in the U.S. (in a naturalistic setting). Among L1 learners, variations in gender and number, tense and mood, and person were measured and recorded over time. L2 English learners in the U.S. were found to exhibit similar inflectional morphological acquisition patterns where unclear, tenseless forms were replaced by tensed forms before person morphology appeared. Armon-Lotem applies her findings to predict L2 Hebrew morphology acquisition among learners in the Diaspora. Based on her previous work, she predicts that L2 learners will follow a similar course of acquisition with similar types of beginning, overgeneralized errors.

Still on the topic of grammar, Shmuel Bolozky examines the merits of explicit instruction of grammatical rules, normative as well as colloquial, compared to a functional, indirect approach that reflects real-life situations and assumes that grammatical generalizations are best acquired through induction from a lot of authentic input. He considers the circumstances under which direct instruction of grammar may be appropriate and proposes a new framework for grammar teaching that integrates the existence of normative rules and non-normative realities, providing guidelines as to which rules should be taught explicitly. Such discussions of grammar instruction fit into a larger question of Israeli culture beyond the scope of the article: which grammatical phenomena appear in the speech of "average" Israelis (a concept in itself impossible to define)? How do we adequately convey "authentic" Israeli speech to L2 students?

The next chapters continue the exploration of authenticity in teaching Hebrew, particularly in terms of culture. Brenda Malkiel outlines the complex nature of translation, and specifically Hebrew-English and English-Hebrew translation. Using principles of translation theory and examples from books, film, and the media, Malkiel describes the difficulties of expressing cultural nuances in a new language. She offers practical suggestions for including translation study in L2 classrooms to increase academic content and cultural awareness.

Further, Edna Amir Coffin demonstrates the ability of literature and poetry instruction to connect L2 learners to the target culture. In her chapter, she discusses methods of teaching reading and the importance of motivating students to study literature. She provides a lesson outline that addresses pre-reading activities, an analysis of the title and last line, structure, words and synonyms, and intertextual comparisons of Yehuda Amichai's poem שֶׁלְוָה גְדוֹלָה: שְׁאֵלוֹת וּתְשׁוּבוֹת.

The goal of intercultural connection is amplified in Vered Shemtov's chapter on technology in the Hebrew language class. Shemtov widens the parameters of communicative language teaching and learning to include communicative competence on the Web. Framing technology not only as a pedagogic means but also a goal, Shemtov shows how the classroom may be more than one space as students can be immersed in Israeli culture through course management systems, the Internet, and various computer technologies, and can function meaningfully and communicatively in Israeli culture on the Web.

Miriam Isaacs' chapter further explores the diverse realities of Israeli Hebrew. She studied language behaviors as identity assertions in the linguistic and cultural situation of Hebrew-Yiddish bilingual Haredi communities in Israel. Individuals in her study maintained Yiddish to segregate and define themselves as different from the majority Israeli community. Isaacs uses the case of Israeli Haredi communities to discuss a larger issue of the relationship between group identity and language preservation and attrition, a theme also relevant to the sub-groups of Hebrew speakers and learners in North America.

In the book's final chapter, Bernard Spolsky looks at Hebrew teaching within a theory of language policy that considers the actual practices of a speech community, its beliefs about language, and efforts to manage beliefs and practices. In Israel, Hebrew is taught in a context of ideological national monolingualism, a continuation of the revival of Hebrew as a central feature of the Zionist movement; it is affected by waves of immigration seen as threats to the hegemony of the language, and challenged by the existence of significant linguistic minorities and a growing support for pluralism and multilingualism. In the United States, itself marked by tension between English monoglot ideology and practice on the one hand and liberal pluralism on the other, the Hebrew language is maintained mainly by Israeli immigrants and its teaching is seriously threatened by the greater use and status of English within the Jewish community.

As we move forward toward an objective of communicative second-language classes, we must continually consider realities of authentic, modern Israeli language, multifaceted and diverse ethnic and cultural identities both in Israel and in the Jewish Diaspora, new modes of modern communication, and the official and cultural policies and social norms under which we live. Additionally, in order to understand processes of second language Hebrew learning and the culture in which Hebrew is spoken by the majority, it is helpful to examine studies from Israel of first language acquisition of normative and non-normative language features. Each of these chapters displays how varieties of Hebrew are developing naturally in individual Hebrew speaking communities, at times moving away from normative language and previously held definitions of the "standard" target language of Hebrew and its native speakers—categories that are by no means monolithic and in fact, must be re-characterized to accurately define their complexities.

I would like to thank my co-editors, Professors Sharon Armon-Lotem and Bernard Dov Cooperman for their insights, direction, and commitment to this project. Finally, I would like to acknowledge the support of the University of Maryland's Gildenhorn Institute for Israel Studies, the Joseph and Rebecca Meyerhoff Center for Jewish Studies, and the Louis L. Kaplan Chair of Jewish Studies.

A note on an editorial decision: Hebrew transliteration varies from chapter to chapter based on standard conventions from authors' individual disciplines.

JEWISH INTRAGROUP CONVERGENCE AND DIVERGENCE IN THE UNIVERSITY HEBREW CLASS

לו שֶׁל הַגַּל קוֹרֵ;

תוֹ – שֶׁאָבוֹא אֲנִי

ב

וְ|י א|שו, וְ|וְּ'|וּ י

וֹת, אָמֵן אָמֵן סֶלָה"

Avital Feuer

University of Maryland

AS A HEBREW LANGUAGE TEACHER and language acquisition researcher living in North America, I have found myself thinking deeply about how my commitment to the Hebrew language affects and creates my sense of Jewish identity. I spent time as a young child in Israel, where I was immersed in the Hebrew language and Israeli culture. When I eventually returned to Canada with my family, the ability to communicatively function in modern Hebrew marked me as different from my peers. Using a qualitative, ethnographic methodological framework based in emergent, grounded theory (Glaser and Strauss, 1967), I investigated the attitudes and feelings of individuals who participated in an advanced, undergraduate modern Hebrew class at a large Canadian university.[1] How did others living in the Canadian Jewish Diaspora negotiate their dual linguistic, national, and cultural loyalties?

I entered the research field with three key questions. First, what framework of ethnic identity did participants structure in their lives? Rather than define identity specifically as Jewish identity, I chose the term "ethnic identity" to ensure freedom and flexibility in defining senses of self while limiting the subject area to the notion of shared ancestry, lineage, or heritage. Second, I asked how Hebrew language fit into participants' frameworks of ethnic identity. Because the students, professor, and I committed time and effort to the study, teaching, or practice of the language, it clearly held a place of priority in our lives, and, I hypothesized, our ethnic identities. Third, I wondered

---

1. See Feuer, A. (2008). *Who Does This Language Belong To? Personal Narratives of Language Claim and Identity.* Charlotte: Information Age Publishing.

7

how these perceptions of the importance of Hebrew would be manifested in social interactions in the Hebrew classroom. In retrospect, I realize that underneath these initial questions, I was truly interested in how participants viewed Hebrew in negotiating a life in the Diaspora; more specifically, whether these individuals managed to build a sense of comfort, satisfaction, and belonging in Canada with my assumption of their deep connection to the Hebrew language and its indelible link to Israeli culture.

Position of the Researcher

I entered the field with a decidedly emic, or insider perspective (Trappes-Lomax, 2004). While I was unfamiliar with the particular experiences and dynamics of those in the Hebrew class, I had an understanding of the Diaspora and Israeli Jewish communities, and of the experience of being a Hebrew learner and teacher. After moving from Israel as a young child, I attended and graduated from a Canadian Jewish day school. I moved to Israel after graduation where I worked, studied, and solidified my mastery of the Hebrew language. As a child, I had felt a sense of difference because I perceived that those in my community did not know or particularly care about the daily routines, traditions, customs and problems of Israelis; most had never visited Israel, and even those who did connected to Israel in a more abstract and symbolic way through monetary donations, political support, and views of the country as the abstract spiritual and cultural homeland. In Israel, my Hebrew fluency was a membership key to the society of Israelis that allowed me to experience and share their cultural knowledge. I was eager to elicit the feelings and attitudes of those in similar positions who likewise, placed Hebrew in a primary role in the constructions of their Jewish identities.

Theoretical Basis and Review of Literature

Johnson's (2004) dialogic sociolinguistic theory was the theoretical impetus for this work. Combining elements of Vygotsky's sociocultural theory (1981) and Bakhtin's literary theory (1981), Johnson offered a new model of second language learning that emphasizes the importance of communicative dialogism in acquiring a new language. The Vygotskyan notion that social language interactions develop and influence thought combines with Bakhtin's theory of dialogism that states that all language exists in response to expectations and assumptions about the interlocutor, and is shared by others based on context, culture, and relationships. Moving forward from this point, I posited that not only does language acquisition depend on the linguistic and social interactions with others within and outside of the group, but that the construction of *identi-*

ty (and in this case, Jewish identity) is similarly *acquired*, like language, through social dialogue and interaction. Dialogues with others both in and outside of the minority community dictate how we impose identities on others, and these dialogues are employed in how we understand our senses of self.

There have been no prior studies that specifically and empirically examine the complexities of identity formation among Hebrew language learners. However, several studies in second and foreign language contexts provide a useful background to frame the present study.

Tse (1998; 2000) examined the ethnic identity rejection and repossession among Asian American heritage language speakers who inhabit a stage prevalent in childhood and adolescence of "ethnic ambivalence" or "ethnic evasion." Alvarez, Bliss, and Vigil (2001) determined a similar sense of confusion among Cuban Americans who expressed a connection to their Spanish heritage language, among other cultural artifacts of their community, but felt disconnected from the oppressive Cubans governing their homeland.

Interviews of 100 Chilean-Swedish teens and their parents by King and Ganuza (2005) found that participants had a "double identity" based on their language switching between Spanish among family and friends and Swedish with members of the dominant linguistic group. Schecter and Bayley (1997) determined that Mexican-American bilingual children defined themselves according to Mexican or American allegiances based on the value placed upon the languages by their parents, and by their relationships with minority and majority group members.

Whereas several studies analyzed elements of hybrid identity between ethnic and dominant monoliths, the following studies probe more deeply into in- and out-group complexities of identity. Lotherington's (2001) study observed complex identities of Chinese teachers and students due to differences in country and region of origin, connection to Chinese, and ability in the Chinese language and specific dialects. Auer (2005) suggested a broader framework in social group identification among Turkish-German bilinguals in Germany. He noted that a particular group of females who spoke German-Turkish code-switch were not necessarily a homogenous group as typically discussed in previous studies. For example, one Persian female spoke German-Turkish code-switch as a *Muslim* (rather than Turkish) identifier among members of her social group.

There is a lack of empirical, and more specifically, qualitative sociological research examining the experience of Hebrew language learners in the Diaspora. Although several scholars have presented think-pieces with prescriptive offerings regarding improving the state of modern Hebrew teaching in the United States (Raphaeli, 1993; Jacobson, 1993; Zisenwine, 1997; Morahg, 2002), these works do not present the voices and attitudes of those participating in Hebrew study. Meanwhile, research among Israelis demonstrates the function of the Hebrew language as a marker of identification and group membership (Auron, 1997; Kaufman, 2000). According to Kaufman, Israeli immigrants to the United States usually do not establish communal ties to organizations and most do not participate in religious activities. Thus, Hebrew is their primary means of Jewish identification.

In wide-scale surveys of Jewish identification, survey protocol often includes categories determining levels of religiosity such as ritual, holiday and Sabbath observance, adherence to laws of the Torah and oral law; those related to the nation such as familiarity and attachment to Israel; and questions regarding cultural or ethnic connections such as membership in communal organizations, and association with Jewish philanthropies (Cohen, 1986; 2005; Schiff 1997; 1999; Auron, 1997). These studies attempted to describe and define the state of the American Jewish identity or to demonstrate a correlation between Jewish education and subsequent strong adult Jewish behavior and identification. These studies generally grouped modern Hebrew ability with attachment to Israel or did not mention it at all. In the present study, participants placed a high value and priority on modern Hebrew language study; thus it was evidently an important part of their lives (and possibly the only or one of the only markedly "Jewish" activities in which they were involved). Yet, some may have identified as strongly committed Jews despite being unaffiliated with various elements included in the term "Jewish life" mentioned in previous scholarly texts. Survey protocol, the criteria that determine strong Jewish identity, are constructed according to the perspective of surveyors, and with no room for participant explication of the reasons behind their responses.

The present investigation aims to elucidate the previously unheard voices of those committed to the advanced study and usage of Hebrew and to understand how ownership of the language contributes to Jewish identity constructions.

Methodology

The Hebrew class consisted of ten female and five male students. Most students were 19 or 20 years old, and one student was 26. The course was held twice a week, for two hours. The professor closely followed the textbook *'ivrit: havanah vehaba'ah* (Veyl, Piurko, and Farstei, 1983), and throughout the semester, each student was required to prepare an oral lecture on any academic topic of choice. The study included one semester of participant-observation,

an in-depth, semi-structured, focus group interview, and individual interviews with ten students and the professor. I conducted the individual interviews with the nine students who attended the class in which the focus group
interview was held, and then purposely selected Seth, the tenth student participant, to represent a broader range of experiences. This student was selected
because of his religious observance and American background. I then interviewed the professor of the course. I obtained consent from all classroom
members and wrote detailed notes as I observed classes, and structured
questions based on linguistic and social behaviors of the students and professor. Throughout the study, I emphasized that participants could communicate with me in Hebrew or in English, and followed the lead of the students
in choosing my language of communication. After recording discussions with
participants, I transcribed and coded their responses. Using the constant
comparison method (Glaser and Strauss, 1967), I continuously re-analyzed
transcripts in relation to others and returned to participants for clarification
or additional information. I coded observation notes and transcripts to create
and analyze the emerged themes.

First Impressions in the Field

An abundance of cultural nuances and social rules shaped the atmosphere and
content of the class. Students sat in divided social and language groups, and
throughout the class, conversations were conducted in diversely accented
Hebrew and English, and Hebrew-English mixes or code-switch. Students
in this class were Canadian-born graduates of Jewish day schools; former
USSR-born immigrants to Canada who lived previously in Israel; children
of Israeli emigrants; and students born in Canada or elsewhere with no or
limited previous elementary or secondary formal Hebrew education who
progressed to an advanced level in university. In addition to the varieties of
nationalities, levels and denominations of religious observance were similarly
diverse among students. There existed a sharp physical and psychological
divide as the class was separated by labels that would later emerge: "Israeli"
and "Canadian."

Upon entering the field, I took note of these two distinct groups in the class.
My groupings were based on features of their speech: the Israelis spoke quickly, fluently, and unconscious of their language, which they used as a means
of expression. The Canadians spoke slowly and laboriously in Hebrew with
much English code-switching and pauses, aware and distracted by the
mechanics of their language. However, the Canadians' literacy levels were
usually stronger than those of the Israelis. Particularly, day school graduates

and the observant students who devoted time each week to biblical and rabbinic textual study possessed high literacy proficiency. Those who called themselves and were called Israelis spoke a sort of "teenager" Hebrew: a non-standard form that seemed to be fossilized at the time they left Israel as early teenagers. For example, several females repeated the following phrase: "*yesh male anashim baḥeder*" [There are full of people in the room] rather than "*haḥeder male anashim*" [The room is full of people] or "*yesh harbeh anashim baḥeder*" [There are many people in the room]. When the professor corrected them, they stubbornly refused to change these speech idiolects; instead, they seemed to cling to these fossilizations as speech characteristics of their particular Jewish sub-groups. Although I originally classified several students as "Russian," I later retracted this category because though they spoke with what I perceived to be Russian phonological accent features, they did not mention their Russian identity in group discussions and did not explicitly refer to themselves using this label. Instead, they frequently asserted their Israeli identities:

> Yana (student): *tishm'i—* [Listen—]
> Aviva (professor): *tishm'i? ani poḥedet mimekh* [Listen? I'm scared of you].
> Yana: [LAUGHTER] *kitah shel israelim* [A class of Israelis].

At this point, Yana motioned to students Marina and Tatiana who sat beside her, attributing her forceful manner of speaking to her Israeliness. Interestingly, though declared to be Israelis among their classroom peers, in individual interviews, several of these students defined themselves as primarily Russian or Russian-Israeli. This aligns with postmodern perception of identity as fluid, constantly changing, and contextually relative.

Although among the "Canadian" students were one American-born and one South-African born student, those in the class constantly referred to the Canadian/Israeli dichotomy. National labelings of "Canadian" and "Israeli" referred not entirely or necessarily to nationality, but often to linguistic communicative ability. These two groups of students sat on opposite ends of the room and rarely spoke to members outside their respective sub-groups. After observing identities asserted in classroom interactions and the focus group interview, I asked participants individually to define their ethnic identifications for purposes of triangulation (Denzin and Lincoln, 1994). The following chart provides background information on this study's participants:

TABLE 1

NAMES, BACKGROUNDS, STATED ETHNIC IDENTITIES,
AND PRESENTATION TOPICS OF INTERVIEWED PARTICIPANTS.

NAME	BACKGROUND	STATED ETHNIC IDENTITIES	PRESENTA-TION TOPICS
Meg	– Born in South Africa – Moved to Canada at age 5	1. Jewish 2. Jewish from South Africa 3. Canadian	The relationship between the state of Israel and Jews in the Diaspora
Yana	– Born in former U.S.S.R. – Moved to Israel at age 6 _ – Moved to Canada at age 14	1. Russian-Israeli 2. Israeli	The religious movements of Judaism and the religious vs. secular rift
Ravit	– Born in Israel – Moved to Canada at age 11	1. An Israeli who has been Canadianized	The effect of army service on Israeli youth
Amy	– Born and raised in Canada	1. A secular Jew	Palestinians' perspectives on Zionism
Naomi	– Born and raised in Canada	1. A Jewish Canadian with very strong ties to Israel	Anti-Semitism in France
Marina	– Born in former U.S.S.R. – Moved to Israel at age 5 – Moved to Canada at age 17	1. Israeli 2. Jewish 3. Russian ("not Canadian")	Holocaust deniers
Tatiana	– Born in former U.S.S.R. – Moved to Israel at age 7 – Moved to Canada at age 14	1. Russian 2. Israeli 3. Canadian	Representations of Jews in American films
Moshe	– Born and raised in Canada	1. One who is struggling to be a religious, observant Jew	ḥasidut (Hasidism) and the Ba'al Shem Tov

Adam	– Born and raised in Canada	1. Jewish 2. Zionist	Why U.S. Republicans are most supportive of Israel and most deserving of U.S. Jews' political support
Seth	– Born in New Jersey – Raised in Canada and the U.S.	1. American Jew	Controversial issues in *hala-khah* (Jewish rabbinic law)
Prof.: Aviva	– Born and raised in Israel – Moved to Canada after marriage in her 20s	1. Jewish-Israeli 2. Canadian	

Results

After data collection and coding was complete, analysis of the records yielded two primary themes in relation to language and identity formation. The first, more peripheral theme was that of convergence of identities. In this case, Hebrew was used as a tool to unite as a worldwide Jewish community, or as a membership key for unique Jewish sub-groups that will be discussed later in the chapter. More dominant was the theme of divergence of identities, in which Hebrew communication or learning determined specific definitions of being Jewish, typically through Othering those in opposing sub-groups.

Though the only criteria for the assigned oral presentation were that the topic be academic and spur discussion, every student in the class, with one exception, chose a Jewishly themed topic (the one exception was a student who was not interviewed and attended class sporadically—he majored in biology and discussed stem cell research). During discussions after presentations on topics such as anti-Semitism in France, Holocaust deniers, and the Palestinian perspective of the Israeli-Arab conflict, the class united against who they perceived to be the common "enemy" or external force of oppression. When students at this largely left-wing, politically active school viewed the mock "Israeli Apartheid Wall" demonstration in the school's main rotunda, or saw necklace pendants in the shape of the state of Israel with "Palestine Forever" written inside for sale in the hallway, they passionately rallied in class and their identities converged: in unanimous agreement, they were all Jews.

However, within the more prevalent theme of divergence of identities, sub-groups of "Jews," defined based on varied and at times conflicting characteristics, emerged. When asked to define their ethnic identities in in-depth, individual interviews, all of the students placed in the "Canadian" group (named in spite of some birthplaces in the U.S. and South Africa, and explicit and reiterative statements that they did not feel a primary connection to Canada as Canadian) defined themselves primarily as Jewish. Jewish was at times modified with other sub-group definitions: "a secular Jew," or a "Jew with strong ties to Israel." The Israelis defined themselves primarily in terms of nation: Israeli or Russian-Israeli.

Denomination and religiosity played a role in the Canadians' definitions of being Jewish. Naomi said, "I have always considered myself to be Conservative, but they would probably consider me Reform here." Seth, who was the son of a Conservative rabbi, was engaged in more religious activities. He studied at a Conservative yeshiva in Israel for one year,[2] participated in biblical text study groups, and presented a lecture on aspects of Jewish law. He was considered to be "Orthodox" or "religious" by the Israeli students. In fact, in group discussions, the Israelis often stereotyped all of the Canadian students as Orthodox or religious. When I asked the Israelis why they thought the Canadians were in the Hebrew class, several assumed that they wanted to improve their proficiency to better read biblical and rabbinic texts.

Although Amy defined herself as a "secular Jew," she structured her connection to Judaism communally through her past Jewish day schooling, youth group participation, and Jewish Education degree. Amy did not view secularism as a label that annulled Jewishness. She described her view of the Israelis' religious frameworks:

> They grew up in a country where a lot of their parents couldn't grow up being Jewish, so being Jewish is a totally different definition than what being Jewish is for me. And also growing up in Israel, the weird thing about being in Israel is that you can be Jewish without being Jewish. It's like in Canada, you can be Christian without being Christian. The Israeli people are not typically as Jewish, they're just more culturally Jewish.

When I asked the Israelis to define their ethnic identities, several from the former U.S.S.R. emphasized that they were not Jewish, explicit in Yana's comments:

---

2. A yeshiva is a Jewish institution for Torah study.

bate'udat zehut sheli katuv 'lo mezuhah' baqet'a shel hadat ki ima sheli notsrit ve'aba sheli yehudi. yesh harbeh aflayah, vehem bodqim et hate'udat zehut ve discriminate against me [On my identity card it says 'unidentified' in the religion section because my mother is Christian and my father is Jewish. There's a lot of discrimination, and they check my identity card and discriminate against me].

When asked to define her ethnic identity, Tatiana stated, "I wouldn't put Jewish because I'm not religious, so Russian, Israeli, Canadian." Tatiana equated Jewishness as religious Orthodoxy, yet when she was probed, discussed her connection to Judaism primarily as a connection to family members who were killed in the Holocaust.

Yana had a very complex way of thinking about her Jewishness: "I'm actually not technically Jewish. My mother is Christian and my father is Jewish. So they're not religious at all. It was never, no tradition, very *mamash mishpaḥah ḥilonit* [a really secular family]." However, later in her interview she stated: "I feel a connection to Judaism because obviously, it's in my blood, even though I'm not fully Jewish. I do feel that way because I grew up in Israel." Yana seemed to first view the state of being Jewish as equivalent to observing Orthodox traditions while later defining her Jewishness as her connection to Israel. This latter association was elucidated in the group discussion during a controversial exchange:

> Yana: *im yesh benadam, ken, vehu lo medaber 'ivrit veein lo shum qeshser lasafah, ken? ani lo yoda'at, keilu ani lo* [If there's a person, yes, and he doesn't speak Hebrew and doesn't have any connection to the language, yes? I don't know, like, I don't—] I don't control him, but I don't really accept him to be Jewish. He's Jewish, but like, I think that if you're Jewish you have to know Hebrew. If you don't then I'll still accept you as Jewish, but the way I'm going to feel about you is different. I'm not going to feel the same connection with somebody that doesn't understand the language.
>
> Amy: Well, that's your connection to Judaism.

Here, Yana acknowledged an assumed general definition of Jewishness but believed that the true meaning of the term pertained to fluency in Hebrew, and possibly Israeliness. Amy's comment showed her open-minded understanding of various connectors to Judaism that create personal definitions of identity. After the class, Moshe, who was an observant Jew, voiced his concern to me about Yana's comments. He felt that her judgment of others' Jewishness was unfair, especially because others did not discriminate against her based on her definition of Judaism and lack of religious involvement.

A further layer of complexity arose upon examination of Meg's comments. Meg defined herself as a religious Jew, with spirituality playing a large role in her life. She grew up in a "Conservadox" home and attended an Orthodox Hebrew school, but described an awakening in her life as she came to a personal relationship with God through a movement that believes in Jesus as the Jewish messiah. Whereas other participants mentioned a communal and social aspect of their connection with Judaism, Meg spoke of a personal spirituality as her foremost connection:

> For me, Judaism was a little more individual. Whether or not people accept you, you know who you are. I took a year off, and thought, 'Let's—I'm going to find myself', right? I had family overseas who believed in *yeshua*[3] and I always figured, all right, that's for them, they're just not very good Jews. And I went there, and I heard the testaments in their lives. And to hear that it was not just only about rules and traditions but that they were really experiencing a personal relationship with God through scriptures—that they would hear back. God of the scriptures was still alive today in a very real way.

Although Meg would not be considered "religious" by some in the Jewish community, she structured a deeply devout religious life for herself: she expressed a level of spirituality voiced not even by the most religiously observant students.

Discussion

After conducting this research in order to understand the complexities of Jewish identity formation, it became clear that participants used modern Hebrew as a way to negotiate and balance their lives in the Diaspora as both a unifier, connecting all Jews, or as a modifying identifier that marked them as different from others in the Jewish community. Additionally, I determined that Hebrew language and participating in the Hebrew class was a social activity. It was a component in the ways they structured their Jewish identities: how they fit into the larger Jewish community and separated themselves into smaller sub-groups. For the Israelis, speaking fossilized Hebrew was an exclusive membership key to the Israeli sub-group of the Canadian Jewish commu-

---

3. *yeshua* is believed to be the Hebrew name for Jesus.

nity. For the Canadians, it was part of a larger framework of Jewish life they constructed to distinguish themselves from the majority culture, and to more abstractly and symbolically connect as Jews. Both groups, at times, stereotyped and viewed the opposing sub-group as the Other. Although Hebrew wasn't often used to communicate, the simple act of learning the language was a Jewish identifier.

This phenomenon logically fits into the historical narrative of the Jews. Jews have a history of heteroglossia: speaking several languages in different contexts. Jews have always simultaneously strived to integrate with the majority culture while facing ethnic obliteration, either by dominant forces or from forces within the community. Jews have created sub-groups and stereotypes for the purpose of intragroup Othering and to strengthen individual and subgroup statuses. In the case of this study, participants asserted their and Others' identities through *language claiming*. Similar to land claims in which aboriginal peoples assert authentic ownership of a plot of land over a majority group to maintain minority group survival, these students claimed that the Hebrew language as more authentically "ours" rather than "theirs."

Because of students' complex backgrounds in which many were ostracized and felt a sense of not belonging in the mainstream Jewish community, they often clung to markers of difference such as language, secularity, religious denomination, or nationality to proclaim a marked difference from the conventional. The term "Jewish" took on many meanings, relative to personal experience and relative context or situation. Internal, intragroup Othering and division into Jewish sub-groups was related to the speaking or learning of Hebrew, as the language was being used as a tool to strengthen intragroup statures and cement self- and other-identifications as true, authentic Jews.

REFERENCES

Alvarez, C., L. Bliss, and P. Vigil. 2001. Cuban identity: A preliminary study. Paper presented at the Annual Meeting of the American Educational Research Association, Seattle, April 2001.

Auer, P. 2005. A post-script: Code-switching and social identity. *Journal of Pragmatics* 37, 403–410.

Auron, Y. 1997. Between 'Israeliness' and 'Jewishness'—The attitude of young Israelis toward their Jewish-Israeli identity. In D. Schers and D. Zisenwine, (eds.), *Making a Difference: Jewish Identity and Education* (pp. 157–176). Tel Aviv: School of Education, Tel Aviv University.

Bakhtin, M.M. 1981. *The Dialogic Imagination: Four Essays by M.M. Bakhtin.* M. Holquist (ed.), Austin: University of Texas Press.

Cohen, S.M. 1986. *Ties and Tensions: The 1986 Survey of American Jewish Attitudes Toward Israel and Israelis.* New York: The American Jewish Committee.

————— . 2005. Poll: Attachment of U.S. Jews to Israel falls in past two years. *The Forward.* Retrieved May 5, 2005 from [http://www.forward.com/main/printer-friendly.php?id2770].

Glaser, B. and A. Strauss. 1967. *The Discovery of Grounded Theory.* Chicago: Aldine.

Jacobson, D.C. 1993. Language and culture in the teaching of Hebrew at American universities. In A. Mintz (ed.), *Hebrew in America: Perspectives and Prospects* (pp. 187–208). Detroit: Wayne State University Press.

Johnson, M. 2004. *A Philosophy of Second Language Acquisition.* New Haven: Yale University Press.

Kaufman, D. 2000. Attrition of Hebrew in the United States: A sociolinguistic perspective. In E. Olshtain and G. Horenczyk (eds.), *Language, Identity and Immigration* (pp. 173–196). Jerusalem: The Hebrew University Magnes Press.

King, K. and N. Ganuza. 2005. Language, identity, education and transmigration: Chilean adolescents in Sweden. *Journal of Language, Identity, and Education* 4, 179–199.

Lotherington, H. 2001. A tale of four teachers: A study of an Australian late-entry content-based programme in two Asian languages. *International Journal of Bilingual Education and Bilingualism* 4, 97–106.

Morahg, G. 2002. The question of Jewish identity in Hebrew language teaching. *Hebrew Higher Education* 10, 13–17.

Raphaeli, R. 1993. Toward Hebrew literacy: From school to college. In A. Mintz (ed.), *Hebrew in America: Perspectives and Prospects* (pp. 187–208). Detroit: Wayne State University Press.

Schecter, S.R. and R. Bayley. 1997. Language socialization practices and cultural identity: Case studies of Mexican-descent families in California and Texas. *TESOL Quarterly* 31, 513–541.

Schiff, A. 1997. The Jewish condition and Jewish education: Educational issues in Jewish identity in the United States. In D. Schers and D. Zisenwine (eds.), *Making a Difference: Jewish Identity and Education* (pp. 79–132). Tel Aviv: School of Education, Tel Aviv University.

Trappes-Lomax, H. 2004. Discourse analysis. In A. Davies and C. Elder (eds.), *The Handbook of Applied Linguistics* (pp. 133–164). Malden, Mass.: Blackwell Publishing Ltd.

Tse, L. 1998. Seeing themselves through borrowed eyes: Asian Americans in ethnic ambivalence/evasion. *Multicultural Review* 7, 28–34.

——————— . 2000. The effects of ethnic identity formation on bilingual maintenance and development: An analysis of Asian American narratives. *International Journal of Bilingual Education and Bilingualism* 3, 185–199.

Veyl, T., Fiurko, L., and C. Farstei. 1983. ʿivrit: havanah vehabaʾah. Jerusalem: Academon, Overseas Students Program, Department for Teaching Hebrew to Speakers of Foreign Languages.

Vygotsky, L.S. 1981. The genesis of higher mental functions. In J.V. Wertsch (ed.), *The Concept of Activity in Soviet Psychology* (pp. 144–188). Armonk, N.Y.: Sharpe.

Zisenwine, D. 1997. Teaching Hebrew: A suggestion for Hebrew educators. *Religious Education* 92, 55–60.

Researching Spoken Hebrew and Its Implications for Teaching Hebrew as a Second Language

'לוֹ שֶׁל הַגֹּל קוֹרֵ:
תּוֹ – שֶׁאָבוֹא אֲנִי •

ג

ז בְּרֹאשׁוֹ, וְהָכִּינוּ ז
וֹת, אָמֵן אָמֵן סֶלָה״

Einat Gonen

University of Maryland

THE REALITY OF SPOKEN HEBREW is different from that of normative Hebrew in many respects. There are even those who see it as a different language (Zuckerman, 2007). Hebrew teachers ponder considerably over the Hebrew that is taught. Should we teach only normative Hebrew or also teach the evolving non-standard varieties of today's spoken Hebrew? How do we present the differences between spoken Hebrew and normative Hebrew? And what is considered "correct" when teaching Hebrew in second-language settings?

Many pragmatic teachers try to distinguish between applied normative forms and normative forms that are hardly applied (see henceforth). However, who can determine who applies which forms, and to what extent? Because of the lack of a comprehensive knowledge base, which includes both written and spoken Hebrew, Hebrew teachers and textbook writers are required to make many independent decisions themselves. The difficulty increases when teaching Hebrew abroad, where Hebrew teachers' lives are conducted outside of Israel. Even when they are familiar with the happenings in Israel and update themselves about Hebrew neology and language changes, it is far different from living in a Hebrew-speaking environment in Israel.

For close to thirty years now voices have called for the establishment of an extensive research study of modern Hebrew. Rabin (1964) suggested that the "intermediate Hebrew" ("*haivrit habenonit*") should be described in a scientific, linguistic manner that could aid language teachers and norm setters. In the late 1970s in a Language Academy assembly, Kaddari (1996) called for the description of the normative written language and normative spoken language used by educated people. In addition, Blau (1991) also called for

basing comprehensive grammar on a large base of written and spoken
language alternatives, and not only by rulings based on several native speakers'
language abilities. Bar-Asher (1994) thought that modern Hebrew and its
sections and varieties should be subject to a survey, though he stressed that the
data investigation should not be connected to setting a normative standard.

In this paper, I will discuss one grammatical issue as a model of the implication that field research may have on teaching Hebrew as a foreign language.
The findings of the field research done on the vowel-reduction phenomenon
in spoken Hebrew will be presented,[1] and the implications of this research on
teaching Hebrew as a foreign language will be analyzed.

Reduction of Vowels in Spoken Hebrew

In classic Hebrew, the *qamats* of an open syllable in a noun changes to a
reduced vowel when that syllable is not next to the stressed syllable. For
example, the *qamats* in the word גָּדוֹל (*gadol*, masculine— "big") changes into
a schwa when the word is inflected: גְּדוֹלָה (*g[e]dola*, feminine—"big"). The
qamats in the word שַׁבָּתוֹת (*shabbatot*, "Saturdays") changes into a schwa: שַׁבְּתוֹתַי
(*shabb[e]totay*, "my Saturdays").

This rule of vowel reduction, which is called "the *hituf* rule," has many
exceptions in classical Hebrew, some of which are related to an "a" vowel
originating in a long vowel (Gesenius, 1910; Bergstrasser, 1972; Jouon and
Muraoka, 1993; Blau, 1972; Gadish and Gonen, 2001). The inflection layout
of the *tsere* ("e" sound) is even more complicated since under the same conditions, the *tsere* may remain or may change to a schwa (Jouon and Muraoka,
1993; Blau, 1972; Gadish and Gonen, 2001; Kaddari, 1996).[2]

Nevertheless, the reality of spoken Hebrew today is that its characteristics
are extremely varied and, in many ways, it deviates from normative grammar.[3]

---

1. The research is based on my doctoral dissertation "The Inflection of Nouns in
    Spoken Hebrew: Processes of Vocalic Reduction" (Gonen, 2006), written
    under supervision of Prof. Moshe Bar-Asher. Much gratitude is expressed to
    him for his devoted guidance.

2. In other normative grammar vowels, the Rule of Vowel Reduction is hardly
    relevant to the noun section (except for the upper accent [*mil'el*] nouns, that
    have their own conjugation table). Full vowels do not change in conjugation,
    while the rest of the vowels are in a closed syllable and are not subject to vowel
    reduction.

3. Deviations from the norm in the Bible are documented also in *hazal* texts (for
    example: *saxir-*, *matanot-*, etc.). Additionally, there are cases in which the vowel

Thus, spoken Hebrew includes forms such as *maraqim* and not *meraqim* ("soups"), *lequḥot* or *leqoḥot* and not *laqoḥot* ("customers"), *mishqafey shemesh* and not *mishqefey shemesh* ("sunglasses").[4] All these forms do not follow the norm.

The undermining of vowel reduction in spoken Hebrew has been reviewed in several studies, from both normative and descriptive aspects. However, no extensive research was really done about the conditions in which the rule of vowel reduction applies today.[5] This paper is based on extensive fieldwork that reviews the pronunciation of hundreds of forms in spoken Hebrew, in both read text and natural speech.

Theoretical Background: Phonology of Modern Hebrew

Modern Hebrew morphology is based on biblical morphology (Ben-Hayyim, 1953: 41), yet its phonology is different from the classical phonology (Schwarzwald, 2002: 97; Ravid and Schlesinger, 2001: 372). There are those who see modern Hebrew phonology as a new, separate unit that is not a natural continuation of any previous phase of Hebrew (Wexler, 1990; Bolozky, 1996: 122–123; Zuckerman, 2005). Therefore, while most morphophonological rules apply to the natural pronunciation scheme in ancient Hebrew, in modern Hebrew there is an apparent difference in the new phonologic reality (Schwarzwald, 1981: 13). Such a situation allows in natural speech many deviations from the rules inherited from the biblical and exemplary language rules.

These deviations are evident in the realization of the classic vowel reduction rule in general spoken Hebrew and they are affected by several phonologic changes that occurred from the tradition of the Tiberian Hebrew to modern Hebrew.[6] They include a lack of distinction between *pataḥ* and

---

change occurred where not expected, such as *limqom eḥad*, *avatḥim* (Bar-Asher, 1980: 54–55).

4. In construct form (*smixut*) only the second component is considered to be grammatically stressed; therefore a reduction is expected.

5. The most extensive research done so far reviewed the conjugation of only 30 words (Ravid and Shlesinger, 2001). Other papers on the subject include Bolozky, 1997; Bolozky, 2002; Bolozky and Schwarzwald, 1990. *Ḥituf* issues are also mentioned in works by Bentolila, 1990; Morag, 2004: 186; Shlesinger, Ravid and Sar'el, 1987; Tzvi, 1998: 118, 123–124.

6. For Eastern Hebrew and general Hebrew, see Blanc, 1964: 134–135; Blanc, 1957: 33; Morag, 1959: 248–254; Morag, 1973: 206–207; Bentolila, 1983: 93; Bentolila, 1989:14.

qamats in pronunciation, lack of *dagesh*,[7] and pronunciation of mobile schwa as a full "e" vowel or as zero (and not as the biblical reduced vowel). These changes substantially reduce the motivation for an abbreviating vowel reduction.

Method of Research

The data presented in this paper are based on review and statistical analysis of the research texts. In the full study, relevant forms from natural speech were compiled to form a control group;[8] however, since it did not enable a methodical, empirical discussion, it is not discussed in this paper. This method, commonly used in language research (Schwarzwald, 1981, 16: 39), has considerable disadvantages; yet, because a comprehensive database of native spoken Hebrew had not been established, it would have been difficult to draw a systematic morphology by listening to random texts.

Formation of the Data Base: Reviewed Questionnaires

Three thousand four hundred fifty-nine words were provided in both questionnaires. The words were given as continuous text over fourteen pages in order to mask the fact that this was a linguistic study. The average reading time of each questionnaire was 22 minutes. Approximately 1870 minutes were recorded altogether, which is approximately 31 hours. Pronunciation of over 1110 forms was registered (out of the 2459 words in the two questionnaires). The forms were then sorted into different categories to enable further, more focused, analysis. In 569 forms, vowel reduction was examined specifically.

Each questionnaire was read by 40 informants (with a total of 80 subjects). In the first questionnaire, there was an additional control group of five informants with linguistic knowledge: four scholars of the Hebrew Language Academy, meticulous in following conjugation of noun rules, and a radio broadcaster.[9] Diversity of the recorded interviewees was emphasized in crite-

---

7. Doubling of the BKF consonants affects the way a vowel is pronounced as plosive and not fricative, though it does not cause "doubling" of the consonant. This is not likely to be perceived as such by speakers.

8. The free text was based on recordings taken from the Corpus of Spoken Israeli Hebrew (CoSIH), recordings I made myself or were made on my behalf. Much gratitude is expressed to Prof. Shlomo Izre'el for his willingness to help and his useful advice in writing this paper.

9. My sincerest gratitude to Mrs. Ruth Almagor-Ramon for her efforts and help.

ria such as age, geographic location, ethnicity, prayer customs, and cultural background. All subjects were either high school graduates or high school students.

Each recorded questionnaire was digitally transferred to the computer in order to isolate a specific syllable. It was played in a loop until a conclusion regarding the pronounced vowel was reached.

Presentation of Findings: Level of Normativeness of the Speaker

The purpose of the normative measure of each speaker is to describe the measure of normative reading of the questions that related to the rule of vowel reduction. It should be noted that the questionnaires were specifically prepared for purpose of this research and, therefore, include more difficult and rarer forms than typically appear in authentic texts.

The data examined produced the following findings:

1. The speakers succeeded in reaching a maximum normative measure of 53 percent on the questions relating to reduction of vowels (the "best" reader reached an average measure of 68 percent of the normative forms in relation to the vowel change).

2. Even expert readers, who meticulously followed conjugations of noun rules, did not read perfectly and reached an average 87 percent on the normative measure. This finding clarifies the ambiguity of vowel changing rules, since even the knowledgeable reader who is familiar with language rules may not have full knowledge of the norm. Even if such a person has an erudite knowledge of the rules, he or she might still find their application difficult.

Findings

The data show an obvious tendency to preserve the vowel in conjugation: 61 percent of the forms actually preserved the vowel, whereas, according to the standard, only 33 percent of the forms were supposed to preserve the vowel (almost doubling the number of nouns without reduction). In terms of the normative conjugation, 56 percent of forms with both preserved and changed vowels were normative, whereas 44 percent were not normative.

Vowel Change by Category

The aforementioned data give a general picture of the distribution of the reduced vowels. In order to further analyze the phenomenon, additional data was examined according to the categorical segmentation of the nouns under discussion: singular construct form, plural and conjugation forms, and plural construct form.

Table 1 presents the extent of vowel reduction according to distribution of the examined forms (so that 100 percent is the total distribution in each category, for example, in the singular construct form, in the conjugated form, etc.).[10] The "a" vowel data (94 percent of the forms relevant to the rule of vowel reduction) were separated from the "e" vowel data (6 percent of the relevant forms). In each group we examined whether the vowel changed in conjugation and whether the vowel change or its preservation was normative. Thus, for example, the construct form *sandeley-* (from "sandals"/ *sandalim*) reflects the normative vowel change, whereas *sandaley-*, which preserves the "a" vowel, is not normative. In pronunciation of the construct form *gmaley-* (from *gamal*, as in *gmaley-hamidbar* "desert camels") the form reflects a normative vowel preservation, whereas when pronounced as *gimley-*, it reflects a non-normative vowel change.

TABLE 1: EXTENT OF VOWEL REDUCTION IN EXAMINED FORMS

Base Form	Vowel change			
	Normative Change	Non-normative Change	Non-normative Vowel Preservation	Normative Vowel Preservation
Example	*sandeley-*	*gimley-* (*hamidbar*)	*sandaley-*	*gmaley-*
"a" Vowel				
Singular Construct	38%	3%	45%	14%
Conjugated Plural	41%	12%	10%	36%
Plural Construct	18%	5%	56%	21%

---

10. The data were automatically rounded by the computer program (Excel or Access). This caused some impreciseness (e.g,. adding the percentage in a certain question could be 101 percent or 99 percent). These are very minor deviations that did not affect the conclusion.

"e" Vowel				
Example	*atsat-*	*ḥavruyot*	*etsat*	*ḥaveruyot*
Singular Construct[a]	70%		30%	
Conjugated Plural[b]	55%		40%	4%
Plural Construct[c]	82%			

a. For example: *atsat-* or *etsat-*.
b. For example: *azorim* or *ezorim*.
c. For example: *zikney-* or *zkeney-*; *edey-*. Examples of expected vowel changes in plural were not given (such as *rof-ey-* from *rofi-im*).

Analysis: The "e" Vowel

According to the findings, in most of the "e" vowel nouns the vowel follows the norm. Only in noticeable circumstances, where the *tsere* in the base form follows a guttural consonant and should change into a *ḥataf pataḥ*, is the weakening of the classic vowel-reduction rule noticeable. Thus, for example, we can see the noun "areas (of)" pronounced *ezorey* instead of *azorey*, or the noun "advice (of)" pronounced *etsat* instead of *atsat*, neither according to normative forms.[11]

Several factors are responsible for the preservation of the classic conjugation rules of the "e" vowel in spoken Hebrew:

a. A substantial number of the *tsere* nouns conjugate even by the normative rules by preserving the vowel.

b. Vowel changes are usually manifested as zero or as an "e" vowel; therefore, the vowel e in the base form may be preserved in pronouncing *masmerim* ("nails"), even when the meticulous vocalizer will vocalize the second *mem* with a schwa.

c. *Tsere*, unlike a *qamats*, may change in many cases when in proximity to the stress. Therefore, many of the normative changes already occur in

---

11. Since the questionnaire included many difficult forms, the findings showed a considerable degree of non-standard vowel preservation: 30 percent in the singular construct form (such as *etsat-*) and 49 percent in the plural conjugation (such as *ezorim*). Such nouns are relatively rare in the noun system and, when conjugated, the desire to preserve the absolute form influences the entire conjugation.

plural form, such as *rofe—rof-im* (doctor—doctors), and not only in the construct state or in conjugation. Nouns tend to preserve the vowel change in the most common plural form.

Analysis: The "a" Vowel

Unlike the "e" vowel, the manner in which the "a" vowel behaves in spoken Hebrew is complicated to describe. Vowel changes in spoken Hebrew are well established in the plural form, when the stress moves: 51 percent of the forms given in the questionnaire normatively require vowel change. Forty-one percent of the forms showed a normative vowel change, whereas ten percent did not. In other words, eighty percent were normative and twenty percent were non-normative, which shows a well-established difference. It is interesting to note that many speakers tended to "hyper-vowel reduction," and the actual vowel change (53 percent) was larger than expected (51 percent).

In construct forms this was not the case. Vowel changes were expected in the classic Hebrew construct forms because the construct state is considered to be one unit and the grammatical stress is on the second component (*somex*) of the construct state (Gesenius, 1910, 247; Ravid and Shlesinger, 2001: 390). The status of the construct state changes in modern Hebrew, and we can notice manners that deviate from classical Hebrew, such as making definite the first component (*nismax*) of the construct state (Bentolila, 1990, 274) or preserving the vowel of an open syllable in the first component of the construct state.

Indeed, this is apparent in the research findings. The number of forms in singular construct state where expected vowel changes did not occur was relatively high (45 percent), though the number of the normative conjugations was still a significant 52 percent.

Of 83 percent of the forms in which vowel changes should occur in singular construct state, it occurred in only 38 percent of the forms. In 45 percent of the forms it did not occur (meaning occurrences of only 46 percent). This is substantially lower than the plural vowel changes appearances. Since we can still notice vowel change in the singular construct forms, it seems that when reading text, most speakers connect between the construct form and vowel changes, though less than with the plural construct forms.[12]

---

12. In natural speech, the tendency to preserve the vowel increases. See Gonen, 2006, chapter 4.

The declining tendency in the number of forms in which normative vowel changes occur is even more obvious in the plural construct form: vowel changes should have occurred in 74 percent of the forms given in the questionnaire. Only 18 percent actually showed standard vowel change (or 23 percent of the normative forms out of the total forms in which vowel changes should have occurred). This shows a substantial decline compared to the singular construct form.

How can we explain this finding? If we argue that, unlike the vowel change in plural construct form, the construct form is being undermined and that speakers do not feel that there is such a distancing from the stress that it requires vowel change, then what explanation can be given for the differences between the singular construct form and the plural construct form?

In my opinion, there are two factors that affect the change:

1. Formation of a new phonologic system in which a linkage is made between the plural form and the construct form: a vowel preserved in the plural conjugation most likely will behave similarly in construct form, whereas a vowel that changes in plural will do the same in construct conjugation. For example, *ma-amadotehem* ("their social position") is like *ma-amadot* ("social position"), *tofa-ot-* ("phenomena of") is like *tofa-ot* (plural of *tofa-a*, "phenomenon"), *eqdahey-* ("guns of") is like *eqdahim*, but ne*sixenu* ("our prince") is like *nesixim* ("princes"), and *gdol-* ("biggest of") is like *gdolim* ("big" plural).

   Since most of the vowel changes examined in the singular construct form occur in most cases in the first radical, this first radical changes in the plural form. Thus, the occurrences of vowel changing in the singular construct form will increase more than those in the plural construct form.

2. The syllable prone to vowel change in the singular absolute form will usually be the first syllable, and the vowel change in many consonants will be from an "a" vowel to zero. This change increases the vowel change motivation since it is worthwhile for the speaker: the number of syllables decreases and the word becomes shorter. In the plural construct form, however, the vowel changes (which have not yet occurred in the plural absolute form) will mostly occur in the middle of the word and will manifest themselves by the "a" vowel changing to an "e" vowel (in many nominal patterns, this will occur after the closed syllable—after the schwa in the previous consonant). This change does not decrease the number of syllables; therefore, the vowel

change motivation that involves distancing from the absolute form decreases.

Summary

The "a" vowel change in the different categories can be placed on an axis according to the extent of their appearances:

1. The vowel changes that involve distancing from the stress in the plural and conjugated forms are substantial and significant.
2. The construct forms show an undermining in the occurrences of vowel changes, a certain undermining in the singular construct form, and a more significant undermining in the plural construct form.

From the aspect of grammar rules we may notice a formation of a new phonologic system in which a linkage is made between the plural conjugated form and the construct form: a preserved vowel in the plural is likely to be preserved also in conjugation and in construct state, whereas a vowel that changes in the plural is likely to change also in the construct state.

Unlike the "a" vowel, the "e" vowel is conjugated by a well-established standard, except for special circumstances: when the vowel change should manifest itself in the "a" vowel (*hataf patah*), a substantial undermining occurs in the incidence of the classic rule of vowel reduction, and many times the speakers tend to preserve the vowel of the absolute noun (see "*ezorim*" above).

Teaching Hebrew Grammar to Native Speakers versus Second-Language Learners

The question of the nature of Hebrew studied and taught as a second language has occupied the minds of Hebrew teachers. In this section, I will address whether the grammar of the rule of vowel reduction should be taught and whether the findings of the research have any implication on the instruction of Hebrew as a foreign language.

When discussing the teaching of grammar, it is important to distinguish between native and non-native speakers (NSs and NNSs). Thus far, there is no dispute (yet) about providing NS students in Israel (particularly in higher grades) with proper grammar knowledge, rules, and customs. Whether they choose to make use of the neglected normative forms or avoid them, this understanding is an important cultural value.

The case is different with the second-language (L2) student. Whereas, for the native speaker, rules of grammar usually enrich previously acquired language, for the second-language student, the rules of grammar are an essential cornerstone in acquiring the language. Indeed, the process of acquiring a new language is possible by means of immersion in the target language community without formal studies. However, formal systematic instruction of the rules of the language is often required. Also, whereas native speakers have the tools that enable them to distinguish between registers and acceptable and non-acceptable expressions, the second-language student does not possess such linguistic capabilities. Experienced second-language teachers recall students who spoke normative Hebrew, yet were ridiculed by Israeli speakers who found their correct expression a disruption that proved the speakers' foreignness.

The L2 teachers' work is, therefore, quite complicated. Not only must they impart the language, they are also required to juggle the goals of teaching correct language and facilitating linguistic acculturation, even at the expense of "correct" language.

Indeed, Hebrew language instruction books for foreign-language speakers reflect these conflicts well. Several of the books even explicitly indicate these conflicts in the preface or relevant chapters. The writers of *Israeli Hebrew for Speakers of English* (Ben Horin et al., 1976), for example, expressed:

> It has been the assumption of the authors that the spoken rather than the written language should be emphasized during the initial stages of language learning. In the first two books of the series, we attempt to provide the student with a firm foundation in Israeli Hebrew as it is spoken in informal contexts by educated native speakers. The decision to teach informal spoken Hebrew has led to occasional departures from normative Hebrew. For example, educated native speakers of Hebrew generally say *katavtem* ("you wrote," plural) and not *ktavtem* in informal contexts. Thus, we have taught the form *katavtem* actively and have only mentioned in passing the existence of the more formal *ktavtem*. We believe this to be justified because we wish to prepare our students to speak and understand the Hebrew spoken by native speakers in Israel today.

Mazal Cohen-Weidenfeld, a teacher and linguist, formed her own grammatical principle (2001: 11):

> In the synchronic description itself I have decided to use the spoken forms and not the normative forms where the normative forms are infrequently used, or when the spoken forms reflect a linguistic reasoning and they do not impinge the language rules. Thus, for example, one can see in the *pa'al* conjugation table the forms *katavtem* ("they wrote," masculine), *katavten* (feminine).[13]

Shulamith Hareven, in a discussion regarding the Hebrew that is taught in *ulpan*,[14] outlined a similar rule. In her view, acceptance of the non-normative form should be considered according to the extent to which it interferes with the language's depth structure. According to Hareven, the forms *katavtem* (instead of *ktavtem*) and *otxem* (instead of *etxem*, "you" accusative) do not interfere with the language's depth structure, whereas forms such as *ḥevrot* (instead of *ḥavarot*, "companies") and *erkot* (instead of *araxot*, "kits") should be strongly opposed. Indeed, the perplexity regarding decisions based on the perceptions of linguists and teachers and the conflicts regarding the nature of the Hebrew taught can be seen in the vowel-reduction issue as presented in various grammar textbooks.

The Rule of Vowel Reduction in Hebrew-Language Textbooks

For the purpose of this study, well-known and prevalent textbooks for adult learners published in Israel and North America were reviewed. The books are divided into three groups:

a. Books with instruction supported by a vocalized vowel system (*niqud*).

b. Books that do not deal with issues of vocalization and are not marked.

c. Books with full or partial vocalization in order to clarify certain pronunciation issues.

The manner of dealing with vowel-reduction issues is obvious in the first two groups. Books based on vocalized transcription, which are not frequently used in adult education today, tend to teach normative grammar. This will be manifested, naturally, by pronunciation nuances represented by vocalization; this is done very meticulously and with few exceptions, in extreme cases.[15] Thus, for example, in the textbook *Hayesod* the rule of vowel reduction appears in the conjugation of nouns (*yedidi*, "my friend," p. 136) or in construct forms (*shlom ha-ish*, "the person's well-being," p. 157), and the phenomenon is clearly explained. On the other hand, books devoid of vocalization tend not to discuss the vowel reduction issues, because most of them are not printed with vowels.

---

13. For more about teaching *ktavtem* see *Hed Haulpan* 49 (1986).

14. *Ulpan* is an intensive Hebrew-language school.

15. Noted in the preface to the book *Hayesod*: "In vocaling we did not scrutinize the laxness of the BGD KFT consonants that come after a word ending with one of the vowel letters, since that rule is not customary in speech, except for certain phrases" (Uveeler and Bronznick, 1998, v).

The third group, which sometimes uses vocalization in difficult forms, represents the strong link between the linguistic application and the pronunciation, as well as the need for pragmatic language instruction. The books in the third group also better reflect the authors' conflicting opinions regarding which Hebrew should be represented and how worthwhile it would be to teach grammar in depth.

The vowel change phenomenon in Hebrew is already represented at the beginners level, both in conjugation (e.g., *gadol-gdola*, "big") and in the construct state. A close examination of textbooks shows that vowel change due to the rule of vowel reduction is not systematically discussed in most of the books. Vowel changes in the plural are taught early in the learning process. However, when teaching the more advanced construct state, teachers frequently avoid teaching the systematic grammar rule. Often, normative conjugation examples are given with vocalization (בְּנֵי יִשְׂרָאֵל, "the sons of Israel") with no explanation of the vowel change[16] or any other descriptive explanation or reasoning of the phenomenon.[17] Several books refer to the vowel changes that occur in construct states, yet only to those manifested by changes in more than one vowel (*milḥama* changes to *milḥemet-*: "war," "war of-").[18] Few books include a grammatical discussion in the chapters' footnotes, which in any case are not usually part of the classroom lesson.[19]

In more advanced levels, systematic grammar instruction is usually given more consideration. It enables an in-depth discussion about the structure of the construct state, including a discussion regarding the rule of vowel reduction (demonstrated in pronunciation). However, it seems that many of the textbooks in use today continue to disregard the subject. Even when examples are given with standard vocalization, there is no grammatical explanation provided (for examples, Bras and Delshad, 2003; Lev and Livne, 2001).

It is particularly noticeable when style and norm issues, yet not vowel changes, are discussed. The book *Combined Syntax* (Lanzberg), for example, lists goals of imparting normative rules and style matters. It discusses the definite article (*he haydi-a*) in the first component of the construct state as a style feature, yet the vowel changes are not mentioned.[20] Even in a book

---

16. See Ringvald (2005), 7, 26, 297; Chayat, Israeli, and Kobliner (2007), 295.

17. See Amir Coffin (1986), 35.

18. See Cohen (2002), 39; Bliboim (2005), 40.

19. Chayat, Israeli, and Kobliner, 2007, 138.

20. "In spoken Hebrew and in slang, making the construct state distinct before the

designated for advanced students, the vowel changes are mentioned with no explanation further than: "The other changes occur only in the vowels and thus will mostly be manifested vocally: *maqom* ('place') becomes *meqom miqlat* ('shelter')."[21] It's important to note that in this book there are discussions of norm matters such as common disruptions: "At times we come across attachment of two components to the first one in a construct state: for example *morey umnahaley ha-ulpanim* ('the *ulpans*' teachers and administrators'). The normative phrase should be *morey ha-ulpanim umnahalehem*."

There are many reasons why teachers choose not to systematically teach the vowel changes. First, in the lower levels, the vowel changes are learned by way of demonstration and repetition (e.g., *gadol—gdolim; maqom— meqomot*), with no necessity for a grammatical explanation. The students internalize the norm without learning the grammatical rule.

The second reason relates to the Hebrew student's goals: vowel changes in construct states might be perceived as a style feature of sophisticated Hebrew, which is not necessary for the beginner student. Thus, for example, in the Hebrew Proficiency Guidelines (1990) distinctions are made between mistakes of Hebrew-language students with no special reference in the guide on matters of pronunciation and particularly the rule of vowel reduction. The guidelines describe errors at the "superior" level:

> Mistakes may technically be the same as those at lower levels, but they occur only sporadically and at much higher levels of morphology, syntax and vocabulary....Such errors rarely disturb natives or cause miscommunication. (28)

It seems here that most Hebrew teachers do not perceive the rule of vowel reduction as disturbing the native speaker or interfering with communication.

Additionally, there is inconsistency regarding this issue in the textbooks for various levels. It seems that at the beginner levels, which provide the students with the basic language communication skills, the teachers do not attempt to overload the student with complicated rules of grammar. Also, pronunciation matters, even the common ones, are not diligently or explicitly taught. At the advanced levels, however, teachers assume that the students are equipped with

---

first component is common, for instance: *habeit sefer* ('the school'), *haheder-oxel* ('the lunch room')...use of such phrases in writing indicates a low register style or imitation of spoken language" (Lanzberg, pp. 29), but when a full noun conjugation table is provided, it is fully vocalized, in different context, the vocalization differences are indicated (31).

21. Bliboim (2005), 39–40.

a basic knowledge of Hebrew and that various issues, such as reduction of vowels in conjugation, have already been learned (either theoretically or in practical studies). Thus, this rule falls between the cracks and is not taught systematically. Perhaps if there existed an extensive series of textbooks covering five or six levels and composed by one author, there would be a more systematic discussion on the subject, whether at the beginner level or at the advanced level.

It seems that a major consideration in not teaching the rule of vowel reduction in an organized way stems from the nature of teaching and evaluating. Both in Israel and abroad, current teaching trends do not emphasize vocalization. Although many of the books set a goal of developing oral skills, some emphasize it more than others and the most popular approach is to teach without vocalization in accordance with most written Hebrew texts today. Furthermore, it seems that in Israel, the *ulpan*'s final-level exam is what affects curricula and not vice versa. In a discussion on noun conjugation, for example, Lanzberg wrote: "On the level exam students are not required to display knowledge in vocalization. Therefore, they can focus on writing the pronominal suffixes correctly, and not deal with vocalization and pronunciation of words. Dealing with correct pronunciation is suitable for students who already know the pronominal suffixes, as it enables them to acquire new knowledge through review of the material" (Lanzberg, *Combined Grammar*).

Research and Teaching: An Application

The findings of the study on the rule of vowel reduction, which were presented in the first part of this paper, suggest a stratified reality in which the rule of vowel reduction applies in an indeterminate regularity. This makes learning the rule difficult, since the instances of fully teaching its derivatives (normative or actual) are rare. It seems that at the basis of these rules are lexical and metrical principles linked to the language stratum from which the word stems. And yet, the findings show that there is a common presence of vowel reduction in quite a number of forms, such as *anshey-* ("men of"), *artsot-* ("countries of"), *meqor-* ("source of"), *bnotehem* ("their daughters"), *yemey-* ("days of") and many other forms, in such a way that increases the need for teaching this subject.

However, the question of how the teacher will deal with the inconsistency of the rule remains unchanged. I find it appropriate at this point to distinguish between two types of teachers: the purist teacher and the pragmatic teacher. Many may think of the purist teacher's work as being more difficult. While his or her pragmatic colleagues gracefully skip over rules that are difficult to teach or over lists of irregular forms (e.g., *ktavtem* ["you wrote"], *e-ene* ["I will answer"], *ishan* ["I will sleep"], *lirkov* ["to ride"]), the purist accepts all standard rules of grammar and is obligated to impart them to students. Nonetheless, I find that regarding the issue of vowel reduction, the purist teacher's work is in fact easier, since all that has to be done is to teach the basic rules of vowel reduction and hand the students a list of the irregular forms. Even if they are not able to memorize them all, there is a good chance that their mistakes will be easily understood, or even commonly and largely made by native speakers. The pragmatic teacher's work, however, is more compli-cated. How will the pragmatic teacher present the anomaly that is manifested in reality?

In light of the research findings and contrary to the way most reviewed textbooks deal with this issue, I suggest that teachers should not neglect teach-ing the rule of vowel reduction since it is actively used in the plural forms, in conjugations of nouns, in possessive suffixes, and in many construct forms. Moreover, my experience as a Hebrew teacher leads me to conclude that most students are interested in hearing grammatical explanations regarding phenomena that they have thus far learned. Such teaching may shed light on the unique traits of Hebrew conjugation and clarify forms that might be heard in meticulous speech. At the beginner level, I suggest that teachers illustrate the common conjugation (e.g., plural or conjugated forms that randomly appear in texts) and give a short explanation of the grammatical rule. At the advanced level, further elaboration about the rule is suggested.

It is important to note that this does not stem from a purist point of view. My interest is not in the normative or "wholeness of Hebrew," but in the language skills that will be provided to the adult student who has completed advanced Hebrew studies in an institute of higher learning and is ready to enter the educated, Hebrew-speaking community. It is appropriate to expose students to "sophisticated" Hebrew spoken by highly educated people. Therefore, I suggest establishing a new standard that, according to the findings of our research that were discussed at the beginning of this chapter, more accurately describes what is prevalent in the language:

> There is a tendency in Hebrew to change vowels in conjugated nouns and verbs, especially in the "a" and "e" vowels, when a syllable is added and the stress in the word moves from the vowel.[22] The vowel

---

22. In advanced levels the teacher may add: the "e" vowel might change also when close to the stress. This can be distinguished from the "a" vowel, which changes in the noun only when removed from the stress.

might change to zero or an "e" vowel (if looking at vocalization: the *qamats* or *tsere* changes into a schwa). For example: *gadol* ("big," masculine), *gdola* ("big," feminine), *gdolim* ("big," plural); *shomer* ("guard"), *shomrim* ("guards"); *malon* ("hotel"), *melonot* ("hotels" since *mlonot* is difficult to pronounce in Hebrew).

In classical Hebrew, the construct state was perceived as a phrase with only one grammatical stress, in the second component of the construct state. Thus, vowel change often occurs in the first component of the construct form. For example: *shana* ("year"), *shnat-* ("the year of"); *mismaxim* ("documents"), *mismexey hamnahalim* ("the documents of the managers").

However, in spoken Israeli Hebrew the occurrence of vowel changes in conjugation decreases, mostly in the construct state. Accordingly, in conjugation the vowel change behaves like it would in the plural form: a preserved vowel in plural (due to its proximity to the stress) is preserved in conjugation. For example: *ma-amadotehem* ("positions," like *ma-amadot*, and in normative Hebrew: *ma-amdotehem*); *binyaney-* ("-buildings," like *binyanim*, and in normative Hebrew: *binyeney-*).

On the other hand, when in plural form, vowel change occurs when moving away from the stress; it usually happens in conjugation as well. For example: *nesixenu* ("our prince," like *nesixim* in plural); *shvur-lev* ("brokenhearted," like *shvurim* in plural). There are cases, mostly in nouns prevalent in traditional Jewish sources, in which vowel change occurs in conjugation and in the first component of the construct form even if in the plural the vowel was preserved. For example: *bney Israel* (from *banim* ["boys"]); *yemey hahanuka* (from *yamim* ["days"]).

Why should we teach this intricate and difficult rule and its many exceptions? Because this is a pronunciation issue that usually does not have any implication in spelling, it should be taught, if only in advanced-level Hebrew. Advanced students invest considerable time in learning rules, conjugation tables, irregulars, exceptions, and derivatives. Here we have a grammatical rule that can shed light on the way a whole system behaves. The discussion may contribute to the development of the student's linguistic sensitivity to practical Hebrew use—meaning change or preservation of vowels common in everyday speech—and to official Hebrew, as well, represented in the media and by meticulous speakers. Furthermore, by systematically ignoring pronunciation issues the advanced student is denied the potential to fully function in

Hebrew without being identified as a recent immigrant or a person who regularly speaks using a simple linguistic style.

Summary

In this article I have illustrated the implications of a study of Israeli Hebrew grammar for teaching Hebrew as a second language. In the first part I presented research findings regarding vowel reduction. In the second part I discussed teaching Hebrew and the rule of vowel reduction. In reviewing textbooks for teaching Hebrew as a foreign language I found that the issue of vowel reduction is hardly taught in a systematic manner. Most of the books are not vocalized, many ignore pronunciation issues, and others relate to pronunciation issues but only for clarification and not in order to fully teach the Hebrew rules of grammar. Thus, the Hebrew learner is left with a confusing linguistic reality. Even though the rules of vowel reduction are complex, I suggest teaching the reasoning behind them in order to provide the L2 student with language skills that will enable a linguistic acculturation that includes familiarity and comfort with intellectual strata of the language.

References

Amir Coffin, E. 1986. *Lessons in Modern Hebrew, Level II*, Ann Arbor: University of Michigan Press.

Bahat, E. 2002. The subject of registers in Hebrew language: Theory and practice in teaching a second language. *Hed Haulpan HeHadash* 84, 7–13.

Bar-Asher, M.1980. Tradition of the Mishnaic language of Italian Jews. *Eda Velashon* 6.

————. 1994. Forty academic years. *Leshonenu La'am* 45, 117–118.

Ben-Hayyim, Z. 1953. Ancient language in a new reality. *Leshonenu La'am* 4, 1–85.

Bentolila, Y. 1983. Hebrew accents used in a settlement of Moroccan descendents in the Negev: A segment in social morphology. Untitled doctoral dissertation, Hebrew University of Jerusalem.

————. 1989. Corpus of Montreal French. *Hebrew Linguistics* 27, 13–28.

————. 1990. The spoken Hebrew. *Leshonenu La'am* 40–41, 266–278.

————. 1999. Mishniac language in the French-Italian tradition. *Eda Velashon* 31.

Bergsträsser, G. 1972. *Hebrew Grammar*. Translated to Hebrew by Ben-Asher, M., Jerusalem: Magnes.

Blanc, H. 1957. Segment of Israeli Hebrew speech. *Leshonenu* 21, 33–39.

————. 1964. Israeli Hebrew texts. In H.B. Rosén (Ed.) *Studies in Egyptology and Linguistics in Honor of H. J. Polotsky* (pp. 132–152). Jerusalem: Israel Exploration Society.

Blau, J. 1972) *Torat Hahege Vehatsurot*. Tel Aviv: Hakibbutz Hameuchad.

————. 1991. Modern Hebrew grammar. *Leshonenu* 55, 149–157.

Bliboim, R. 2005. *Syntax+ [for Teachers and Advanced Students*. Jerusalem: Academon.

Bolozky, S. 1996. Israeli Hebrew as a Semitic language: Genealogy and topology. *Language Studies* 7, 121–134.

————. 1997. Israeli Hebrew phonology. In A.S. Kaye and P.T. Daniels (Eds.), *Phonologies of Asia and Africa, Vol. 1* (pp. 27–311). Winona Lake, Ind.: Eisenbrauns.

————. 2002. Phonologic and morphologic diversity in spoken Hebrew. *Document 18: Speaking Hebrew*, 239–278.

Bolozky, S. and O. Schwarzwald. 1990. On vowel assimilation and deletion in casual modern Hebrew. *Hebrew Annual Review* 12, 23–48.

Brandeis University 1990. *The Hebrew Proficiency Guidelines*. Waltham, Mass.: Brandeis University.

Chayat, S., S. Israeli, and H. Kobliner. 2007. *Hebrew From Scratch, Part I* Jerusalem: Academon.

Cohen, M. 1992. *Legendary Language (Agada Shel Safa)*. Academon: Jerusalem.

Cohen-Weidenfeld, M. 2000. *Po'oley Binyan*. Jerusalem: Rehlim.

Diskin-Ravid, D. 1995. *Language Change in Child and Adult Hebrew*. Oxford: Oxford University Press.

Gadish, R. and E. Gonen, 2001. Rules of noun inflection. *Leshonenu La'am* 51–52, 4.

Gadish, R. (Ed.). 2006. Academy resolutions about grammar. *Leshonenu La'am* 55, 1–2.

Gesenius, W. 1910. *Gesenius' Hebrew Grammar*. E. Kautzsch (Ed.), second English edition revised by A. E. Cowley, Oxford: Oxford University Press.

Gonen, E. 2006. *The Inflection of Nouns in Spoken Hebrew: Processes of Vocalic Reduction*. Unpublished doctoral dissertation, Hebrew University: Jerusalem.

Izre'el, S., B. Hary, and G. Rahav. 2002. Towards establishing a pool of Hebrew spoken in Israel. *Leshonenu* 64, 265–287.

Izre'el, S. 2002. The corpus of spoken Israeli Hebrew (CoSIH): Examples of texts. *Leshonenu* 64, 289–314.

——————— . 2004. Study of spoken Hebrew – First step: About transcription of speech for purpose of research. *Leshonenu La'am* 54, 106–119.

Jouon, P. and T. Muraoka. 1993. *A Grammar of Biblical Hebrew (Second Edition)*. Rome: Pontifical Biblical Institute Press.

Kaddari, M.S. 1991. The position of grammar in teaching Hebrew as a second language. In R. Nir (Ed.) with A. Noibach, *Teaching Hebrew Language and Hebrew Literature at an Academic Level* (pp. 33–20). Jerusalem: International Center for Teaching Culture in Universities.

——————— . 1996. The urgent need for a survey of the existing literary Hebrew. In J. Blau (Ed.), *The Hebrew Language, Evolution and Regeneration* (pp. 127–147). Jerusalem: Israel Academy of Sciences and Humanities.

Kantor, H. 1999. Ma nora ha"nora" haze (What's so terrible about "terribly"). *Hed Haulpan HeHadash* 77, 18–20.

Lanzberg, G. *Combined Syntax. Hebrew for the Advanced Hebrew Learner Combined with Semantics, Style and Expression, for the Fifth Level*. Jerusalem: Jerusalem Institute for Education (MILA).

Lauden, E. 2000. Teachers' position survey taken in the Hebrew studies department in the Tel Aviv University. *Hed Haulpan HeHadash* 81, 30–37.

Lev, B. and R. Livne, 2001. *Grammatic Structure*. Dyunon: Tel-Aviv.

Morag, S. 1959. Planned and unplanned development in modern Hebrew. *Lingua* 8, 247–263.

——————— . 1973. Several remarks on the description of the spoken Hebrew vowel system. *Leshonenu* 37, 205–214.

——————— . 2003. About grammatical errors and ways for uprooting them. In M. Bar-Asher, Y. Breuer, and A. Maman (Eds.), *Review of Hebrew by Generations* (pp. 177–205). Jerusalem: Magnes.

Muchnik, M. 2002. Is there a place for slang in the ulpan? *Hed Haulpan HeHadash* 84.

Rabin, C. 1964. The problems of correct Hebrew language in view of linguistics. *Leshonenu La'am* 16, 161–173.

Ravid, D. and Y. Shlesinger. 2001.Vowel reduction in modern Hebrew: Traces of the past and current variation. *Folia Linguistica* 36, 371–397.

Ringvald, V. et al. 2005. *Brandeis Modern Hebrew*. New Lebanon, N.H.: University Press of New England.

Rom, M. and R. Refaeli. 1989. *Learning Third Level Hebrew*. Jerusalem: Academon.

Rosén, H.B. 1979. Trends and development in the living Hebrew and its implications on work in the ulpan. *Hed Haulpan* 30–31, 16–18.

Schwarzwald, O. 1981. *Grammar and Reality of the Hebrew Verb*. Ramat Gan: Bar-Ilan University.

—————— . 2002. *Studies in Hebrew Morphology*. Tel Aviv: The Open University.

Shlezinger, Y., D. Ravid, and Z. Sar'el. 1987. *The Normative and the Linguistic Reality Represented in the Qamats*. Jerusalem: Ministry of Education and Culture (Department of Teaching Certification).

Sovran, T. 1999. Use, norm, theory and cognation – the case of 'regarding' (legabei). *Hed Haulpan HeHadash* 77, 27–35.

Uveeler, L. and N.R. Bronznick. 1988. *Hayesod – Fundamentals of Hebrew*. Jerusalem-New York: Feldheim.

Wexler, P. 1990. *The Schizoid Nature of Modern Hebrew: A Slavic Language in Search of a Semitic Past*, Wiesbaden: Otto Harrassowitz.

Zip, T. 1998. Mistaken vocalization and living Hebrew. *Helkat Lashon* 25, 115–129.

Zuckermann, G. 2005. Pretty language Hebrew, Ho! – Literature Periodical, 2nd issue [retrieved from http://www.nrg.co.il/online/5/ART/945/896.html].

—————— . 2005. A new vision for 'Modern Hebrew': Theoretical, cultural and practical implications of analyzing Israeli as a Semite-European mixed language. [retrieved from http://www.zuckermann.org/pdf/gz6.pdf].

—————— . 2007 [submitted]. 'Realistic prescriptivism': The Academy of the Hebrew language and its campaign of 'good grammar' and espionage. [retrieved from http://www.zuckermann.org/pdf/realistic.pdf].

Uprooting the Root

or

Sociolinguistics and the Modern Hebrew Teacher

Lewis Glinert

Dartmouth College

לוֹ שֶׁל הַגַּל קוֹרֵ׳

תוֹ – שֶׁאָבוֹא אֲנִי

ד

ז בְּרֹאשׁוֹ, וְהָכִּינוּ ז

וֹת, אָמֵן אָמֵן סֶלָה״

STRANGE THINGS CAN HAPPEN when one asks Israeli *'ivrit*[1] teachers why they teach the expression *meayin atah?* although few Israelis ever say it, or why they teach that *binyan pi'el* is intensive when they know full well that they can find only a handful of *pi'el* verbs that are more "intensive" than their *qal* counterparts (see Glinert, 1979). I have heard teachers insist that speakers really do use Hebrew this way, or launch into a lament that speakers *don't* use Hebrew this way ("Most Israelis don't know Hebrew"), or occasionally concede that they teach these things because the textbook says it (and why, after all, get into a fight with the book?).

For the American language teacher, who for two generations or more has taken it as axiomatic that foreign-language teaching must be based on the vernacular and on a linguistic descriptivism of the vernacular, the attitude of most Israeli teachers to *'ivrit* may be disconcerting but it is something one learns to live with. After all, most *'ivrit* teaching is perforce in the hands of Israelis, for the apparently incontrovertible reasons that the native speaker teaches it best and that no one else wants to teach it anyway. Sadly, however, the educational establishment both here and in Israel has done little to professionalize the training of *'ivrit* teachers to meet the demands of foreign-language teaching in the Diaspora. The textbooks in common use are a token of this and, indeed, perpetuate the problem. So too are the bilingual dictionaries, which rarely indicate such everyday realities as the word for "to carry"

---

1. *'ivrit* means "Hebrew."

(*saḥav*) or the use of *kaf hayad* for "hand," whereas *yad* denotes the entire lower arm (Glinert, 1994).

Thirty years ago, the reason for this situation appeared to be the normativism that dominated the study of Hebrew in Israeli academia (Rabin 1983), derived from classic conceptions and descriptions of the language predating the Revival. Even as Israel welcomed millions of *'olim*[2] and presumed to be teaching them a practical Hebrew to absorb them into society and the workplace, its teachers and policy-makers labored under a cognitive dissonance about modern Hebrew: it was still, they thought, being revived. Any features that diverged from the norms of biblical or rabbinic Hebrew were aberrations or, at any rate, temporary; the language had not, after all, had a chance to settle down. When Aharon Rosen, author of the classic 1950s *ulpan*[3] primer *Elef Millim*, incorporated negations of the form *ani lo mevin* (rather than *eineni mevin*), this was a daring compromise with the norms. If a linguist dared to suggest that Hebrew teachers should teach the reality altogether as it was, he or she was still roundly condemned. As a consultant on *ulpan* curricular development to the Israel Ministry of Education Adult Education Division in the 1970s, I became convinced that the *ulpan* profession was torn between two incompatible goals: equipping their students to function in Hebrew and heroically reviving the language.

Surveying the scene now, I have the eerie feeling that little has changed. True, in the past twenty-five years Israel has seen communicative goals, student-centered teaching, linguistic descriptivism, and anti-elitism sweep the board in English-language teaching. And true, much of the old respect for the Classic Hebrew canon and Classic Hebrew pedagogical tradition has dissipated and Zionist/national values have retreated on all fronts. Scholars writing for the Hebrew-teaching profession regularly highlight the contemporary realities (Fruchtmann, 2006). But still, teachers of Hebrew cling to their lofty norms. The texts in the textbooks may nowadays be racy or amusingly trivial, the vocabulary thick with hi-tech and cool, but some of the rules are the same pedantic, even archaic, rules taught fifty years ago, explained in the same "Alice in Wonderland" terms as they always have been. Thus, Ora Band's *'Ivrit Shalav Gimel* (1983: 209) would have us express the superlative of the adjective (e.g., "the tallest of") in one of the following four ways, of which only the last is actually in colloquial use:

---

2. *'olim* are new immigrants to Israel.

3. *ulpan* is an intensive Hebrew-language school.

> *ha'ets hagavoah baya'ar*
> *ha'ets hagavoah beyoter baya'ar*
> *ha'ets hayoter gavoah baya'ar*
> *ha'ets hakhi gavoah baya'ar*

Similarly, the *Brandeis Modern Hebrew* textbook (Ringvald et al., 2003: Unit 3) requires agreement for gender between the numerals 11–19 and their head noun, even though this is, again, not a general colloquial practice.

If it is no longer normativism that is driving these practices, it must be the sheer inertia of the Hebrew-teaching profession. Sociolinguistic consciousness is just one of many advances in language teaching in the past thirty to forty years. Others are error analysis, communicative needs, and motivation theory (Celce-Muria, 1991). Some structures are simply much harder than others, some are more functional than others, and success in learning is critically dependent on wanting to learn. Hebrew teaching has still to apply these lessons in earnest.

Let me give an example from a grammatical phenomenon that figures early on in so many *'ivrit* course-books: masculine-feminine agreement for numerals. The Israel Ministry of Education 1976 *ulpan* curriculum provided for teaching this distinction for the absolute numerals 1–19 at an early stage of the language-learning process. Similarly, Ora Band's course has agreement for 11–19 in *Shalav Bet*, unit 9; Edna Amir Coffin (1992) has agreement for 1–10 at Level 1, unit 7; and the Brandeis Hebrew course demands it for 1–10 in unit 2 and for 11–19 as early as unit 3. In the widely used *Ivrit Min Hahathalah* (1990, vol. 1), designed for one academic year and divided into 28 language lessons, agreement for 1–10 is taught in lesson 10 and for 11–19 in lesson 18, in other words, just a little after half-way through the first year curriculum and at a stage when study of the verb has been limited to the present tense of *pa'al, pi'el,* and *hif'il,* and a little taste of the past tense. Teaching numeral agreement in this fashion flies in the face of the following realities:

a.   The average Israeli no longer employs gender agreement for the numerals 11–19 in casual speech. The "feminine" form of the numeral is used with both masculine and feminine nouns, thus *shteim 'esreh baqbuqim, shlosh 'esreh hadarim* rather than *shneim 'asar baqbuqim, shloshah 'asar hadarim.*

b.   In casual speech, gender agreement is sometimes ignored even for the numerals 2–10, particularly for *shtei.*

In terms of pedagogical considerations per se,

    c. Few Hebrew learners make a gender distinction for 11–19 in their own mother tongue.

    d. Failure to make this gender distinction in no way impedes comprehension.

Nonetheless, virtually every Modern Hebrew textbook and dictionary I have examined insists on gender agreement for the numerals 1–19.[4]

This is in no way to suggest that *'ivrit* teaching should teach nothing but the colloquial. But an elegant brand of Hebrew should be taught for what it is, on its own terms. Instead, it is being smuggled into the colloquial Hebrew class.

Perhaps the three holiest cows in Hebrew grammar teaching are these:

    a. All verbs and nouns are based on 3-letter or 4-letter roots

    b. Roots generally have clear and tidy meanings.

    c. *binyanim* generally have clear and tidy meanings.

To cite the three course-books mentioned earlier: Ora Band (*Shalav Bet*, Unit 5) refers to *binyanim* as "meaning classes": "Each *binyan* describes a certain type of action: simple, causative, passive, reflexive etc. Each *binyan* tells us that a verb expresses a special type of action related to the basic meaning of the root." Taking as her first example the root k-t-v, Band describes the *qal* and *nif'al* as "simple" (whatever that may mean), the *pi'el* and *pu'al* as "intensive" (sic!), the *hif'il* and *huf'al* as "causative," and the *hitpa'el* as "reflexive or reciprocal," but then confesses: "The word *kitev* is no longer in common use." She later backtracks further, revealing just how conflicted a leading Hebrew educationalist could still be in the 1980s about telling the truth about Hebrew (p. 122): "Today, the relation between the *qal* and the *pi'el* is much less clear. Most common *pi'el* words seldom or never appear in the *qal*." Similarly, Edna Amir Coffin was not considering a large portion of the Hebrew noun inventory when she stated (p. 96): "A root is a sequence of consonants that form the basis of all verbs and nouns."

The Brandeis Hebrew course introduces unsuspecting students to the root in a similar vein (Unit 2, p. 59): "All words in Hebrew (verbs and nouns) are based on a 3-letter root system that determines their meaning." Hardly anything in this statement is correct. How, one wonders, would the editors

---

4. For more details on the contemporary Hebrew numeral system, see Glinert, 1989 and 2005.

of the Brandeis course have tackled the roots of a sentence like *haikar qilel et hatraqtor hamequlqal?* Regarding *binyanim*, they state: "*hif'il* verbs are very often used as causative verbs" (p. 415) and "*hitpa'el* verbs often have a reciprocal or reflexive sense" (p. 468), but make no statement about the *pi'el* and its important de-nominative role.

There is an obvious attraction in teaching a sweeping generalization. It provides students and teachers alike with a sense of security and, when pressed, a good teacher can always provide a fanciful fudge or plead that there are "exceptions." But it was not a lack of intelligence that prevented grammarians before the eleventh century from teaching a 3-letter root theory. There have always been major difficulties with it, as with the notion of semantically unitary roots and *binyanim*. Thus, the seminal tenth to eleventh-century Sephardi grammarians Ḥayyuj and Ibn Janaḥ had to posit an unarticulated and generally unseen middle consonant (*alef* or *vav*) for the so-called "*'ayin-vav*" root and their contemporary Rashi, in his less systematic mode of presentation, had to posit (Genesis 49:19 on *gad gedud yegudenu*) a doubling of the final consonant of the "*'ayin-vav*" root for the *pi'el* and *hitpa'el*. Similarly, regarding the meaning of roots, Ibn Janaḥ emphasized in his introduction to his dictionary *Sefer HaShorashim* (Berlin 1896: 4) how diverse a set of meanings they could convey, and in the entries he duly moved from one meaning to another without ado and without the slightest attempt to conjure up creative connections between them. (See, e.g., the entries *'ayin-zayin-bet*: "leave/strengthen" and *'ayin-tet-peh* "beseech/cover.")

The varied meaning of the biblical or post-biblical root is only to be expected. The semantics of a language never stop changing, even when it is just used for written purposes—metaphors or euphemisms may intervene, as well as sheer drift—and, as a result, what were once closely related ("polysemous") uses of a word may become distinct homonyms. This may help explain families of words with the "same" root such as *taqa'* "blow (an instrument), thrust," *lava* "loan," *liva* "accompany," *aval* "mourn," *aval* "indeed," *yashan* "old," *yashen* "sleep," *diber* "speak," *midbar* "desert," *dvorah* "bee," *'arev* "pleasant," *'arav* "guarantee," *'erev* "evening," *'erav* "mix."

Pinning a simple and consistent meaning on the *binyanim*, by contrast, has always been a credo of grammarians—until quite recently. David Kimhi (*Sefer Michlol*, twelfth century, *Sha'ar Diqduq Hapealim*), perhaps the most widely studied of the medieval biblical grammarians, offered sweeping semantic labels for each of the derived *binyanim* (ed. Chomsky 1952: 86). He described *pi'el* and *hif'il* of a transitive *qal* as causative, *pi'el* or *hif'il* of an intransitive *qal* he adjudged intensive (*ḥizuq hape'ulah*), and *hitpa'el* was reflexive or at least non-transitive. An example of this kind of procrustean thinking is the verb *hithalekh* (Gen 6:9), which he seeks to explain as denoting walking alone, all to oneself. Kimhi only adduced a few examples for each of these—and this is hardly surprising, since the statistics of biblical Hebrew hardly support these generalizations. Thus, Arnold and Choi (2003:47f) offer four basic, and hardly related, meanings of the *hitpaʿel*: reflexive, reciprocal, iterative, and denominative. Similarly, on the *piʿel*, they endorse Joosten's conclusions (1998: 227) that the various functions of the *piʿel* simply cannot be reduced to one underlying function. However, it is still hard to break out from the comforting generalization of Gesenius-Kautzsche (1910, §52f) that "the fundamental idea of *piʿel*, to which all the various shades of meaning in this conjugation may be referred, is to *busy oneself eagerly* with the action." It is this kind of generalization that has left the deepest mark on *ʿivrit* teaching in the modern era.

Meanwhile, in Israeli Hebrew, the status of roots and *binyanim* is even more problematic. A number of factors have been at work. First, Israeli Hebrew drew on a lexicon laid down over two millennia of continued change, and has gone on to add to it frenetically. Second, borrowing and loan-translation from related or unrelated languages has massively enriched the mixture, further diluting the semantic identity of the root, some examples: *shakhaḥ* "forget" and (from Aramaic) *shakhiaḥ* "frequent"; *geshem* "rain" and (from Aramaic) *gashmi* "material"; *tipes* "climb," *tofes* "form," and (from Greek) *tipusi* "typical"; *nakhon* "correct," *makhon* "institute," and (echoing the European word for "machine") *mekhona* "machine"; *kaf* "spoon" and (from Arabic) *kef* "fun," *kiyef* "have fun." Third, changes in pronunciation have obscured old connections between words. New Israeli pronunciation norms disregard various distinctions that were part of the medieval Tiberian pointing rules, such as single versus doubled consonants (the *dagesh ḥazaq*) and the vowels *qamats* versus *pataḥ*, and the student is equally unlikely to be aware of them on the printed page. As a result, many of the cues to old root identities have been lost, affecting hundreds of words. Note, for example, the verbs *lehaziq* "to harm" and *lehaziz* "to shift." As pronounced today they would appear to belong to the same verbal pattern and thus to the same type of root. But, in fact, most grammar books, mindful of the Tiberian pointing rules, derive *lehaziq* from the root n-z-q and *lehaziz* from the root z-u-z. Similarly, the nouns *mashav* "draft" and *teshuvah* "response" would be derived by the dictionaries from n-sh-v and sh-u-v respectively. I shall return to this issue shortly.

One might add that even more fundamental changes in Hebrew pronunciation have taken place, wiping out several ancient consonantal distinctions (such as *sin/samekh* and *quf/kaf*) and thus conflating hundreds of roots in the spoken language. But since these distinctions are still retained in writing they can be regarded as not affecting the teaching of the Hebrew root to any serious extent.

How, then, is the teacher to present the Israeli Hebrew root and its associated patterns of vowels and affixes (*binyanim* and *mishqalim*)? It might appear self-evident that the teacher should present a realistic picture of the type of Israeli Hebrew that the student wishes to learn. But what kind of reality do they have? It is clear that all verbs are constructed on a skeleton of consonants (a "root") and that *piqadti, mefaqed, afaqed* "to command" share the same root p-q-d. But do *hifqadti, mafqid, afqid* "to deposit" also share that same root p-q-d? In terms of formal grammar, they surely do, but in semantic terms this seems to be doubtful.

It is instructive to compare the Hebrew root-and-*binyan* system to the Latin-based prefix-and-stem system in English. As we can note in the use of stems such as *-vent, -nounce, -fect* and prefixes such as *in-, per-, pre-, re-* as in *invent, prevent, circumvent; announce, denounce, renounce;* and *infect, defect, perfect, affect,* there is clearly a formal-grammatical pattern. This is what enables English speakers to build sets of derived words in fairly regular fashion, e.g., *invention, prevention, circumvention.* However, one can detect little if any *semantic* identity in these prefixes or stems (unlike, perhaps, their Latin ancestors). At the same time, English has a second, smaller set of prefixes that have a very clear and consistent meaning and that can be prefixed fairly freely to verbs (rather than to mere stems) with quite predictable semantic effect. Two examples are *re-* in the sense of "again" and *pre-* in the sense of "prior": "deploy/redeploy," "fashion/refashion" and "package/prepackage," "board /pre-board." As we shall see, the Hebrew root-and-*binyan* system has similarities to both the prefix-and-stem and the prefix-and-verb system of English.

Indicators of linguistic reality are of two main kinds: direct, using the actual data of the language, and indirect, using psycholinguistic experimentation. Language data, in turn, must be handled with care. Are they sociolinguistically representative of formal Hebrew or casual Hebrew? Do they need to be statistically weighted to mirror common usage? And—a question that probably does not have direct bearing on language teaching—do they represent productive trends or are they "fossilized"?

The data for Modern Hebrew show very clearly that the root plays a major role as a grammatical formative. Indeed, the verbal system is constrained to use the root—every Hebrew verb form is a combination of a root and *binyan* affixes. The same is true for a large proportion of adjectives and nouns, combining roots and so-called *mishqal* affixes. One can sometimes even see *semantic* roots being created productively, with clear and consistent meanings, in the extraction of the consonants from some nouns to coin new verbs. Thus, *maqom* "place" yields m-q-m to create a verb *miqem* "to locate," *torpedo* yields t-r-p-d to create the verb *tirped* "to torpedo," *pnim* "interior" yields p-n-m to make a verb *hifnim* "to internalize." At the same time, a sizable part of the noun inventory—and a small part of the adjective inventory—is not built around roots at all. I am referring, first and foremost, to the large number of non-Semitic loans (e.g., *traqtor, musiqah, debili, shateni*), but also to native words. A few examples out of hundreds are: *av, em, tsafon, tsalaḥat, delet, rosh.* It should be added that where a noun has been subjected to affixation, e.g., *delet ~ dalti,* it may be better to speak of a stem + affix (*delet* + i) rather than a root d-l-t.

The picture for the contemporary Hebrew root is thus mixed and reminiscent of the situation for English: semantic identity in parts and purely grammatical identity elsewhere.

Statistics for the meaningfulness of the *binyanim* have been reported by Ornan (1979), using Even-Shoshan's Modern Hebrew dictionary—though without any sociolingustic discrimination or weighting for frequency. What he found concerning the *pi'el* and the *hif'il* is of particular significance. Taking all *binyan qal* verbs, starting with the letters lamed, mem, and nun (n = 257), he found that two thirds had a counterpart *pi'el* verb from the same root. Of these, no less than 40 percent had the same meaning in *qal* as in *pi'el*; for a further 29 percent, the *pi'el* verb had a totally unrelated sense. This left just 31 percent of the *qal-pi'el* pairs related by a semantic modulation of any sort. And this 31 percent broke down into 18 percent causative (e.g., *lamad~limed*), 5 percent intensive (e.g., *nafats~nipets*), and 3 percent multiple actions. Thus, of 257 *binyan qal* verbs, just eight or nine had an intensive *pi'el* counterpart. To test for the *hif'il*, Ornan took all *qal* and *hif'il* verbs with an initial root *alef*, 118 in total. Just half of them provided a *qal~hif'il* pair, and of these just one quarter involved a causative (i.e., *hif'il* as causative of *qal*). Thus, giving all the verbs in the Even-Shoshan Dictionary equal weight, the chances are low that a given *hif'il* verb will be the causative of a *qal* verb (of the same root). I would add that the *hif'il* is occasionally causative of a *nif'al* verb, e.g., *nikhn'a ~hikhni'a, ne'elam~he'elim,* but this does not improve the chances by much. Ornan's findings are hardly an endorsement of what so many students are taught.

On the other hand, a study of high-frequency verbs (Schwarzwald, 1981) found that most of the *binyanim* indeed frequently had clear and consistent meaning. Another kind of study by Bolozky (1978), based on new coinages and word-coining experiments, also suggested that ordinary Israelis do feel that most *binyanim* have meaning. But the key phrase is "most *binyanim*." This applies to the *nif'al*, *hif'il*, *huf'al*, *pu'al*, and *hitpa'el*, but not to the *qal* and *pi'el*.

Ignoring the semantic issues entirely and focusing on how to teach the morphological minefield of Hebrew inflections as logically as possible, Ornan proposed a radical new phonologically based framework as early as 1978.

Drawing upon the available research on Modern Hebrew usage, I summarized the role of the root and the *binyanim* in my full reference grammar (Glinert, 1989: 459ff.) and then again—in a form more accessible to learners—in Glinert 2005 (Ch. 24–32):

1. Many roots have a well-defined meaning, holding across several *binyanim* and *mishqalim*. An example is r-t-v in *ratuv* "wet" (adj.), *rotev* "gravy," *nirtav* "get wet," *hirtiv* "make wet," *hitratev* "get wet." As mentioned earlier, however, any root is liable to yield words whose relationship to the root meaning is blurry, possibly for the speaker as well as for the analyst. Thus, one wonders if the Israeli speaker connects *rotev* "sauce" to *ratuv*, any more than an English speaker connects "fed up" to "to feed" (even though Israeli speakers, faced with an unfamiliar word, have been shown to plumb their knowledge of root meanings in an attempt to interpret the word).

2. Many roots do not have one well-defined meaning. One meaning may hold across two or three *binyanim* or *mishqalim* while in others quite different or related but unpredictable meanings may be present (see Even-Shoshan's *Yalqut ha-Shorashim*, an appendix to his *Hamilon Hehadash*, bearing in mind that Even-Shoshan includes a large number of words that are now obsolete or recherché). An example is b-sh-l: *bishel* "to cook," *hitbashel* "become cooked," *tavshil* "dish" versus *bashel* "mature, ripe," *hivshil* "ripen," and *hitbashel* "to mature."

3. Most of the *binyanim* are meaningful, but just for some roots, and always as part of a relationship with another *binyan* or *mishqal*. The main meanings are:
    –   *nif'al* as the passive of *qal*
    –   *hif'il* as the causative of *qal*
    –   *hif'il* as the inchoative ("becoming") of an adjective (e.g. *hishmin* ~ *shamen*)
    –   *huf'al* (almost automatically) as the passive of *hif'il*
    –   *pi'el* expressing "doing something to some object" (e.g. *qilef* ~ *qlipa*)

— *pu'al* (almost automatically) as the passive of *pi'el*
— *hitpa'el* as the intransitive of *pi'el* (e.g., *hishtalem* ~ *shilem*)
— *hitpa'el* as the inchoative of *qal* or an adjective (e.g., *hityashev* ~ *yashav*,
     hitqarev ~ *qarov*)

In comparison to these last two uses of *hitpa'el*, the reflexive *hitpa'el* is statistically less important. Furthermore, none of these semantic relationships is limited to one *binyan*. Thus, for "reciprocal" we may find *pi'el* ~ *hitpa'el* or *qal* ~ *nif'al* (e.g., *pagash* ~ *nifgash*). Similarly, for intransitive versus transitive we may find *hitpa'el* ~ *pi'el* or *qal* ~ *hif'il* (e.g., *qatan* "become smaller" ~ *hiqtin* "make smaller").

A further constraint on the use of the root in teaching Hebrew—and again, one that many teachers and textbooks are reluctant to confront in its contemporary realities—is the formal obscurity of some root types (the traditional "weak *gzarot*"). By "formal," I mean the grammatical form of the root as opposed to its semantics.

Consider the so-called *peh-nun* roots. *hipil* "drop," *hapalah* "abortion," *mapal* "fall," and *mapolet* "landslide" are justifiably derived from n-f-l, given the existence of *nafal* "fall." Similarly *hisi'a* "drive (someone)," *hasa'ah* "lift," *masa'* "journey" are from the same root as *nasa'* "travel." But what about *hibit, higia', hikir, hitir, lehagid*? There is no related verb or noun with an initial nun (the semantic connection between *hibit* and *nevatim* or between *higia'* and *naga'* is a remote one) and, indeed, Israeli speakers do not feel that these verbs have *peh-nun* roots, despite what most dictionaries say about them. Might it not be better to treat them as having two-letter roots? True, this goes against the instincts of anyone brought up in the spirit of *diqduq*, but this is a small and steadily decreasing band of brothers. The sociolinguistic reality is that the overwhelming mass of Hebrew speakers just learns a word like *hikir* or *mabat* "as is"—without any theory of a dropped letter nun—which is no doubt why even educated people often alternate between *makir* and *mekir* and between *mevin* and *mavin*. It behooves the foreign-language teacher to respect sociolinguistic realities, particularly when they make for simpler teaching (as they so often do).

Many grammatically trained teachers, of course, will object that we need to posit an initial nun in *hikir* or *hibit*, in order to explain the *dagesh* in the *kaf* and the *bet*. To which I would respond: Does any teacher seriously use this kind of argument to explain the *dagesh* in *yikanes, yitapes*? We just teach it "as is."

This same disregard for roots guides us when we teach the *'ivrit* noun. No one worries over the root of *ribah* "jelly" or *gvinah* "cheese," and no one asks if *maraq* relates to *lemareq* "to scour" or *basar* to *levaser* "to announce." The *dagesh* in the inflections *tsahov* ~ *tsehubah* and *dov* ~ *dubah* is just taught as "one of those things," and the same should apply to all those nouns that the grammar books once upon a time obscurely derived from double-letter roots, such as *ḥoq*, *kol* (classically from ḥ-q-q, k-l-l).

Sociolinguistic training (call it "social realism") and sheer loyalty to the contemporary goals of language teaching must, therefore, be a top priority today for Hebrew educators. The old grammatical ways of thinking are still holding on tenaciously and must be confronted. To think about Hebrew in the way we think about English is not a threat to the language. To rethink our roots and *binyanim* can only provide a more solid and honest foundation for the Hebrew learner.

References

Arnold, B. and J. Choi, 2003. *A Guide to Biblical Hebrew Syntax.* New York: Cambridge University Press.

Band, O. 1983. *Ivrit Shalav Gimal.* Behrman House.

Bolozky, S. 1978. Word formation strategies in the Hebrew verb system: denominative verbs. *Afroasiatic Linguistics* 5: 111–136.

Celce-Muria, M. (ed.) 1991. *Teaching English as a Second or Foreign Language.* Boston: Heinle and Heinle.

Chayat, S., S. Israeli, and H. Kobliner. 1990. *Ivrit min ha-hathalah.* Jerusalem: Academon.

Chomsky, W. (translator and editor) 1952. *David Kimhi's Hebrew Grammar (Mikhlol),* New York: Bloch Publishing Company.

Coffin, E. 1992. *Encounters in Modern Hebrew.* University of Michigan Press.

Fruchtmann, M. 2006. *ha-'ivrit ha-meduberet: hebetim umegamot (skira). Hed HaUlpan HeHadash* 89.

Gesenius, W. 1910. *Gesenius' Hebrew Grammar edited and enlarged by the late E. Kautzsche.* 2nd English ed. revised in accordance with the twenty-eighth German ed. 1909 by A. E. Cowley. Oxford: The Clarendon Press.

Glinert, L. 1979. Linguistics and language teaching: The implications for modern Hebrew. *Hebrew Annual Review 3:* 105–127.

———— . 1989. *The Grammar of Modern Hebrew.* Cambridge: Cambridge University Press.

———— . 1994. Modern Hebrew lexicography: The last hundred years. *Jewish Book Annual* 52: 37–58.

———— . 2005. *Modern Hebrew: An Essential Grammar.* New York: Routledge, 3rd ed.

Joosten, J. 1998. The functions of the semitic D stem: Biblical Hebrew materials for a comparative-historical approach. *Orientalia* 67: 202–230.

Ornan, U. 1978. *netiyat ha-po'al keytsad*. *Orahot* 10: 47–68.

——————— . 1979. *od al hora'ot ha-binyanim*. In C. Rabin and B-Z.Fischler (Eds.) *Kodesh Jubilee Volume*. Jerusalem: Council on the Teaching of Hebrew.

Rabin, C. 1983. The sociology of normativism in Israeli Hebrew. *International Journal of the Sociology of Language 41*: 41–56.

Ringvald, V. et al. 2003. *Brandeis Modern Hebrew*. Waltham, Mass.: Brandeis University Press.

Schwartzwald, O. 1981. *Dikduk u-metsi'ut ba-poal ha-ivri*. Ramat Gan: Bar-Ilan University Press.

לוֹ שֶׁל הַגַּל קוֹרֵ׳
תוֹ – שֶׁאָבוֹא אָנִי
ז בְּרֹאשׁוֹ, וְהֵכִינוּ ז
ּוֹת, אָמֵן אָמֵן סֶלָה׳׳

THE ACQUISITION OF
VERBAL MORPHOLOGY IN
FIRST AND SECOND LANGUAGES

Sharon Armon-Lotem

University of Maryland

THE ACQUISITION of the Hebrew verbal system, with all its conjugations and inflections, poses a challenge for learners of Hebrew as a second or foreign language, whereas the acquisition of Hebrew as a first language does not. This article examines how children acquire verbal morphology in the natural setting for first and second language, that is, when a child is exposed to the language and no instruction is involved. Comparing Hebrew and English, this essay discusses the similarities and differences between first- and second-language acquisition of different languages and discusses possible implications for language teaching.

First-language acquisition involves some innate knowledge of what is possible in human languages. This knowledge helps children to decipher and acquire the language they are exposed to. Within the generative tradition (Chomsky 1986; Crain 1991; Pinker 1984, among others) this innate knowledge is referred to as Universal Grammar (UG). The question of whether the process of second-language acquisition is similar to that of first-language acquisition boils down to the question of access to this kind of knowledge by second-language learners.

Three hypotheses for second-language acquisition have different views of the relation between the first language (L1) of the second language learner and the target (second) language (L2). According to the Full Transfer/No Access (FT/NA) hypothesis, no aspect of Universal Grammar (UG) is available to the learner of a second language (cf. Bley-Vroman 1989; Clahsen 1988). This makes the two processes totally distinct. The second-language learner has to rely only on her knowledge of L1 and on some learning strategies. Since UG is not available to the learner, similarities to the process of first-language acquisition will be viewed as artifacts, which might reflect the influence of L1, rather than evidence for access to UG. The No Transfer/Full Access (NT/FA) hypothesis for second-language acquisition (e.g., Epstein, Flynn, and Martohardjono 1996) suggests that UG in full constrains L2 acquisition, whereas L1 does not affect the process. These assumptions entail a similar course of acquisition for L1 and L2.

The findings discussed in this essay comply with neither Full Transfer/No Access nor No Transfer/Full Access, but rather with the third hypothesis: Full Transfer/Full Access (FT/FA). Proponents of the Full Transfer/Full Access hypothesis (cf. Eubank 1994; Schwartz and Sprouse 1996) assume that rules of L1 grammar constitute the initial state for the L2 learner. However, UG is accessed in L2 acquisition in order to move from this initial state to the target L2 grammar. The duality of FT/FA predicts that the development of the grammar of English as L2 will follow a similar path to the one seen in the development of English as L1. Any divergence from this path necessarily is attributed to the L1 influence. Moreover, all intermediate grammars of the L2 learner should conform with UG, being possible grammars of human languages.

Since this article follows the reasoning of the third hypothesis, we will be looking at first- and second-language acquisition of Hebrew and English. The focus on Hebrew makes it necessary to start with a background on the Hebrew verbal system. Next, we will compare children's acquisition of verbal inflections in Hebrew as a first language to English. This will be followed by a description of children's acquisition of verbal inflection in English as a second language. The essay concludes with a discussion of the predictions for the acquisition of verbal inflection in Hebrew as a second language.

Hebrew Verbal System in a Nutshell

Hebrew verbs are constructed in one of five morphological patterns, called *binyan* conjugations. Each *binyan* conjugation associates prefixes, as well as interdigited vowels, with a set of root consonants. Table 1 shows the distribution of two verb roots, *g-d-l* "grow" and *k-t-v* "write," across five verb patterns.

Some of these patterns are associated with particular functions, such as, reflexivity (*hitpa'el*) or causativity (*hif'il*). However, there are numerous lexical gaps and semantic inconsistencies between *binyan* form and function in Modern Hebrew, setting this system in the domain of word-formation (derivational morphology) rather than grammatical inflection.

TABLE 1: THE DISTRIBUTION OF TWO VERB ROOTS
ACROSS FIVE VERB PATTERNS

Pattern	*g-d-l*	Gloss	*k-t-v*	Gloss
P1 *pa'al*	*gadal*	"grow, Intr"	*katav*	"write"
P2 *nif'al*	—	—	*nikhtav*	"be/get written"
P3 *pi'el*	*gidel*	"grow, Trans"	*kitev*	"captionize"
P4 *hitpa'el*	*hitgadel*	"self-aggrandize"	*hitkatev*	"correspond"
P5 *hif'il*	*higdil*	"enlarge"	*hikhtiv*	"dictate"

Some of these patterns are associated with particular functions, such as, reflexivity (*hitpa'el*) or causativity (*hif'il*). However, there are numerous lexical gaps and semantic inconsistencies between *binyan* form and function in Modern Hebrew, setting this system in the domain of word-formation (derivational morphology) rather than grammatical inflection.

Hebrew verbs are also inflected for five mood/tense categories:

1. Infinitives are marked by a prefixal *l-*, which takes a different vowel depending on the nature of the following syllable (*li-, la-,* or *le-*).

2. Imperative forms are historically based on future tense stems, but children generally use the forms common in everyday colloquial usage, a future stem without the 2nd-person *t-*prefix (Berman 1985; Bolozky 1979).

3. Present tense verbs that are also participial.

4. Past tense verbs.

5. Future tense verbs.

Table 2 shows the alternation of verbs across the five categories of mood/tense. The examples in Table 2 show verbs in the three *binyan* patterns with highest frequency of usage, in adults' and children's speech. The three "finite" forms—present, past, and future—are listed in the morphologically simplest form of masculine singular, 3rd person.

In addition to these tense/mood alternations, finite forms and the imperative, which is derived from the future tense, are also marked for agreement. Verbs in the present tense and the imperative agree with their subjects in

TABLE 2: ALTERNATION OF VERBS
ACROSS FIVE CATEGORIES OF MOOD/TENSE

Root	Pattern	Gloss	Infinite	Imper-ative	Present	Past	Future
g-m-r	P1 *pa'al*	"finish"	*ligmor*	*gmor*	*gomer*	*gamar*	*yigmor*
t-q-n	P3 *pi'el*	"fix"	*letaken*	*taken*	*metaken*	*tiken*	*yetaken*
g-d-l	P5 *hif'il*	"enlarge"	*lehagdil*	*hagdel*	*magdil*	*higdil*	*yagdil*

number and gender. This yields four forms per verb. For example, in the present tense, masculine singular has a zero morpheme, feminine singular is marked with unstressed -*et,* masculine plural with stressed -*im,* and feminine plural stressed -*ot.* Verbs in past tense and future tense agree with their subjects in number, gender, and person. This yields up to nine forms per verb. For example, in past tense affixes are added to the masculine singular stem: -*ti* 1st singular, -*ta* 2nd masculine singular, -*t* 2nd feminine singular, -*a* 3rd feminine singular, -*nu* 1st plural, -*tem* 2nd masculine plural, -*ten* 2nd feminine plural, and -*u* 3rd person.

Children's Acquisition of Verbal Inflections in Hebrew as a First Language

Children acquiring Hebrew as a first or second language should master both the derivational morphology—the *binyan* conjugations—and the inflectional morphology—the tenses and agreement patterns. This essay offers a comparative analysis of the acquisition of Hebrew as a first language and the acquisition of English as a second language. It focuses on the common denominator, the inflectional morphology, showing how the acquisition of this chunk of knowledge follows similar patterns in first- and second-language acquisition across languages.

The acquisition of verbal morphology starts with the earliest verbs. Berman and Armon-Lotem (1996), in a study of the twenty earliest verbs of six Hebrew-speaking children prior to their second birthday, show that early verb usage is characterized by unclear forms or aspectually limited use of particular verbs. Phonetically, most forms are reduced, non-adult forms, e.g., *tse* for *rotse* "want," *ito* for *lištot* "to drink." Syntactically, over 80 percent of the verbal forms look like infinitives without the infinitival morpheme *le-* "to." Past forms are used only with perfective actions, e.g., *fal* for *nafal* "fell," and present tense forms are used for durative actions, e.g., _khel_ for _okhel_ "eating." Morphologically, all non-infinitival forms are singular, with some nonproductive variation between masculine and feminine forms, e.g., _khi_ "you, feminine, take" is used both for female and male addressees. Finally, there is no overt person morphology on the verbs.

Armon-Lotem (1996) analyzed the acquisition of verbal morphology by toddlers aged eighteen to twenty-four months. She found that the first morphological knowledge children manifest is subject-verb agreement in gender (and sometimes number). Gender is the prevalent grammatical feature in the verbal and nominal systems. This knowledge is applied, in a limited fashion, to third-person forms in the present tense and second person in the imperative. Initially, this is a formulaic rather than a productive use, which shows no agreement with the subject, using a verb with feminine inflections for a masculine subject and vice versa. Soon, however, the child converges on the grammatical use of gender.

In our research sessions, Smadar, an eighteen-month-old girl, started using gender marking equally for masculine and feminine. This was mainly in the imperative, with one past form in the default 3rd-person masculine. For the first few sessions, it was a formulaic rather than a productive use, which showed no agreement with the subject. Within the next month, Smadar's use of gender agreement extended to five imperative forms, as shown below:

1. _sim / sími_   "put!" (ms. / fm.)
   kaḥ / khi   "take!" (ms. / fm.)
   vi / abí'i   "give (me)! bring!" (ms. / fm.)
   ten / tni   "give!" (ms. / fm.) and
   šev / švi   "sit!" (ms. / fm.)   [Smadar 19 mos.]

FIGURE 1: BREAKDOWN OF GENDER AND NUMBER

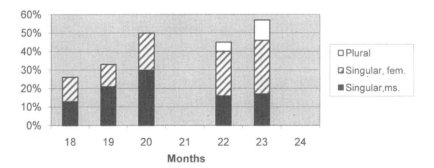

Thus, the imperative, in which second person is the default, already seems adult-like with gender and number morphology, e.g., *zuz/zuzi/zuzu* "move!" (sg. ms. / sg. fm. / pl.) [Lior 19 mos.]. Another girl, Lior, at eighteen months and thirteen days, showed similar alternations in the imperative, as well as a possible alternation in the present tense form *pes*(?) / *péset* "climbs" (ms.(?)/ fm.); and a month later (nineteen months and sixteen days) Lior also used present tense *bokhé* / *bokhá* "cries" (ms. / fm.). Since person is not marked in Hebrew present tense, children appear to use these forms properly at this point. However, the forms they use are still aspectually limited, i.e., the same verbs do not occur in the past form.

About a month after gender is used productively, a sharp increase in the use of past and present tense forms is observed. For example, whereas Smadar at age nineteen months used only one form of the verb "eat," at twenty-two months the same verb shoed the following breakdown:

2. *le'ekhol* "to eat," *okhélet* "eating" (sg., fm.), *akhá(l)ti* "I ate," *tokhlí* "you will eat" (fm.), also colloquial imperative "eat!"

Figure 2 shows the breakdown for tense/mood categories in Smadar's verb usage at this point for the three major classes of forms she used: unclear forms, irrealis forms, which combine infinitives and imperatives, and finite forms, which combine present, past, and future. Figure 2 reveals an explosion of finite forms (mainly present and past) at age twenty to twenty-two months.

FIGURE 2: BREAKDOWN OF TENSE/MOOD

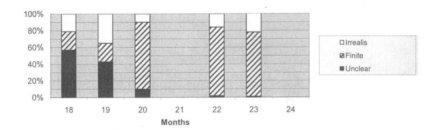

A comparison of the use of unclear forms, irrealis forms (infinitives and imperatives), and finite forms (present, past, and future) shows a remarkable change. This increase in tensed forms correlates with a decrease in the percentage of unclear forms. For example, at age nineteen months tensed forms constituted only 22 percent of Smadar's verbal forms, and these were aspectually limited, whereas one month later, by age twenty months, and especially at age twenty-two months, tensed forms constituted 80 percent of her verbal forms (45 out of 55), and unclear forms were very few. That these verbs indicated tense rather than (lexical) aspect was evident by the use of the same lexeme both in past and present tense, as well as by the use of durative verbs in the past and unaccusative (perfective) verbs in the present tense.

The last acquisition during this period is of first- and second-person marking. For the first few months, though agreement in gender and number, as well as tense, are acquired, children make only a sporadic use of person agreement. Figure 3 gives the breakdown for first, second, and third person in Smadar's verb usage during the same period. Though verbs are inflected for number in Hebrew, for ease of presentation, we have combined the categories of number and person, neutralizing for number so that person applies to both singular and plural (the equivalent of both "I" and "we," and so on for 2nd and 3rd person, as well). This seemed legitimate since the children generally used few plural forms and the pattern is not substantially affected by separating out the category of number.

FIGURE 3: BREAKDOWN OF PERSON

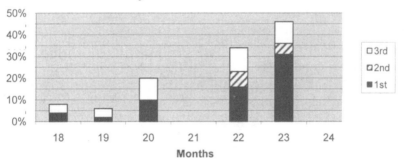

Smadar, for example, used first-person singular in the past, once per month over the first three months in what looks like rote-learned forms (Berman 1986), whereas Lior used just one verb in second person in the past tense: *asit* "made," for the first two months, adding one more verb in the second person over the next two months. Lior used both *asit* and *(na)falt*, which have second-person morphology, to refer to herself in a first-person sense. However, by twenty-three months, person became a robust phenomenon that was used productively, and second person was used with the proper referent, as shown below for the verb "finish":

> 3. *gamárti* "I finished," *gamárta* "you finished" (ms.), *gamart* "you finished" (fm.), *gamárnu* "we finished" [Lior 23 mos.].

By acquiring person inflection, children complete the acquisition of the inflectional verbal morphology of Hebrew. There are many irregularities in the verb forms that they still have to master, but none of them involves different inflections.

Figure 4 shows that the order of acquisition of the three inflectional categories that are morphologically marked in Hebrew verbs—gender/number, tense/mood, and person—is the same for all the children studied.

Moving away from early verb usage, for each of the children gender marking was the first to emerge. This was followed by an explosion of tensed forms marking tense/mood distinctions; whereas (past tense) suffixes and (future tense) prefixes marking first person in contrast to second and third person are the last to be acquired.

FIGURE 4: AGE OF ACQUISITION OF AGREEMENT
AND TENSE/MOOD INFLECTION

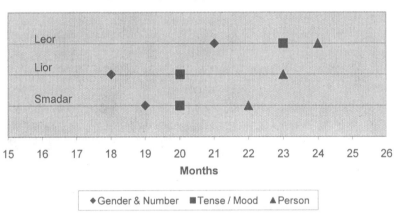

Children's Acquisition of Verbal Inflections in English as a Second Language

Brown (1973) reports a similar order for English as a first language. He asserts that English-speaking children first acquire the progressive -ing and then the perfective -ed. They use the third-person marker -s only after auxiliary verbs appear. But are we to expect similar order for English second-language acquisition? Would the order discussed for Hebrew as a first language be relevant for the acquisition of Hebrew as a second language? What in the acquisition of English as a second language is relevant for the acquisition of Hebrew as a second language? Are similarities to be expected in L2 acquisition of different languages, as is the case for L1 acquisition?

As a start, in this section the acquisition of inflectional morphology in English as a second language is shown to take a similar route to the acquisition of this system in English as a first language, as described by Brown (1973) and others. Moreover, as suggested above, this seems to be the same route proposed for the acquisition of Hebrew as a first language in the previous section. This crosslinguistic similarity between first- and second-language acquisition seems to support at least some access to universal grammar in second-language acquisition, enabling us, in the conclusion, to make predictions for the acquisition of Hebrew as a second language.

A study of two children, aged 5 and 7, acquiring English as a second language (Armon-Lotem 1997) focuses on the acquisition of the English verbal morphology. When the children started using verbs, after three month of exposure to English in the United States, their early verbs consisted of over 80 percent infinitival forms, as below:

(4) a. *I go*   for   *I went*
    b. *He go*   for   *He goes*

This kind of utterance, which contains root infinitives (Rizzi 1994; Wexler 1994)—i.e., infinitival forms in root, matrix, sentences—has been widely studied for first- and second-language acquisition, suggesting many similarities between the two processes (see Haznedar and Schwartz [1997]; Prevot [1997] among others). None of the monosyllabic unclear verbal forms found in L1 acquisition shows in L2 acquisition, since the phonological limitations of L1 learners are irrelevant for somewhat older L2 learners. The remaining 20 percent of early verbs are rote-learned past forms that are used equally for past and present. At this point, as in first-language acquisition of English, there are no auxiliaries and no modals.

Since gender and number are not available in English verbal morphology, the first and major change over the first six months in the child's acquisition of English as a second language is a marked growth in the use of past forms in past context. Figure 5 gives the breakdown for past forms versus irrealis (nonfinite) forms in past tense context over a period of six months. The analysis is limited to past tense, since the only way to distinguish tensed from untensed forms in the present tense is by person morphology, which shows up later.

Though past forms are used from the first month, Figure 5 shows an increase in the use of past forms in the past tense, from 36 percent in the first month to 72 percent in the sixth month. This growth is similar to what we found for the acquisition of Hebrew as a first language.

FIGURE 5: USE OF PAST TENSE IN PAST CONTEXTS IN L2 ACQUISITION

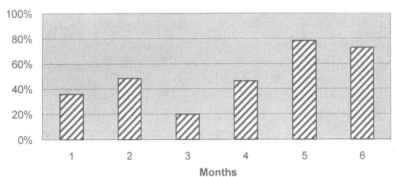

Whereas tense stabilizes by the end of the sixth month, person continues to be used sporadically, far into the end of the first year. This follows the pattern noted earlier for first-language acquisition. Just as person is the last distinction to be acquired both in Hebrew and in English as L1s, so is third person in the present tense the last to be acquired in acquiring English as a second language. In sum, a similar course of acquisition of verbal inflections emerges for first and second language of English and for first-language acquisition of Hebrew, in which unclear tenseless forms are replaced by tensed forms before person morphology emerges.

Predictions for the Acquisition of Verbal Inflection in Hebrew as a Second Language

These similarities show the relevance of a crosslinguistic study of the acquisition of verbal inflections, and make it possible to predict the acquisition of verbal morphology in Hebrew as L2. This concluding section has a more stipulative nature and opens the way for further research, since it tries to predict the course of natural acquisition of Hebrew as a second language by children, as well as discuss possible implications for Hebrew instruction in the classroom. Children who acquire a second language are not subjected to the same phonological limitations that show in first language. Thus any monosyllabic unclear verbal forms are not expected, as was found for the English L2 learners. However, assuming that children's earliest verbs should resemble the phase of early verb usage, infinitival forms, as in (5a), and agreement errors, as in (5b), are expected:

(5) a. *ani lalekhet* "I to go"
    b. *hi nafal* "she fell" (m.)

Moving beyond this phase, subject-verb agreement in gender should emerge, making distinctions both in present tense forms, as in (6a), and in past tense forms, as in (6b):

(6) a. *okhel* "is eating" (m.) versus *okhelet* "is eating" (fm.)
    b. *nafal* "fell" (m.)   versus   *nafla* "fell" (fm.)

Plural marking might show up at the same time, but the same verb will not be inflected both for past and present tense during this period.

After gender and number morphology stabilizes, an extensive use of past and present forms is expected. During this phase, paradigms like *hu akhal* "he ate" versus *hu okhel* "he eats" will emerge, but errors like (5b) will persist. Finally, first- and second-person morphology will emerge, creating full paradigm for each verb. Verifying these predictions is beyond the scope of this paper.

How is all this relevant for second-language teaching? Should language learners be exposed to partial paradigms following the naturalistic production or should they be exposed to full paradigms as is the natural learner? Research on second-language learning suggests that generalizations of learning take place in the direction of the less-marked structure. Eckman, Bell, and Nelson (1988) showed that, for relative clauses, teaching more complex relative clauses (according to Keenan and Comrie's [1977] hierarchy), such as those modifying an indirect object, facilitates the use of less complex ones, such as those modifying a subject or a direct object, but not vice versa. This argues for introducing the richer data. The full paradigm carries more information about the inflectional system, but is it parsable information for a beginning learner?

These deliberations are only food for thought. There is no conclusive proposal in this article for teaching the verbal morphology of Hebrew as a foreign language. This essay merely shows what seems to be more accessible in natural acquisition of languages. If it is more accessible in natural acqui-sition, it might be the same for learners of Hebrew as a foreign language, but checking this is subject for future research.

References

Armon-Lotem, S. 1996. "A Parametric Approach to Functional Heads and the Acquisition of Hebrew." Ph.D. dissertation. Tel Aviv University.

————— . 1997. "Root Infinitives in Child Second Language Acquisition." In S. Montrul and R. Slabakova, eds., *GASLA "97 Proceedings, McGill Working Papers in Linguistics*. Montreal: McGill University.

Berman, R.A. 1985. "Acquisition of Hebrew." In D.I. Slobin, ed. Pp. 255–371.

————. 1986. "A Step-by-Step Model of Language Learning." In I. Levin, ed., *Stage and Structure: Re-opening the Debate*. Norwood, N.J.: Ablex. Pp. 191–219.

Berman, R.A. and S. Armon-Lotem. 1997. "How Grammatical Are Early Verbs?" In *Les Annales Littéraires de l'Université de Besançon*. Besancon, France.

Bley-Vroman, R. 1989. "What Is the Logical Problem of Foreign Language Learning." In J. Schachter and S. Gass, eds., *Linguistic Perspectives on Second Language Acquisition*. Cambridge: Cambridge University Press.

Bolozky, S. 1979. "The New Imperative in Colloquial Hebrew," *Hebrew Annual Review* 3: 17–24.

Brown, R. 1973. *A First Language: The Early Stages*. Cambridge: Harvard University Press.

Chomsky, N. 1986. *Knowledge of Language*. New York: Prager.

Clahsen, H. 1988. "Parameterized Grammatical Theory and Language Acquisition: A Study of the Acquisition of Verb Placement and Inflection by Children and Adults." In S. Flynn and W. O'Neil, eds., *Linguistic Theory in Second Language Acquisition*. Kluwer.

Crain, S. 1991. "Language Acquisition in the Absence of Experience," *Behavioral and Brain Sciences* 14: 597–650.

Eckman, F., L. Bell and D. Nelson. 1988. "On the Generalization of Relative Clause Instruction in the Acquisition of English as a Second Language," *Applied Linguistics* 9: 1–20.

Epstein, S.D., S. Flynn, and G. Martohardjono. 1996. *Second Language Acquisition: Theoretical and Experimental Issues in Contemporary Research*. Behavioral and Brain Sciences. Cambridge University Press.

Eubank, L. 1994. "Optionality and the 'Initial State' in L2 Development." In T. Hoekstra and B. Schwartz, eds., *Language Acquisition Studies in Generative Grammar*. Amsterdam: John Benjamins Publishing Co.

Haznedar, B., and B.D. Schwartz. 1997. "Are There Optional Infinitives in Child L2 Acquisition?" *BUCLD* 21.

Keenan, E. and B. Comrie. 1977. "Noun Phrase Accessibility and Universal Grammar," *Linguistic Inquiry* 8: 63–99.

Pinker, S. 1984. *Language Learnability and Language Development*. Cambridge, Mass.: Harvard University Press.

Prevost, P. 1997. "Truncation in Second Language Acquisition." Ph.D. dissertation. McGill University.

Rizzi, L. 1994. "Early Null Subjects and Root Null Subjects." In Hoekstra and Schwartz. Pp. 151–76.

Schwartz, B. and R. Sprouse. 1996. L2 Cognitive States and the Full Transfer/Full Access Model. *Second Language Research* 12.

Wexler, K. 1994. "Optional Infinitives, Head Movement and the Economy of Derivation in Child Grammar." In D. Lightfoot and N. Hornstein, eds., *Verb Movement*. Cambridge, Mass.: Cambridge University Press.

לוֹ שֶׁל הַגֹּל קוֹרֶ׃
תוֹ – שֶׁאָבוֹא אֲנִי

ד

ז בְּרֹאשׁוֹ, וְהָכִּינוּ ז
 וֹת, אָמֵן אָמֵן סֶלָה״

GRAMMAR IN THE CLASSROOM
THE CASE OF ISRAELI HEBREW

Shmuel Bolozky
University of Massachusetts/Amherst

MOST TEACHERS of a foreign language (FL) recognize that there is little correlation between the structures taught or drills performed in class and what is actually acquired by the student. Regardless of how many times one may teach and drill a particular grammatical structure, the average student's performance will not improve in direct relationship to the degree of instruction. Clearly, one should not conclude from this state of affairs that instruction must be totally excluded from second-language learning; claims that it is irrelevant appear to have been based on measurement or testing that is not methodologically sound (Doughty 1991). However, the inefficiency of drilling grammar leads most instructors and textbook authors to believe that texts introduced in class should not be restricted to the structure one wishes the students to acquire. Rather, one should select texts representing real-life situations, aimed at specific types of proficiency, in which the structures that need acquiring are included, but not in a disproportionate ratio to their share in normal, natural discourse. The assumption is that, given sufficient comprehensible input (e.g., Krashen 1985), most FL structure can be acquired inductively.

One may argue for minimizing grammar instruction in an *ulpan*[1]-type, immersion environment, while concentrating on comprehensible input. Saturation, particularly with reinforcement from the linguistic environment

---

1. An *ulpan* is an intensive Hebrew school in Israel, designed for new immigrants.

outside the classroom, is very likely to be effective in such circumstances, even when direct instruction of grammar is minimized. However, avoidance of grammar instruction can hardly be realistic in FL instruction in the United States, given the limited exposure the typical American student has to the FL taught. Furthermore, students' individual capabilities and inclinations vary, and some find (or at least claim) that they learn FL best by acquiring its grammatical rules directly. So a certain degree of direct teaching of grammar is unavoidable. The question is how to do it most economically and most effectively.

1. *Principles Determining the Desirability of Direct Instruction of Grammar*

Pica (1985) and others have demonstrated that, for English as a second language, classroom instruction can accelerate acquisition of linguistically simple morphology, such as plural -*s*, but retard the learning of the linguistically more complex progressive -*ing*. Instruction of rules followed by deductive usage is straightforward when dealing with simple structures, whereas direct teaching of complex grammatical rules is tedious, confusing, and inefficient. It is more efficient for students to acquire complex structures by induction from the output. For teaching Hebrew as FL, Bolozky (1995, 1989) similarly argues for direct instruction of simple grammatical rules. Bolozky suggests that a grammatical rule may be taught when it applies widely, and that instruction of grammatical rules may be beneficial when regularities are formulated not in terms of underlying structure, but rather by means of transparent surface generalizations, even if such generalizations do not reflect natural linguistic phenomena. One may also consider teaching simple didactic tools that may not reflect actual linguistic processes, but are, nevertheless, based on some linguistic principles as a means to achieve instructional goals. Bolozky (1986) also argues that the benefits of grammar instruction may be considered when linguistic phenomena in the target language have (simple) parallels in the first language, and pointing to the similarity (or difference) may help in acquiring and internalizing such phenomena.

Although each of the principles involved can be motivated on its own, there is still the question of whether notions such as "rule complexity," "transparency," and "rule scope" can be more specifically defined, and whether it is possible to quantify them. Furthermore, one needs to ask whether first- and / or second-language acquisition can throw any light on the issue of "grammar in the FL classroom," and to consider the differences between processing or comprehending a grammatical structure in FL, and its role in production.

Learning FL is quite different from first- or even second-language acquisition in many respects. First-language acquisition involves children, with
their innate capacity to acquire readily any language within the window of
opportunity naturally available to them. That inborn capability is so powerful,
that even with limited input, children can extract language structure and
constantly modify it without requiring much feedback and correction. What
is typically referred to as "second-language acquisition" also often involves
children and, even if adults are concerned, the exposure to the second language is considerable and consistent. On the other hand, learners of FL are
usually adults and their exposure to the target language tends to be minimal.
That they are adults obviously means that the window of opportunity for first-
language acquisition type is long gone. At the same time, however, it also
means that the learners are at a mature cognitive stage, which may enable
them to process structures children find difficult. Perhaps the most important
difference is that first-language acquisition, and often second-language acquisition, is triggered by natural-language input, whereas in the FL classroom the
input is not only limited, but is also arbitrarily imposed by the teacher. Conse-
quently, it is questionable whether one may even consider a "natural" order
of acquisition of FL structure, since introduction of FL structures is more
dependent on teacher judgment than on what could potentially constitute a
natural sequence of acquisition for the student.

This does not mean that there are no similarities between first/second-
language acquisition and that of FL. There do exist some parallels, occasionally even in the acquisition order itself. Clark's (1980, 1993) "simplicity principle," for instance, would account for Hebrew-speaking children often
adding the plural suffixes +im and +ot without modifying the stem and regardless of normative gender, as in:

[1]   kapitim "teaspoons" (cf. normative kapiyot < kapit "teaspoon")
       simlot "dresses" (cf. smalot < simla "dress")[2]

or having all future paᶜal forms with the stem-vowel o, in analogy with the
majority of paᶜal future forms:

[2]   yilboš "he will wear" (cf. normative yilbaš)
       yilmod "he will study" (cf. normative yilmad)

(see Berman 1986). Later, children learn to adapt and modify these over-
generalizations to conform to normative usage, identifying classes of excep-

---

2. *Simlot* is acceptable only in the construct state.

tions as well as idiosyncratic exceptions that must be memorized individually. Simplicity-motivated over-generalizations also can be documented for beginning learners of Hebrew as FL, in forms like *yilboš* and *yilmod*,[3] as well as in:

[3] *ḥanutim* "stores" (cf. normative *ḥanuyot* < *ḥanut* "store")
studenṭot "students"(f.) (cf. normative *studenṭiyot* < *studenṭit* "student"(f.))

This suggests that simplicity may be just as important in FL acquisition. But there is a basic difference. It does not take long before children modify their over-generalizations, since they are constantly exposed to given forms of words in certain linguistic and/or pragmatic contexts, and thus readily acquire "familiarity with how classes of items pattern in a certain way on the basis of phonological, morphological or word-class, or semantic types of commonalities" (Berman 1986: 360). On the other hand, since the exposure of students of Hebrew as FL to Hebrew input is very limited, over-generalized forms may be irreparably internalized. So should we teach students of FL simplified rules that capture broad regularities, but will later be contradicted by exceptions and classes of exceptions? To circumvent the problem, texts could be introduced that do not contain exceptions, but those would not be natural, authentic texts, and as such would constitute bad models.

The fact that the principle of simplicity is at work in FL learning, as it is in first- and second-language acquisition, does not automatically guarantee its effectiveness as a teaching tool. It may be argued, for instance, that methodologically, it would be better to start with more complex structures, assuming that the capability to process related simpler ones would follow as an automatic corollary. Some research has shown that a proven accessibility hierarchy that is based on markedness may contribute to more efficient teaching of a second language. That is, if we know that a marked structure (or category) is less accessible than a related one, teaching the marked structure first may facilitate the learning of the related simpler, unmarked structure, in a sense providing it free. Keenan and Comrie's (1977) "noun phrase accessibility hierarchy" posits a scale of relative-clause antecedents, from subject (least marked) to genitives or objects of comparison (most marked). Second-language researchers, such as Eckman et al. (1988), Gass (1979, 1982), and

---

3. Note that even non-native linguists can over-generalize here. Chomsky and Halle (1968: 356) quote *yilmod* as a prototype for the unmarked stem vowel of the imperfect. In Biblical Hebrew *yilmod* is marginally attested, but should be the last verb to use as a prototype.

Doughty (1991) claim that generalization of learning tends to occur in the direction of the less marked structure: teaching the more marked structures (e.g., relative clauses in which the antecedent is genitive) automatically improves the student's performance on the unmarked ones (e.g., relative clauses in which the antecedent is subject). But it is unlikely that similar procedures would benefit teaching of FL, because the learning circumstances and intermediate goals are different. If the learner is saturated with input, communication is achieved even when that input is complex. However, should the exposure to FL input be minimal, proficiency in the language and communication capability could take very long to establish if the initial input is complex. By resorting to simple inputs and simple instructional devices, minimal communication capability can be established right from the start, enabling the student to conduct simple conversations about himself, read, write, and understand simple texts, building up immediate self-confidence and realizing that he may, indeed, be able to reach a level of functioning in the target language. Overshooting with complex texts and structures is liable to destroy self-confidence and belief in one's capability to ultimately function in the language learned.

This all-important goal of building up self-confidence is also affected by negative feedback. Experienced instructors of FLs take care not to over-correct student oral errors, so as not to shake student confidence and retard whatever fluency has already been attained. Correction is exercised in measure; it is more appropriate in written work, where fluency is not as relevant. Even in writing, it is preferable to correct indirectly, hinting at how the student can correct on his own, by rewriting. There should be less effort to correct errors in reading and in listening comprehension, where fluency is also less of an issue. Comprehension versus production is also relevant to the question of direct instruction of simple grammatical rules, for a number of reasons. Whereas production starts from scratch, comprehension uses a good model, and there are facilitating contextual and grammatical clues. Also, as will be shown below, generalizations based on surface observations are often simple and straightforward; their production counterparts tend to be more complex. It is thus usually more efficient to teach surface generalizations for comprehension than it is to state production rules. And as noted above, to reduce the detrimental effect on fluency and self-confidence, correcting production errors involving generalizations that have been taught, particularly in oral production, should be minimized. Bolozky (1987, 1989) discusses one type of production error in detail. He asserts, in particular, that one should avoid correcting oral production errors that are also found in Israeli speech, owing to their naturalness, in possessive sentences, such as:

[4]   *haya lo be^{c}ayot* "he had problems"
      there was (m.s.) to him problems (f.pl.)

cf. normative:

   hayu lo be^{c}ayot
   there were to him problems

   haya lo ḥaverim "he had friends" (m.pl.) vs. normative *hayu lo ḥaverim*

in demonstrative pronoun agreement, as in:

[5]   *ze ʾiša* "that's a woman" vs. normative *zot ʾiša*

or in numeral gender agreement, as in:

[6]   *šéva^c šéqel*   "seven(f.) shekels(m.)" vs. normative *šiv^{c}a šqalim*
      "seven(m.) shekels(m.)"

so that student fluency and confidence can be maintained. Cataphoric reference of the *hayu lo be^{c}ayot* type is marked, and is normally avoided even in Biblical Hebrew. Gender agreement in numerals is marked as well (at least beginning with the number "3"), and the neutralization of the suffixed with the unsuffixed one in colloquial Hebrew is expected (see also Bolozky and Haydar 1986).

Thus, the special circumstances and needs of FL support the suggestion in Pica (1985) and in Bolozky (1989, 1995) that direct teaching of grammatical generalizations (and even invented didactic tools) be restricted to ones that are simple and transparent, and that such generalizations be ranked by scope and by the likelihood of their being contradicted by exceptions. Otherwise, grammatical structures should be introduced by induction from ample illustration through natural authentic input. The proposal made here is that the primary evaluation measure for simplicity/transparency/saliency be the number of steps involved in the presentation of a grammatical structure or generalization. Evaluation by number of steps also enables one to account for processing of FL structure being easier than its production, and could suggest different treatments of structure for didactic purposes, depending on whether production or processing is involved. It should be emphasized, however, that the teaching of structure is dictated by its occurrence in authentic natural texts, regardless of how complex the structure might be. If it happens that the sequence of introduction in FL corresponds to the order of first-language acquisition, we may regard it as supporting evidence for the naturalness of that order, but first-language acquisition does not have direct implication for the FL situation *per se,* nor does relative simplicity. Simplicity as used here has relevance only to the question of whether to teach through deduction or induction, and merely suggests where the shorter deductive route may be taken when the opportunity arises—nothing more. It does not necessarily dictate order of presentation, for instance. If complex structures occur in the authentic input used at an early instructional stage, they will not be removed. They may or may not be referred to, but the generalizations involved will not be taught directly, owing to their complexity. In time, they will be arrived at by induction. Below are a few illustrations, some of which are taken from Bolozky (1995).

2. *Some Cases in which Direct Instruction of Grammar/Structure May Be Considered*

2.1. *Adverbs*

Adverbs are not subject to any gender or number agreement (i.e., are invariable):

[7] ʿoved/ʿovédet/ʿovdim/ʿovdot   qašé "work (any person/number/
                                                gender) hard"
work, m.s./f.s./m.pl./f.pl. hard

This is a one-step generalization, with no exceptions regardless of whether processing or production is involved.

2.2. *Nouns Ending in +a*

Nouns ending in +a are feminine. This is also a one-step generalization. The only exception students may encounter is *láyla ṭov* "good night."[4] A related observation: gender marking is always regular in adjectives, even when the noun itself is marked irregularly—thus, a rule of thumb: adjectives reveal the "true" gender of a noun, and if the student is familiar with a noun phrase like *láyla ṭov,* it reveals the gender of the head noun.

Note that the generalization is that nouns ending with +a are feminine, not that feminine gender is marked by +a, since there are other feminine endings, such as +it, +et, and +ut, and numerous feminine nouns that are not marked by any suffix. Thus, while for processing or comprehension, only one step is

---

4. For instance, *šulya ḥaruẓ* "diligent apprentice," belongs to a higher register than what students are likely to encounter.

involved, production may involve more, since to form a feminine noun–adjective NP, for instance, the learner must use the lexicon to determine the proper feminine suffix for that noun (null suffix included). The same applies to characterizing feminine marking in the verb system. In the present tense, for instance, +*et* marks a verb form as feminine, but in production there are other realizations: the +*at* variant of the gutturals and the +*a* of roots with a middle glide and of those with a final *yod*.

2.3. *Unmarked Plural Suffixation*

The generalization that the plural of the masculine is marked by +*im* and that of the feminine by +*ot* is perfect for the present tense paradigms in the verb system, where it has no exceptions: *kotvim* "write" (m.pl.) / *kotvot* "write" (f.pl.), *medabrim* "speak" (m.pl.) / *medabrot* "speak" (f.pl.), etc. It is obviously somewhat problematic in the noun system, owing to the numerous exceptions. +*im* is less of a problem; of the frequent words these students may encounter, there are only a handful of exceptions in which +*im* marks a feminine noun:

[8]

F.S.	GLOSS	PL.	F.S.	GLOSS	PL.
ʔiša	woman	našim	mila	word	milim
šana	year	šanim	páʕam	(one) time	peʕamim
beẓa	egg	beẓim	ʕir	town, city	ʕarim

However, there are many more common masculine nouns that are marked for plural by +*ot*; such as:

[9]

M.S.	GLOSS	PL.	M.S.	GLOSS	PL.
šulḥan	table	šulḥanot	kise	chair	kisʔot
ḥalon	window	ḥalonot	ʔaron	cupboard	ʔaronot
qir	wall	qirot	reḥov	street	reḥovot
maqom	place	meqomot	ʔav/ʔába	father	ʔavot
ʕiparon	pencil	ʕefronot	šavúaʕ	week	šavuʕot
maḥaze	play	maḥazot	rúaḥ	wind; spirit	ruḥot
lúaḥ	board	luḥot	maqel	stick	maqlot
ḥalom	dream	ḥalomot	malon	hotel	melonot
ʔor	light	ʔorot	bor	hole	borot

For these exceptions, identifying the correct gender involves at least two steps. In forms such as

[10] SING.	GLOSS	ADJ.	GLOSS	PLURAL NP	GLOSS
šulḥan	table	ḥum	brown	šulḥanot ḥumim	brown tables
ʾor	light	ḥazaq	strong	ʾorot ḥazaqim	strong lights

linear processing identifies the gender of the noun as feminine on the basis of the ot-suffix. When the following adjective suffix is +im, the gender identification is corrected to masculine. This in itself consists of two steps. The process involves an additional small step when vowel reduction is involved, since the singular noun form and/or the singular adjective form need to be identified in sequences like *meqomot reḥoqim* "distant places":

[11] SING.	GLOSS	ADJ.	GLOSS	PLURAL NP	GLOSS
maqom	place	raḥoq	distant	meqomot reḥoqim	distant places
maqel	stick	kaved	heavy	maqlot kvedim	heavy sticks

Admittedly, reconstruction from the reduced form is easy, but in cases of suppletion, the singular base may become quite opaque and difficult to identify:

[12] SING.	GLOSS	ADJ.	GLOSS	PLURAL NP	GLOSS
ʾiša	woman	qaṭan	little	našim qṭanot	little women
ʿir	town, city	gadol	big	ʿarim gdolot	big cities

Despite the relative complexity caused by exceptions to the +im/+ot generalization, it is still worth teaching directly, particularly owing to its very wide scope, which, as noted above, also covers all plural forms of the present tense paradigms in the verb system. For the majority of items, this is still a one-step rule. The exceptions in the noun system need to be memorized and, at least insofar as +im is concerned, seldom does the average student need to internalize more than the above list of exceptions. It is not clear whether it is worth bothering to define subclasses of exceptions with +ot so as to enable the student to predict at least some of them. For instance, many of the nouns ending with +e that are derived from a root with a final *yod*:

[13] *maḥaze* "play" > *maḥazot*

  maḥane "camp" > *maḥanot*

  maʿale "uphill incline" > *maʿalot*

  but note *maʿase* > *maʿasim*.

2.4. *Derived Adjectives Ending in +i*

In the adjective realm there is a clear case in which first-language acquisition order, or what a child might find to be complex, should not affect our decision as to whether to teach a particular morphological generalization directly. Adjectives derived by appending the *i*-suffix to nouns, the so-called *nísba*-type adjectives,[5] are acquired quite late by Hebrew-speaking children, who master the passive participial resultative adjectives (*meCuCaC, CaCuC, muCCaC*) earlier, in spite of their greater morphological complexity. *Nísba*-type adjectives usually belong to a higher register, and apparently involve a higher degree of abstraction. There are good reasons, however, for early teaching of *i*-affixation to learners of Hebrew as FL. Although the most commonly used adjectives are not of the *nísba*-type, enough of them would occur in natural basic texts to justify introduction of the simple, one-step suffixation of +*i* to almost any type of base. Bolozky (1999) shows that in the noun/adjective system, *i*-suffixation is the most productive derivation device. If the target meaning involves a verb, *meCuCaC* is more productive, but in the noun/adjective system as a whole *i*-suffixation has no equal in productivity. Learners are quite likely to encounter +*i* that is appended to gentilic nouns (e.g., *ʔameriqáʔi* "American," *yisreʔeli* "Israeli," *ʔangli* "English," *germani* "German") quite early in their study and across many others as their learning progresses. For adults with developed cognitive capability +*i*-adjectives are very easy to learn: it is the most general device characterizing the quality of the base to which it is appended, and the suffix is prominent and clearly identifiable. Although *i*-suffixation is neither automatic nor totally predictable, semantically the end result is fairly predictable, and the linear derivation is simple, even when concomitant reduction is involved (as in *maqom* "place" > *meqomi* "local").

2.5. *The Construct State and Abstract Nominalizations*

There are two other types of structures that are acquired late by children, owing to their relative complexity and (often) relatively high register: the construct state[6] and abstract nominalization patterns of verbs. The construct state involves changes in the structure of the first nominal component, as in:

---

5. *Nísba* is a term from Arabic that refers to adjectives formed by +*i* suffixation for "minimal" attribution, generally denoting "having the characteristic of..." the base to which the suffix has been appended.

6. This is generally true of the construct state, but not necessarily. The construct

[14] *ḥaverim   šel/be   kibuẓ > ḥavrey kibuẓ* "kibbutz members"
      members of/in   kibbutz

  ha-ʔíša   šel   ha-nasi > ʔéšet hanasi "the president's wife"
  the-wife of   the-president

Conceptually, the analytical alternative of having a preposition such as *šel* "of" between the two nouns makes the relationship between the two nouns much more transparent. Although the construct state does not necessarily present a problem for mature FL learners, it is not sufficiently simple to merit direct instruction. Exposure to a sufficient number of cases in natural texts and inductive learning may prove to be more effective. The relationship between abstract nominalizations and their related base verbs is also somewhat opaque. There is little point in actually deriving the nominalization *CCiCa* from its verbal base *CaCaC*, for instance, although it is possible to simply state that the two patterns are related and describe the nature of the relationship. Even then, one should be careful, since the relationship is not automatic. One obviously cannot always predict actual occurrence nor guarantee that the noun would be a proper gerund-type. Often, the nominalization would have a gerundive meaning, as well as a more specific, unpredictable one that is much more common, as in:

[15] *CCiCa*   *yašav* "sit" ~ *yešiva* "sitting; session; Yeshiva"
            yaẓa "come out" ~ *yeẓiʔa* "coming out; exit"
            qana "buy" ~ *qniya* "buying; purchase"

  CiCuC   *diber* "speak" ~ *dibur* "speaking; speech; utterance"
            ṭipel "take care, treat" ~ *ṭipul* "taking care, treating; treat-
                        ment"
            ṭiyel "take trip, walk around" ~ *ṭiyul* "taking a trip,
                        walking around; a trip, a walk"

  haCCaCa *hisbir* "explain" ~ *hasbara* "explaining; propaganda"
            hik̲htiv "dictate" ~ *hak̲htava* "dictating; a dictation"
            hik̲hnis "let in" ~ *hak̲hnasa* "letting in; income"

---

state is common in fused compounds such as *beyt sefer* "school (= house of book)," as well as in common collocations with heads such as *ḥavrey...* "members of...," *naᶜaley...* "shoes of...."

Methodical introduction of such nominalization patterns might be effective at advanced levels, but at lower levels learning particular cases individually
would be more effective.

Nominalizations ending with *+ut* would be better candidates for direct
instruction. Although such patterns are also acquired late by children—as all
nominalizations are—they have the advantage of a salient *+ut* suffix, as well
as a reasonably transparent morpho-phonological relationship with the verb.
Normally (see Bolozky 1999) *+ut* is a productive marker of abstract nouns in
forms that are not verb-related; children already use non-verb-related *+ut*
productively at the age of four (Berman and Sagi 1981):

[16]   *ẓmiʾut* "thirst"   (< *ẓame* "thirsty")
       mazʿiut "sweating (N)"   (< *maziaʿ* "sweating")
       keʾevut "being in pain"   (< *keʾev* "pain")
       raʿut "wickedness"   (< *raʿ* "bad, wicked")
       qosmut "magic"   (< *qosem* "magician")

When the *+ut* form is derived from a verb, *CiCuC* is a serious competitor
of *+ut*, particularly when there are reasons to assume a relationship to *piʿel*. But
+ut gerunds related to other verb bases are reasonably productive. In some of
the patterns concerned *+ut* nominalization is a one-step process, as in:

[17]   Nominalizations ending with *+ut*, no change in the stem

       niCCaCut: *nifqad* "(be) absent"   > *nifqadut*
                     nivʿar "ignorant"   > *nivʿarut*
       meCuCaCut: *mehuyav* "obliged"   > *mehuyavut*
                     meyutar "redundant"   > *meyutarut*
       maCCiCut: *mazkir* "secretary"   > *mazkirut*
                     manhig "leader"   > *manhigut*
       muCCaCut: *mugbal* "restricted"   > *mugbalut*
                     mufraʿ "disturbed"   > *mufraʿut*

In others, vowel deletion is involved, resulting in a two-step process:

[18]   Nominalizations ending with *+ut*, a stem vowel is deleted

       hitCaCCut: *hitqadem* "advance"   > *hitqadmut* "advancing; progress"
                     hitnageš "collide"   > *hitnagšut* "colliding; collision"
       hiCaCCut: *(le)hikanes* "enter"   > *hikansut*
                     (le)hitaqel "bump (into)" > *hitaqlut*
       CoCCut: *honekh* "trainer"   > *honkhut*
                     hoveš "dress wound"   > *hovšut*

meCaCCut: *meyaled* "obstetrician"   > *meyaldut*
    mefaqed "commander"   > *mefaqdut*[7]

Again the more specific, unpredictable meaning may overshadow the gerundive one, and many occurrences belong to a relatively high register. So direct instruction of verb-related +*ut* gerunds is a possibility, but should still be considered with caution.

2.6. *Generalizations Involving Cataphora*

Generalizations involving cataphora are always more complex than ones involving anaphora, since, in linear processing, cataphora requires a two-step process. Once the linearly farther referent is identified, the learner has to go back and reinterpret the pronoun, as in the possessive sentence (*hayu lo be⁽ayot* "There were to him problems" = "He had problems") or demonstrative pronoun agreement (*zot ᵓiša* "This(f.) is a woman") noted in Section 1 above, and in other possessive structures like:

[19] *ᵓišt-o* *šel* *ha-nasi*
   wife-his of the-president
   "the president's wife" ~ *ᵓéšet hanasi* ~ *haᵓiša šel hanasi*

   maskurt-am *šel* *ha-sarim*
   salary-their of the-ministers
   "the ministers' salary" ~ *maskóret hasarim* ~ *hamaskóret šel hasarim*

Such possessive structures are at least as complex as their construct state variants, *ᵓéšet hanasi* "the president's wife" and *maskóret hasarim* "the ministers' salaries," respectively. It is thus doubtful that it would be advantageous to teach them directly.

2.7. *The Future Stem Vowel in* pa⁽al

In the *pa⁽al* verb pattern, the future stem vowel is *a* if the second or third radical of the root is guttural:

[20] *tišᵓal* "you will ask"   *tinhag* "you will drive"
   /*tišma⁽*/ > *tišma* "you will hear" *tišlaḥ* "you will send"

A limited number of *a*-verbs (including some stative verbs that are too few to characterize as a separate group) will have to be memorized as such:

---

7. All *meCaCCut* items are considerably less natural than all other +*ut* nominalizations.

[21]   *tilmad* "you will learn"
       tiškav "you will lie (down)"
       tirkav "you will ride"
       tiqṭan "you will be/become small"
       tigdal "you will be/become big, you will grow"

Otherwise, the future stem vowel is *o*, which accounts for the majority of *paʕal* verbs. Essentially, we have two one-step generalizations, which definitely merit direct instruction. The desirability of identifying and teaching additional subgroups would depend on student level and teacher judgment. Such additional subgroups include: *e* for most cases in which the first or last radical is *y*, as in *tešev* "you will sit" and *tiqne* "you will buy," respectively; *u* for bi-radical roots such as *taqum* "you will get up" (*i*-cases like *tasim* "you will put" are too few to justify direct instruction).

2.8. *Regularities Involving Spirantization*

The spirantization rule (*beged kefet*), if it is to be taught at all, should be introduced on the basis of surface distribution rather than as a pseudo-phonetic process attempting to recreate the historical alternation. Originally, the stops *p, t, k, b, d, g* simply became fricative after a vowel (i.e., *f*, θ, *x*, *v*, $\tilde{G}$ γ, respectively)—an assimilation of continuity from the vowel that was blocked only by gemination (the doubling marked by a *dageš forte*). In Israeli Hebrew, however, the process has lost most of its productivity, owing to considerable opacity caused by phoneme merger and loss, loss of gemination, etc. All one can do—if one chooses to do so—is speak of frequency of fricatives in certain (surface) environments that can be characterized by one-step generalizations, as at the end of the word:

[22]

SING.	PLURAL	GLOSS	SING.	PLURAL	GLOSS
rav	*rabim*	much, numerous	*ʔarokh*	*ʔarukim*	long
kaf	*kapot*	tablespoon	*ẓahov*	*ẓehubim*	yellow
rakh	*rakim*	soft	*ʕeẓev*	*ʕaẓabim*	nerve

in the second segment of an initial consonant cluster:

[23]   *švira* "breaking"   *sfira* "counting"   *škhuna* "neighborhood"

after a prefix ending with a vowel (with some classes of exceptions, e.g., the future/imperative of *nifʕal*: *yibane* "will be built"):

[23] PAST	GLOSS	FUTURE		PAST	GLOSS	FUTURE
baraḥ	run	*yivraḥ*		*pataḥ*	open	*yiftaḥ*
katav	write	*yikhtov*		*biqeš*	request	*yevaqeš*
piṭer	fire	*yefaṭer*		*kibes*	launder	*yekhabes*

and in certain *mišqal* configurations, for instance, the second consonant in *CiCCon+ot*, the plural of *CiCaC+on*, as in:

[24] SING.	PLURAL	GLOSS
zikaron	*zikhronot*	memory, mémoire
ʿiparon	*ʿefronot*	pencil

Even in these environments there are a good number of exceptions, but most are characteristic of the casual or substandard register.

2.9. *The ʾet Rule*

Another option can be considered. For the typical American student who has never been taught basic concepts such as "definite" or "direct object," one might introduce a generalization involving a simpler surface observation regarding *ʾet*: "insert *ʾet* after a verb and before either a noun with #*ha*+ 'the' or a proper noun."

2.10. *Economical Representation of Vowel Marks when Needed*

The next case concerns orthography. Bolozky (1990, 1995) proposes a simplified didactic tool that, though not capturing a particular linguistic structure, is, nevertheless, based upon linguistic principles. At the initial stages of instruction—and at any later stage in the dictionary/glossary component—one can use partial vowel marking in which *plene*-writing is used for any *i* (*yod*), *o* (*vav*), or *u* (*šuruq*).[8] *Segol* and *ẓere* are still marked to designate *e*, but any unmarked non-final consonant is interpreted as a transition to the vowel *a*, and a *šva* as the absence of a vowel. If it is difficult to pronounce a consonant cluster with *šva*, it will be realized as *e* (the minimal vowel of Israeli Hebrew). The proposal is based on the observation that *a* is the unmarked vowel of Hebrew and constitutes at least one-third of all vowel realizations in Israeli Hebrew. This proposal entails a number of advantages, primary of which is

---

8. To distinguish *o* from *u*, one can mark the *vav* for either of them. Since *o* is more common, we could mark *u* with the *šuruq* dot, to distinguish it from unmarked *vav*, representing *o*. *Vav* that stands for [v] is relatively rare (except for the conjunction *ve*+ "and"); its instances can be memorized individually.

getting beginning students used to the idea that an orthographic non-final consonant usually consists of a consonant-plus-vowel, and that as such there is a good chance that it will be realized as a consonant-plus-*a*, unless it is followed by *yod* or *vav* (the number of syllables with *e* is relatively small). The use of *šva* as the absence of a vowel, i.e., only as a zero, will not only inform the student where to close the syllable or to form a consonant cluster, as in

[26]   *katva* "she wrote"   *ktiva* "writing"   *katavt* "you(f.s.) wrote"

but will also—and this is its main advantage—provide us with the natural pronunciation of the *šva mobile* when required. In Israeli Hebrew one is naturally led to pronounce the orthographic *šva* as a vowel when a consonant cluster is formed that is hard to pronounce because of violations of sonority sequencing.[9] The vowel *e*, the modern counterpart of the *šva mobile*, splits such clusters:

[27]   *yladim* "children" > *yeladim* (cf. *klavim* "dogs")

   mtuqa "sweet" (f.s.) > *metuqa* (cf. *ptuḥa* "open" (f.s.))

   lvanim "white" (m.pl.) > *levanim* (cf. *qtanim* "small" (m.pl.))

   nmukhim "short" (m.pl.) > *nemukhin* (cf. *gnuvin* "stolen" (m.pl.))

   t͑ufa "aviation" > *te͑ufa* > *teufa* (cf. *tšuva* "answer." Although the historical *͑ayin* is not realized, it is useful to regard it as a consonant slot)

   tilmdu "you(pl.) will learn" > *tilmedu* (cf. *tiqnu* "you(pl.) will buy")

   meṭalfnim "phone" (V), (m.pl.) > *meṭalfenim* (cf. *medabrim* "speak" (m.pl.))

Note that the instruction to the students to "pronounce an unpronounce-able zero *šva* as *e*" is linear, following the progress of reading. Thus, in the case of /*tilmdu*/, the first *šva* is read as zero, resulting in *til*. Since the *šva* under the *mem* is unpronounceable as zero, *m* is realized as *me*, just as the *y* in /*yladim*/ becomes *ye*. All the generalizations the student needs to remember, then, are that the *šva* is zero and that any unmarked, non-final consonant is pronounced C*a*.

The only disadvantage of this efficient method is the contradiction the student will face when using some standard dictionaries in which the zero *šva*

---

9. In sonority sequencing within a syllable, consonants rise in sonority from the beginning of the onset toward the nucleus, and decline in sonority from the nucleus to the end of the coda.

is often not represented. The teacher should consider whether the benefits of the proposed system outweigh this shortcoming.

2.11. *The Furtive-Pataḥ Rule*

In the partial vocalization system proposed above, there is no need for any of the symbols for *a*. One of them, however, may be reserved initially for a special use: the *pataḥ*, to signal the *pataḥ gnuva*, the furtive-*pataḥ* rule, simplified so as to facilitate its introduction to the student. It makes no sense to recapture the historical rule, which inserted the low vowel *a* before a word-final guttural (which is also low, like *a*) if that guttural was preceded by a non-low vowel. The rule itself is complex, and if one considers that the low consonants concerned are no longer low, or may not even exist, it would be easier to invent a simple rule of thumb: if you see a *pataḥ* under the last consonant of the word, pronounce it as if it had an *ʾáleph* before it, which would result in an insertion of *a*, as in *rúaḥ* or *noséa*.

3. *Generalizations Involving Comparison to the Learner's Native Language*

The following are generalizations made valuable by pointing to similarities with, or differences from, the learner's native language.

3.1. *Word Order within a Noun Phrase*

The instructor may point out that the Hebrew word-order within a noun phrase (noun–adjective–adverb) is equivalent to the organization of similar noun phrases in English (adverb–adjective–noun), except that it constitutes its mirror image:

[28]   *sefer*   *ṭov*   *meʾod*   "(a) very good book"
      book   good   very

3.2. *Some Parallels between Inchoative and Causative Marking in English and Hebrew*

One should also consider the desirability of drawing a parallel between markers of causation and inchoativity ("becoming…") in Hebrew and their English counterparts, say, for instance, between causation through *binyan* membership (be it *hifʿil* or *piʿel*) and English +*ize*# or +*ify*#:

[29]   *muḥaši* "concrete"   ~ *himḥiš* "concretize"
      yafe "beautiful"   ~ *yipa* "beautify"
      šamaᶜ "heard"   ~ *hišmíaᶜ* "vocalize"
      pašuṭ "simple"   ~ *pišeṭ* "simplify"

and on the other hand, show that there are also cases, as in English, in which causation and inchoativity may be realized in the same surface form, as in some English verbs with the +*en* suffix:

[30] *hišḥir* "blacken" (tr./int.)
      hilbin "whiten" (tr./int.)
      hišmin "fatten" (tr./int.)

3.3. *Hebrew Consonant Clusters Occurring in English Fast/Casual Speech*

It is also possible to facilitate the pronunciation of Hebrew clusters that do not occur in English by pointing to their existence in the casual/fast register of English. Thus, for instance, the clusters *pt, tm,* or *bn* normally are not allowed as syllabic onsets, and some English-speaking students find it difficult to pronounce them in words such as:

[31] *ptuḥim* "open" (m.pl.)   *tmuna* "picture"   *bney* "sons of"

It might be helpful to point out to them that such clusters do exist in their own English casual/fast speech:

[32] p[ar]ticular p[o]tato t[o]mato b[i]noculars

3.4. *Strong-Verb Patterns in English as* mišqalim

An insightful illustration in this category is the comparison between discontinuous patterns of root-plus-*mišqal* and the so-called strong-verb patterns in English, which are also discontinuous.

[33] Discontinuous word formation patterns in the English verb system:

speak-spoke-spoken, freeze-froze-frozen, steal-stole-stolen, weave-wove-woven;

swim-swam-swum, drink-drank-drunk, shrink-shrank-shrunk, sing-sang-sung, sink-sank-sunk, ring-rang-rung, spring-sprang-sprung, stink-stank-stunk;

grow-grew-grown, blow-blew-blown, know-knew-known, throw-threw-thrown;

bind-bound-bound, find-found-found, grind-ground-ground, wind-wound-wound;

drive-drove-driven, write-wrote-written, ride-rode-ridden, rise-rose-risen, arise-arose-arisen, strive-strove-striven, smite-smote-smitten, bestride-bestrode-bestridden;

take-took-taken, shake-shook-shaken, forsake-forsook-forsaken.

Thus, for instance, in the first group, the discontinuous related *mišqalim* would be *C(C)īC-C(C)ōC-C(C)ōCn*, and the roots *spk, frz, stl, wv*. Students can be told that had English contained more patterns of the strong verb type, with many more items realized in each, its morphology would have been closer to (discontinuous) Hebrew word-formation.

Some instructors of Hebrew have doubts regarding the usefulness of comparing aspects of the target language to the native language. They feel that, instead of helping the student, pointing to structural similarity may, in fact, be detrimental. It could either confuse the learner, who is hardly aware of the structure of his own language, or it might legitimize additional, inappropriate dependence on structures from the native language, resulting in the transfer of unwanted, wrong constructions. Neither has happened in my experience, but proper testing—with control groups, in a number of colleges and over a number of years—is certainly called for.

4. *Conclusion*

The question of whether to teach grammar directly or not does not have a simple yes-or-no answer. It depends on a variety of considerations, such as complexity, scope of application, degree of surface transparency, saliency, methodological usefulness/efficiency, and the existence of parallels in the native language. Most importantly, it should be tailored to the specific audience and the instructional context in general. Some of these notions, particularly simplicity, transparency, saliency, and efficiency may also be quantified according to the number of processing steps necessitated by the proposed rule.

REFERENCES

Berman, R.A. 1986. *The Acquisition of Hebrew*. Part 3 of *The Cross-linguistic Study of Language Acquisition Vol. 1: The Data*, D.I. Slobin (ed.). Hillsdale: Erlbaum.

Berman, R.A. and I. Sagi. 1981. *ᶜAl darkhey tezurat ha-milim ve-ḥidušan be-gil zaᶜir* (Word formation and neologisms at a young age) [Hebrew]. *Hebrew Computational Linguistics* 18: 31–62.

Bolozky, S. 1986. Awareness of linguistic phenomena in the native language and its implications for learning Hebrew. *Bulletin of Higher Hebrew Education* 1/2: 14–17.

————. 1987. On the teaching of gender in Hebrew numerals and other phenomena simplified in semi-standard native speech. *Bulletin of Higher Hebrew Education* 2/1: 7–11.

————. 1989. Grammar simplification strategies in the teaching of Modern Hebrew and the natural approach. *Bulletin of Higher Hebrew Education* 3:1/2: 15–19.

————. 1990. ⁽Al simun hatnu⁽ot a ve-e ve⁽al simun he⁽der tnu⁽a baktiv šel ha⁽ivrit haḥadaša [Hebrew]. *Lashon Ve'Ivrit* 5: 34–37.

————. 1995. Direct instruction of grammatical structure to students of Hebrew as a foreign language. *Bulletin of Higher Hebrew Education* 7/8: 30–38.

————. 1999. *Measuring Productivity in Word Formation: The Case of Israeli Hebrew.* (*Studies in Semitic Languages and Linguistics* 27) Leiden: E. J. Brill.

Bolozky, S. and A.F. Haydar. 1986. Colloquial gender neutralization in the numeral systems of Modern Hebrew and Lebanese Arabic. *Al-'Arabiyya* 19: 19–28.

Chomsky, N. and M. Halle. 1968. *The Sound Pattern of English.* New York: Harper and Row.

Clark, E. 1980. Convention and innovation in acquiring the lexicon. *Papers and Reports on Child Language Development* 19: 1–20.

————. 1993. *The Lexicon in Acquisition.* Cambridge: Cambridge University Press.

Doughty, C. 1991. Second language instruction does make a difference. *Studies in Second Language Acquisition* 13: 431–69.

Eckman, F., L. Bell and D. Nelson. 1988. On the generalization of relative clause instruction in the acquisition of English as a second language. *Applied Linguistics* 9: 1–20.

Gass, S. 1979. Language transfer and universal grammatical relations. *Language Learning* 29: 327–44.

————. 1982. From theory to practice. In M. Hines and W. Rutherford (eds.), *On TESOL "81* (pp.129–39). Washington D.C.: TESOL.

Keenan, E. and B. Comrie. 1977. Noun phrase accessibility and universal grammar. *Linguistic Inquiry* 8: 63–99.

Krashen, S.D. 1985. *The Input Hypothesis: Issues and Implications.* London: Longmans.

Pica, T. 1985. Linguistic simplicity and learnability: Implications for language syllabus design. In K. Hyltenstam and M. Pienemann (eds.), *Modelling and Assessing Second Language Acquisition.* Clevedon: Multilingual Matters.

TEACHING TRANSLATION IN THE HEBREW LANGUAGE PROGRAM

ּלִי שֶׁל הַגַּל קוֹרֵ׳
תוֹ – שֶׁאָבוֹא אֲנִי

ז בְּרָאשׁוֹ, וְהִכִּינוּ ז
ּוֹת, אָמֵן אָמֵן סֶלָה״

Brenda Malkiel
Bar-Ilan University

> Ever since humans first devised writing systems, translators have been building bridges between nations, races, cultures and continents. Bridges between past and present, too. Translators have the ability to span time and space. They have enabled certain central texts—works of science, philosophy or literature—to acquire universal stature. Translators breach the walls created by language differences, thereby opening up new horizons and broadening our vision of reality to encompass the entire world. (Joly, 1995: xiii)

WHY DO AMERICANS watch foreign films with English subtitles when the domestic studios release countless movies every year? Why do they read Sayed Kashua, Gabriel Garcia Marquez, and Umberto Eco in translation instead of Alice Munroe, Charles Dickens, and David Lodge in the original? Translations sweep us into a distant world, one in which the people literally speak a different language.

Translators play an especially vital role in small countries where the *lingua franca* is a language of limited distribution, with Israel as a case in point. Translators working into Hebrew (and Arabic) make it possible for Israelis to operate their Miele dishwashers and Nokia phones, to watch "Six Feet Under" and "Star Wars," and to read *Harry Potter* and *Don Quixote*. Translators working out of Hebrew provide global exposure for Israeli literature and films and enable Israeli firms to conduct business abroad. Without translators, "Beaufort" would not have been nominated for an Oscar, Amos Oz would be an unknown outside of Israel, and Teva Pharmaceuticals would not be traded on the NASDAQ.

At first glance, translation seems to be a somewhat mechanical task, something even a computer can do. To the layperson, translation has little of the allure of its first cousin, interpreting.[1] Rather, translation appears to be a sophisticated form of typing, with the translator reading a text in Language A and simply retyping it in Language B. Little could be farther from the truth. Charles Kraszewski (1998) writes: "The reader will excuse me for stating the obvious here, which I must do in order to prove my point that no translation problem is a simple one and that even the translation of newspaper prose can present the translator with tasks just as complex as those to be found in the most technically complex poetry" (19).

Anyone who has engaged even briefly in translation will agree that Kraszewski is stating the obvious. Professional translators find translation just as challenging as bilinguals and language students do (Gerloff, 1988). Professionals read the source text with a practiced eye and are acutely aware of where their target text falls short.[2] The translation student becomes ever more conscious of how difficult translation is—difficult because of the seemingly unbreachable gap between the source and target languages and the source and target cultures. The teacher in a foreign-language program can exploit the difficulties of translation to underscore the fundamental differences between the native and foreign languages, such that translation is the ideal vehicle for teaching contrastive analysis. Translation reinforces and brings to life the lessons presented in the language classroom, but in a more theoretical and academic manner.

With the benefit of hands-on experience and readings in Translation Studies, students can discuss the merits of statements such as:

- All bilinguals can translate.
- Translations are always flawed.
- A historian is the last person who should translate a history book.
- It is more difficult to translate "happy" than "astrophysics."

---

1. Here the word "translation" refers exclusively to the written modality. Interpreting requires a level of verbal facility that is far beyond the reach of language students. In the theory classroom, students certainly can be introduced to the special problems that arise in English-Hebrew or Hebrew-English interpreting, but having students actually practice interpreting has little purpose.

2. By convention, this paper uses the following terms: source language (the language of the original), target language (the language of the translation), source text (the text to be translated), and target text (the translation itself).

- Better translators produce longer texts.
- "Real" translators don't use dictionaries.
- A good translation doesn't sound like a translation.
- Donut is not an adequate translation for סופגניה.

Teaching Translation

In recent decades, academics have frowned on the use of translation in the language classroom (Schjoldager, 2004). Kirsten Malmkjær (2004) observes that "the reluctance to introduce translation into the language classroom is most acutely felt in Britain and the United States where, also, enrolment in language classes is notoriously low in both secondary and tertiary education" (5). Translation has typically been used as a mechanism for teaching a foreign language and for assessing a student's competence and accuracy in that language. In this approach, translation is a means rather than an end and translation theory is almost irrelevant. However, as Guy Cook (1998) points out, the oft-criticized grammar-translation method "holds no monopoly, and translation may be used both more imaginatively, and as a complement to direct method teaching rather than an exclusive alternative to it" (119).

It is important to stress that bilingual competence is no guarantee of translational competence. In fact, the ability to translate does not appear to depend on the individual's degree of bilingualism (Dornic, 1978: 268). A balanced bilingual does not necessarily have the makings of a professional translator. According to Marisa Presas (2000: 19), one proof that there is a difference between bilingual competence and translational competence is seen in the preponderance of bad translations. The goal in the language classroom is not to make the student a translator, but rather to use translation as a vehicle to teach language skills and an appreciation of cultural and linguistic diversity. The student need not translate Shakespeare or the Bible in order to reap the benefits. In fact, many translation programs focus almost exclusively on non-literary material.

Maria Piotrowska (1997) claims that translation theory is an important key in the acquisition of translation skills. I would extend Piotrowska's argument to say that translation and translation theory are valuable instruments in the acquisition of foreign-language skills. Experience in translation immeasurably improves the students' command of not only their second language (L2) but their first language (L1) as well. This serves the students well in their university career and beyond.

In an ideal world, language students would enroll in both a text-translation workshop and a course in translation theory. A less intensive option would be a single translation course, with the texts carefully chosen to illustrate specific aspects of contrastive analysis and translation theory. A third possibility would be for the language teacher to include a translation module in each lesson.

Translation adds an element of—dare we say the word?—fun to the language classroom, and students typically comment on how thoroughly they enjoy the experience of translation. This is not surprising: translation has been said to have a good deal in common with certain cerebral leisure-time activities, such as chess (Levy, 1967) and Scrabble (Holmes, 1988). These ten snippets demonstrate how challenging and thought-provoking English-Hebrew and Hebrew-English translation can be.

- ¥ Is that dish too hot for you?
- ¥ Course-catalogue listing: (עברי) כיצד לקרוא טקסט
- ¥ Sam's grandparents bought him a lollipop.
- ¥ נו ...
- ¥ Article about underwater photography: Cameras that swim with the fishes.
- ¥ בשבתות וחגים החוזר בשאלה חובש כיפה.
- ¥ I can't get no satisfaction.
- ¥ החיל חטף כדור ביד.
- ¥ Act your age, not your shoe size.
- ¥ שיר אהבה פשוט / פשוט שיר אהבה

Most professionals today translate exclusively into their L1. The assumption in the field is that few bilinguals have the linguistic tools to produce an articulate, natural-sounding target text in L2. Edmund Keeley (2000), a highly regarded professional translator, writes: "Anybody who translates out of the translator's native language—what some call the 'mother tongue'—into a second, adopted language, is reasonably sure to get himself or herself into trouble, unless he or she is a genius. And sometimes even if he or she is a genius" (19).

In certain ways translation into L2 can be less hazardous than translation into L1, for the simple reason that translators are less likely to misunderstand the source text when it is in their native tongue. Nonetheless, translation into L2 can be an exercise in frustration for language students, often more effective for improving their dictionary skills than for anything else. Although most translation should be from L2 to L1, there is no reason language students cannot work on translating very short texts into their second language.

Translation is a bridge between two languages and two cultures. Through the study of translation, the student gains a greater appreciation of and sensitivity toward both the foreign language and culture and the L1. Although the teacher might choose to introduce translation into the language classroom as a means to improve the student's L2, translation can revolutionize the student's entire approach to what language means. In the translation classroom, the student:

- ¥ Learns to closely read a text.
- ¥ Hones his or her L1 writing and revision skills.
- ¥ Understands implications of the fact that different languages "work" in different ways.
- ¥ Is introduced to important concepts in Translation Studies, such as voids, translationese, and gridding.
- ¥ Becomes aware of the intimate connection between language and culture.
- ¥ Appreciates that a certain idea can be expressed in many different ways.

In the traditional translation workshop, students are assigned a text to translate for homework. During class, each student reads a sentence or two from his or her translation. The teacher provides feedback and may ask to hear more than one student's version of the same passage. This method can be used successfully for teaching translation into the L1. There are, however, other ways to profitably introduce translation and translation theory into the language program.

A number of English books have been translated into Hebrew two or more times. Students can examine a short passage from, for example, *Alice in Wonderland*, together with two Hebrew versions. This helps them appreciate the types of strategies that are available to the translator and the fact that there is no one correct translation of a text. Another option is to have the students translate a piece into English at home; in class they can meet in groups of three or four to compare their translations and create a preferred version.

Many Israeli films are available on DVD through Netflix and local rental stores. In class or at home, students can watch a movie, paying close attention to the English subtitles. They can then discuss the difficulty of subtitling in general and with regard to the particular movie. Movies are also an excellent vehicle for exposing the student to contemporary Israeli culture.

Students can be instructed to compose a short English text that contains, for example, voids or false cognates. The text can then be assigned for homework or as an in-class exercise. This project is helpful both for the writer and for the peer translators. Finally, something students find particularly entertaining is spotting the mistakes in a published translation. Beginners can identify where the translator went wrong; more advanced students can suggest a correct version. Unfortunately, there is no shortage of material for this exercise.

Translation demands the closest possible reading of a text. Stratford (1995: 93) writes:

> All the skills of a trained reader are called into play in the act of trans-lation. The translator must have a global appreciation of the text; must be sensitive to its larger rhythms, to its system of metaphor and symbol, to the structure of its events, the interplay of its characters and the quality of its language; and must also be aware of its historical and cultural context. Indeed, all the skills we laboriously acquire and then try to communicate as teachers of literature are used both in serious reading and in translation, and it has always surprised me that more teachers are not translators, so admirably are they equipped for the task.

It is in the translation class that the student learns how to read a text. The language of the source text is largely immaterial—the lessons of reading a Hebrew text apply equally well to English, Swedish, and German. In the class discussion of the source text, the student will revisit familiar topics, such as metaphor, dialect, register, alliteration, ambiguity, and connotation. Since translation is a form of writing, translation students learn to revise and re-revise, revise and re-revise, until they produce a well-written target text.

As a matter of course, translation requires research and students are instructed in the use of reference tools (mono- and bilingual dictionaries, thesauruses, atlases, encyclopedias, concordances, search engines, etc.). These skills benefit the student in his or her history and philosophy courses, when writing a legal brief or an article for *Scientific American*, or when relaxing with E.M. Forster or David Grossman.

Combating Interference

In his seminal work on bilingualism, *Languages in Contact: Findings and Problems*, Yiddishist Uriel Weinreich defines interference as those "instances of deviation from the norms of either language which occur in the speech of bilinguals as a result of their familiarity with more than one language, i.e. as a result of language contact" (1953:1). Although some bilinguals are more susceptible to interference than others, interference is considered a normative feature of bilingual language use (Hoffmann, 1991).

Interference most often occurs from the L1 to L2, such that a native Hebrew speaker will produce sentences such as "Let's invite pizza for dinner" or "I'm regular to that." In translation, however, interference occurs from the source language to the target language, or, more accurately, from the source text to the target text. Since most often translators work into their mother tongue, the direction of interference is from L2 to L1. As a result, when a native English speaker translates from Hebrew into English, the translation will almost inevitably contain certain traces of the weaker language. Translations from Hebrew will therefore contain sentences such as "This book was printed in 1956" and "Teachers and kindergarten teachers are underpaid."

Israeli scholar Gideon Toury has argued that interference is a law of translation, a view that has gained wide currency in Translation Studies. Toury reports: "The analysis of thousands of pages translated into Hebrew and English allows me to claim that virtually no translation is completely devoid of formal equivalents, i.e., of manifestations of interlanguage" (1979: 226). The interlanguage typical of translators and translation is often called "translationese." Although professionals are more adept at avoiding interference than are less-skilled translators, interference remains "the occupational disease of translation" (Newman, 1987: 75).

It is important to note that the translator is not influenced by the source language per se, but by the source language as presented in the particular source text. If the Hebrew source text contains the word פרוטוקול, the translator might translate it as "protocol" rather than "minutes"; if that specific word does not appear, the translator will not be subject to this particular form of interference, but perhaps to another.

False cognates—in translation jargon, *faux amis*—are a common cause of interference. False cognates are "phonologically similar but whose meanings do not overlap, or overlap only in part" (Gernsbacher and Shlesinger, 1997: 123). The translator must ignore the obvious similarity of the false cognate to a target-language word lest he or she make a serious (and embarrassing) error. Hebrew-English false cognates include pairs such as אנגינה-angina (strep throat), לורד-lord (marker), סטפס-steps (tap dance), and וילה-villa (single-family home). To complicate matters, a Hebrew word can be a false cognate in American English, but a true cognate in British English, such as צ'יפס, which should be translated as "french fries" in the United States and "chips" in Britain, and פלסטר "band-aid" in American English and "plaster" in British.

False cognates are a recurrent source of word-level interference for the translator and language learner alike (Anderman, 1998: 43). Brian Harris (1978) explains that people use three elements in word association: sound, meaning, and extra-linguistic references and connotations. With false cognates, "the association by sound is very strong while the difference in meaning is not sufficient to counteract the sound" (425). The association by sound is so strong, in fact, that foreign-language students continue to experience difficulty with false cognates even after repeated instruction (Frantzen, 1998: 243). One would expect that a student who is warned about the risk of mistranslating a false cognate will be better equipped to deal with false cognates in the language classroom.

For the translator, interference is not limited to actual lexical or syntactical errors, but can appear in more subtle guises, such as a skewed statistical distribution of certain grammatical or stylistic features (Chesterman, 1997: 71) or the insufficient utilization of target-language linguistic resources (Klaudy, 2003: 200). The overuse of cognates (Mossop, 2001: 26) is evidence of interference, as is establishing a pattern of cohesion in the target text that reflects source- rather than target-language norms (Blum-Kulka, 1986).

The language learner's errors are both regular and consistent (Corder, 1981: 66) and contrastive analysis can often be used to predict where a language learner will go wrong. Work on reducing interference in the translation classroom will have a beneficial effect on the student's L2 skills as well as his or her translations. One could even go so far as to argue that interference in the translation classroom is a good thing for the language teacher, because it identifies trouble spots and brings home the lessons of contrastive analysis.

The Contrastive Analysis of English and Hebrew

Languages differ in innumerable and often unexpected ways. Here we operate according to the "no pain, no gain" principle. The energy the students are forced to invest in translating a seemingly simple sentence, e.g., "The teacher ate a sandwich for lunch," is a surefire guarantee that they will remember the lessons of gender and conjugation, as well as the fact "sandwich" can be translated in more than one way.

Hebrew is a more condensed language than English. Witness the difference between the pithy שנינו and the word-heavy "the two of us." In the language class, the teacher will treat the kaf-schwa as an equivalent for "about"; in the translation classroom, the students will see how many letters are required to express this idea in English—"about," "so," "approximately," or "some"—and that often the best translation for כתשעים is "ninety." In the opposite direction, it takes an entire word to express the idea of the English comparative -er and superlative -est.

Hebrew often refers to people by their attributes (הסקרנים, החיוורת, השמן), whereas English requires both adjective and noun. In a reading-comprehension class this is a straightforward matter—הצעיר is understood to be a person who is young and male. But the translator must supply a noun, and every possibility has a slightly different connotation: young guy, young male, young person, young man, and so on.

The differences between Hebrew and English (or any language pair, for that matter) can on occasion seem random. Why does Hebrew use the same word for "ticket" and "card"? Why doesn't English have a one-word term for חודשים (two months)? It is clear to the native English speaker that there is a distinction between "less" and "fewer." It is equally clear to the native Hebrew speaker that there is a distinction between עוד and יותר ("more"). These differences are evident when we translate the following sentences into Hebrew:

- ¥ David has less hair than he used to, and soon he'll be bald.
- ¥ Fewer children signed up for camp this year than last.
- ¥ Sarah smiled at her father and asked, "Can I please have more cocoa?"
- ¥ The Library of Congress has more books than the downtown library does.

This is not the forum for an in-depth discussion of Hebrew-English contrastive analysis. Instead, I present some rather obvious differences between the two languages that can complicate the translation process.

In the movie מדורת השבט ("Campfire") a mother sits at the table with her two daughters, the rebellious Esti and the more docile Tami. She says:

אני רק רוצה שתדעו שאתן הדבר הכי יקר בעולם, ושחוסר ההתחשבות שלכם ושיתוף הפעולה שלכם, אני מרגישה שאתן עושות לי דווקא. אני מרגישה שאתן מאשימות אותי שאבא מת, אתן צעירות, אתן לא מבינות, אני גם מקווה מאוד שאתן לא תבינו. אבל אני רוצה שתבינו את זה: אנחנו עכשיו חיות תחת זכוכית מגדלת.

Gloss: I just want you to know that you're the most precious thing in the world to me. I feel like you're being inconsiderate and uncooperative on purpose. I feel like you blame me for your father's death. You're young, you don't understand, and I really hope that you'll never understand. But I want you to understand this: right now we're living under a magnifying glass.

The subtitler translated אתן simply as "you." As a consequence, the English speaker watching the film could logically draw the conclusion that the mother's anger is directed solely at Esti. Other options ("the two of you," "both of you," "you two") can be seen to perhaps overstate the case that the mother is speaking to both daughters.

Later in the movie, the mother says to Tami: "—את יכולה לספר למישהו אחר ליועצת, לפסיכולוגית." This appears in the subtitles as "You can tell someone else—the school counselor, a psychologist." In Hebrew, it is not only understood but stated outright that both the guidance counselor and the psychologist are women. In the English, either or both could be male.

Gender is a problem regardless if Hebrew is the source or target language. The translator working into English has three basic options: to specify gender ("female soldier," "male nurse"), to use a gender-neutral noun ("soldier," "nurse"), or to find another way to indicate that the soldier is actually a woman ("the soldier ... she"). The translator must decide on a case-by-case basis how to treat gender in the English. The gender of the proctologist or gynecologist is apt to be more significant than the gender of the general practitioner.

In contrast, a translator working into Hebrew often must verify if the soldier and nurse are male or female. Coupled with this, something that can be left ambiguous in English must be specified in the Hebrew. If the teenager tries to tell the truth but not the whole truth, she might tell her parents she was at "a friend's house"—an evasion that is impossible in Hebrew.[3]

Compare the difficulty of translating the two following sentences:

- This isn't a life or death matter.
- This is not a life or death matter.

Translators working into Hebrew have to find a way to express the colloquial register created by English contractions. When they work into English, they have to make a concerted effort to use contractions when appropriate, so that their target text sounds like authentic original English. This isn't as easy as it sounds. Maeve Olohan (2003) demonstrated that translations into English typically contain fewer contractions than original English texts.

The fact that English has capital letters and Hebrew does not can make the translator's life a misery. It takes creativity and thought to translate a sentence such as "He was Average with a capital A." David Carr used a capital to create humor in his *New York Times* piece about the screenwriters' strike: "The best lines this year haven't come from David Letterman's writers but from whoever (or Whoever) is whispering in Mike Huckabee's ear." Hebrew has no parallel device.

---

3. I thank my student Yulie Davidovich for this example.

The fact that English employs adjective-noun and Hebrew employs noun–adjective is discussed in the language classroom. The translation teacher will talk about how one translates the ambiguous phrase "organic brown rice and mushrooms" or ספרים ומחקרים חשובים. Although the focus in the classroom is on translation rather than interpreting, this is an appropriate juncture to discuss the tremendous burden the reversal of the adjective and noun places on the interpreter. This is particularly problematic when the source text contains long strings of adjectives, such as "constant, active, conscious, healthy interest or influential, educated, mobile, well off executive" [taken from a source text used by Shlesinger (2000)].

In the language classroom, students are introduced to the Hebrew tense system and drilled on various conjugations. It is in the translation classroom that students fully grasp the difference between how the passage of time is expressed in Hebrew and English. Translator Nicholas de Lange (1993), who works from Hebrew to English, writes: "Older Hebrew, being a Semitic language, does not have tenses as we have them in English. Even modern Hebrew, which is deeply influenced by European languages, treats time with great freedom, often to the translator's despair. We are forced to be definite where the Hebrew is ambiguous, to make choices where there is no one right answer." Translators working into Hebrew have to find mechanisms to express the subtle differences in a passage such as this:

> Scientists have long said the only way to restore Louisiana's vanishing wetlands is to undo the elaborate levee system that controls the Mississippi River, not with the small projects that have been tried here and there, but with a massive diversion that would send the muddy river flooding wholesale into the state's sediment-starved marshes.
>
> And most of them have long dismissed the idea as impractical, unaffordable and lethal to the region's economy. Now, they are reconsidering. In fact, when a group of researchers convened last April to consider the fate of the Louisiana coast, their recommendation was unanimous: divert the river. (*New York Times*)

Principles of Translation Theory: Gridding and Voids

It has become almost a truism that every human language divides up and maps the world differently. It thus comes as no surprise that two languages rarely have exact lexical matches. Between-language lexical differences are so ubiquitous that translation theorist Rosa Rabadán maintains that "the chances of finding perfectly symmetrical correspondents depend on sheer coincidence" (1991: 39). Languages, including English and Hebrew, differ as to how they segment the rainbow, how they express kinship relations, how they divide the parts of the body, and how they relate to weather and the seasons.

The renowned linguist Benjamin Whorf writes: "Hopi has one noun that covers every thing or being that flies, with the exception of birds, which class is denoted by another noun. The former noun may be said to denote the class (FC-B)—flying class minus bird. The Hopi actually call insect, airplane, and aviator all by the same word, and feel no difficulty about it" (1956: 216). As native English speakers, the idea that helicopters and bees could be members of the same category seems rather odd, and the idea that birds are not included in that category equally odd. This is, however, one of the vagaries of language: what seems arbitrary to a native English speaker makes eminent sense to a native Hopi speaker.

Menachem Dagut (1990) also uses the act of flying as an example of how gridding affects our perception of the world. Drawing a distinction between mechanical and natural flying seems natural and right to the native Hebrew speaker. Dagut argues that when the native English speaker mistakenly uses עָף instead of טָס the Hebrew speaker will view this error "as laughably grotesque, rather than just linguistically mistaken" (15). One must ask whether a dentist knows less about medicine than her colleague the רופאת שיניים does.

Gridding differences are much more common than one would think. Even so-called true cognates are not always consistently true. Take the example of "concert" and קונצרט. The English "concert" will be translated in one way if the Philharmonic is performing Mozart (קונצרט) and another if the Rolling Stones are on tour (הופעה). Similarly, the Hebrew קונצרט will be translated as "concert" for an orchestra but as "recital" for a soloist or a music student.

In translation, the difficulty arises when we work from the language with fewer distinctions to that with more. While the translator can work on autopilot when translating "pigeon" or "dove" into Hebrew, he or she must weigh the different options in rendering יונה into English. It requires more energy to translate יד into English than "hand" or "arm" into Hebrew; it is harder to translate "painter" into Hebrew than צייר into English (even before we deal with the question of the painter's gender).

The difference between "house" and בית is a common lesson in the language classroom. The ramifications of "home/house" become clear when a student thinks about how to translate the following paragraph from the *New York Times*:

By 10 a.m. Saturday, more than 700 people filled a hall in the convention center here for what real estate agents say is the largest auction
of foreclosed properties ever in Minnesota, with more than 300
houses or apartments for sale in two days. Opening bids ranged from
$1,000—for a three-bedroom house—to $729,000, for a five-
bedroom house on 11.9 acres. The crowd was standing-room only,
with more waiting to enter. Some were looking for homes, others
for investments.

Depending on the students' Hebrew skills, they might translate the entire
paragraph into Hebrew or translate only selected words. Students at any level
would profit from a discussion of the strategies required to translate "house,"
"home," the dollar sums, and the word "acres." The task can be tailored to
the individual students, something that is particularly helpful when teaching
a heterogeneous population.

At times, translation can be difficult because a term in the source text simply
doesn't exist in the target language, i.e., the target language has a void. One
finds a seemingly endless number of words that are unique to Hebrew or
English. Voids are generally divided into three categories:

- LEXICAL VOIDS: The concept exists in the target culture, but the target
  language does not provide a one-word label for it. English has a one-
  word expression for the act of driving too quickly—"speeding"—
  whereas Hebrew does not. It goes with without saying that drivers are
  as prone to speed in Israel as they are in English-speaking countries.
  At the same time, Hebrew has the one-word expression מחותן, which
  must be rendered in English as "son-in-law's father" or "daughter-in-
  law's father," or some variation thereof.

- REFERENTIAL VOIDS: The target language does not provide a label
  because the referent does not exist in the target culture. Referential
  voids often relate to matters such as religion, geography, and local
  customs. Hebrew has no word for "slush" or "slushy"; English has no
  equivalent for the Middle Eastern שרב.

- MORPHOSYNTACTIC VOIDS: English has the noun "conscience" but
  no one-word equivalent for the Hebrew מצפוני. Hebrew has a noun
  for "pencil," but requires several words to express the English verb "to
  pencil." It can require creativity to translate words such as עקרוני, ערכי,
  and הרקדה.

The translation teacher can discuss voids and translation strategies. A lesson
on voids also provides a springboard for a more theoretical discussion: What
is the relationship between language and culture? What, if anything, can we

learn from the fact that Hebrew has no one-word equivalent for "treif" (non-kosher)? What can the translation of voids teach us about the translation process and the translator's job?

Although authentic texts are generally preferred in the translation classroom, the teacher also has the option of composing a source text to serve a particular purpose, e.g., to work on the translation of idioms. This short source text highlights the translation of voids. It also contains a number of false cognates:

לרוע המזל, נדמה שהחיים בעידן המודרני אינם קלים יותר מהחיים שהתנהלו בעידן האבן או בימי הביניים. מכשירי החשמל הביתיים הנפלאים—מדיח הכלים, מעבד המזון, ותנור הטורבו—כולם נועדו לחסוך עוד יותר את זמנינו, ולהעלות את הסטנדרטים שלנו. פעם נהגנו לקנות את כל מצרכינו במכולת הקרובה, החל מסודה ולחמניות עד למיונז וטונה; כיום, אנחנו נאלצים להידחק בין המוני הקונים בסופר או להיכנס לחמש חנויות שונות כדי לקנות את מצרכינו: לאטליז, למאפייה, לירקן, לפיצוחיה ולחנות למזון אורגני. פעם הסתפקנו בקורת גג מעל לראשינו ובלחם שהרווחנו במו ידינו; כיום, עלו ציפיותינו—מדירה של שני חדרים לקוטג' של שישה חדרים. משישי שבת בחוף הים לטיול ספארי של חודש ימים בחו"ל. מה קרה למסורת הישנה והטובה?

Translating Culture

> The solutions to many of the translator's dilemmas are not to be found in dictionaries, but rather in an understanding of the way language is tied to local realities, to literary forms and to changing identities. Translators must constantly make decisions about the cultural meanings which language carries, and evaluate the degree to which the two different worlds they inhabit are "the same." (Simon 1996: 138)

Not only must the translator be bilingual, he or she must also have an intimate familiarity with both source and target cultures. The translator uses the twin processes of explicitation and implicitation as a bridge between the source and target cultures. Kinga Klaudy (1998) defines explicitation as "the technique of making explicit in the target text information that is implicit in the source text" (80); by extension, implicitation is making implicit in the target text information that is explicit in the source text.

The American will recognize Beantown, Roe v. Wade, and Starbucks; the Israeli ירוחם, סביח, and בני עקיבא. It is the translator's job to supply the members of the target-language audience with the information they lack. The movie "Capote" is called "Truman Capote" in Hebrew; in the subtitles for the film כנפיים שבורות ("Broken Wings") the line אני עובדת ברוצ'לד is translated as "I work at Rothschild hospital." Explicitation is far more common in translation than is implicitation, since, as a matter of course, we are more knowledgeable about our own culture than about a foreign one.

The following text was designed to teach the concepts of explicitation and implicitation. Native English speakers do not necessarily have to translate the text; it is sufficient that they identify the changes that should be made when translating the text for an Israeli reader:

> I grew up in Chicago in the sixties. Once a month my father would take me by El to the Loop where we would stop in a pizzeria to split a large pie and talk about the White Sox. Perhaps my fondest childhood memories are these father-son outings.
>
> With the outbreak of the 1967 Six Day War between Israel and her Arab neighbors, my father became fiercely Zionistic. Not only did we begin to talk about politics instead of sports, he also insisted that instead of eating pizza, we should dine on the typical Israeli street food, felafel, which is deep-fried chick-pea balls served in a pocket bread with finely chopped tomatoes and cucumbers.
>
> To be honest, I enjoyed pizza and the Sox more than felafel and politics, but I understood and respected my father's newfound obsession with the State of Israel.

Umberto Eco (2001) asserts that "*Father* is not a synonym for *daddy*, *daddy* is not a synonym for *papà*, and *père* is not a synonym for *padre ...*" (9). I would argue that even if the owner of an American falafel stand follows his or her Israeli cousin's recipe to the letter, using spices and chickpeas imported from Israel, and even if the most discerning customer couldn't tell which falafel ball was produced in Topeka and which in Haifa, there would still be a difference in connotation between the words "falafel" and פלאפל. In America (and therefore English), falafel is a recent import and has more cachet than, say, a peanut butter and jelly sandwich.

The translator must be sensitive to cultural connotations. At first glance, פנימיה seems to be a fine translation for "boarding school," since both denote a school where the students dorm. But there are vast socioeconomic differences between the students at a פנימיה and those at a boarding school—so vast that it is almost comic to refer to Eton or Groton as a פנימיה. Teaching this disparity helps the student understand how rooted we are in our own culture and the intimate connection between culture and language.

The following excerpt from Jon Krakauer's *Into the Wild* illustrates some of the questions translators wrestle with on a daily basis:

Jim Gallien had driven four miles out of Fairbanks when he spotted the hitchhiker standing in the snow beside the road, thumb raised high, shivering in the gray Alaska dawn. He didn't appear to be very old: eighteen, maybe nineteen at most. A rifle protruded from the young man's backpack, but he looked friendly enough; a hitchhiker with a Remington semiautomatic isn't the sort of thing that gives motorists pause in the forty-ninth state. Gallien steered his truck onto the shoulder and told the kid to climb in.

The hitchhiker swung his pack into the bed of the Ford and intro-duced himself as Alex. "Alex?" Gallien responded, fishing for a last name.

"Just Alex," the young man replied, pointedly rejecting the bait. Five feet seven or eight with a wiry build, he claimed to be twenty-four years old and said he was from South Dakota.

- Will the Israeli reader know that Fairbanks is a city in Alaska? If not, is this information important to convey?
- Should miles be converted into kilometers? Feet and inches into centi-meters? If the translator decides to convert Alex's height into centi-meters, must the miles be converted as well?
- Is "eighteen, maybe nineteen at most" considered to be as young in Israel as in the States?
- Will readers understand from context that Alaska is the forty-ninth state?
- Will an Israeli know where South Dakota is? Does this matter?

The translation of seemingly simple words and sentences can lead to a com-plex understanding of the differences between cultures and the relationship between language and culture. Norms in the United States frequently differ from those in Israel and, as a result, English and Hebrew speakers will differ in their interpretation of basic terms. While בוקר is an obvious translation for "morning" and ערב for "evening," an American and an Israeli would disagree as to when morning and evening begin and end.

This sentence can generate a fruitful discussion in the translation classroom: להגיע לאתר מוקדם בבוקר במצדה חם מאוד בקיץ וכדאי ["Masada is very hot in the summer and you should arrive at the site early in the morning"]. Will "very hot" properly convey how scorching Masada is in the summer? Will the tourist think that a 9:30 arrival time qualifies as early? Will he or she assume that the summer begins in July and ends in August? Miriam Shlesinger provides a related example from the Demjanjuk trial:

...when an American attorney questioned an Israeli police man about "the winter of 1986," the former was referring to the period beginning in November 1986 (by which time winter sets in in the area where he lives) and lasting until about April of 1987, whereas the latter assumed this referred to the period beginning in January 1986 and lasting through March of the year, in line with Israeli climate. (1991: 149)

Just as seasons are problematic, so are the days of the week. Is "Saturday night" the same as מוצאי שבת? Can "weekend" be translated as שישי-שבת? How do we translate the Goodwill slogan "Give people a chance to hate Monday mornings"?

The translator also risks Christianizing a Jewish term if he or she translates בגדי שבת as "Sunday best" or צדיק as "saint." The two main characters in the film האושפיזין have an intimate relationship with God, addressing Him with the Hebrew אבא and the Yiddish טאטע. The subtitler translates both as "Father," which is uncomfortably reminiscent of "Our Father who art in heaven."

The subject of religion is not limited to overtly religious texts or to referential voids such as לולב, מחזור, and חמין. Even texts written by secular Israelis that are not on a religious topic can be sprinkled with talmudic expressions (תרתי משמע, דא עקא, דברים בגו) and Jewish concepts (בל תשחית, פיקוח נפש, למהדרין). It requires time, effort, and knowledge to translate these into English. The translator working into Hebrew must consider how best to translate terms that the traditional Jew might find offensive (bacon and eggs, pigsty, shrimp cocktail). It is tricky to find the proper balance between accuracy and appropriateness.

Translation and the Department of Hebrew Language and Literature

Translation Studies highlights the interrelationship between language and reality. Translation courses create a link between a Hebrew-language program and disciplines such as linguistics, comparative literature, religious studies, psychology, history, and cultural studies—something of great importance in this age of interdisciplinary and multidisciplinary studies.

Israeli scholars have made and continue to make a vital contribution to the field of Translation Studies. *The Translation Studies Reader* (Venuti, 2000), a compendium of the most important writing in Translation Studies, includes contributions from three Israelis: Shoshana Blum-Kulka, Itamar Evan-Zohar, and Gideon Toury. These scholars take their place alongside thinkers such as Jorge Luis Gorges, Walter Benjamin, and Vladimir Nabokov. Many important papers in translation journals and collected volumes use translation into or out of Hebrew as a springboard for a discussion of central issues in translation.

The fact that Israeli scholars have been so active in Translation Studies has important implications for the language program. Language courses typically have little or no academic content and professors have few opportunities to introduce academic materials into the curriculum. There are, however, many fine articles written in English about Hebrew-English or English-Hebrew translation. Topics include the translation of literary dialogue into Hebrew (Ben-Shahar, 1994), the "intranslatability" of Agnon (Aphek and Tobin, 1983), lexicalization in Hebrew-English translation (Shlesinger, 1992), the translation of Lewis Carroll's wordplay (Weissbrod, 1996), and the ideological considerations that influenced the translators who rendered *Ben-Hur* into Hebrew (Ben-Ari 2002). These articles shed light on translation *qua* translation but also on specific features of the Hebrew language, Israeli culture, and the Jewish religion. A course with a translation-theory component can be more intellectually challenging than the typical language course and far more rewarding for student and teacher alike.

REFERENCES

Anderman, G. 1998. Finding the right words: Translation and language teaching. In K. Malmkjær (ed.), *Translation and Language Teaching: Language Teaching and Translation* (pp. 39–48). United Kingdom: St. Jerome.

Aphek, E. and Y. Tobin, 1983. The means is the message: On the intranslatability of a Hebrew text. *Meta* 28, 57–69.

Ben-Ari, N. 2002. The double conversion of Ben-Hur: A case of manipulative translation. *Target* 14 (2), 263–301.

Ben-Shahar, R. 1994. Translating literary dialogue: A problem and its implications for translation into Hebrew. *Target* 6: 195–221.

Blum-Kulka, S. 1986. Shifts of cohesion and coherence in translation. In J. House & S. Blum-Kulka (eds.), *Interlingual and Intercultural Communication: Discourse and Cognition in Translation and Second Language Acquisition Studies* (pp. 17–35). Tübingen: Narr.

Chesterman, A. 1997. *Memes of Translation: The Spread of Ideas in Translation Theory.* Amsterdam/Philadelphia: John Benjamins.

Cook, G. 1998. Use of translation in language teaching. In M. Baker (ed.), *Routledge Encyclopedia of Translation Studies* (pp. 117–120). London/New York: Routledge.

Corder, S.P. 1992. A role for the mother tongue. In S.M. Gass and L. Selinker (eds.), *Language Transfer in Language Learning*, Revised Edition (pp. 18–31). Amsterdam/Philadelphia: John Benjamins.

Dagut, M.B. 1990. Incongruencies in lexical 'gridding'—An application of contrastive semantic analysis to language teaching. In The Contrastive Analysis of English and Hebrew: A Reader for Schools Studying the "Translation Skills" Syllabus (pp. 13–23). Jerusalem: Division of Curriculum Development, Ministry of Education & Culture.

De Lange, N. 1993. Reflections of a translator. Sixteenth Annual Rabbi Louis Feinberg Memorial Lecture in Judaic Studies. Cincinnati: Judaic Studies Program, University of Cincinnati.

Dornic, S. 1978. The bilingual's performance: Language dominance, stress, and individual differences. In D. Gerver and H.W. Sinaiko (eds.), Language Interpretation and Communication (pp. 259–271). New York/London: Plenum.

Eco, U. 2001. Experiences in Translation, trans. A. McEwen. Toronto/Buffalo/London: University of Toronto Press.

Frantzen, D. 1998. Intrinsic and extrinsic factors that contribute to the difficulty of learning false cognates. Foreign Language Annals 31 (2): 243–254.

Gerloff, P. 1988. From French to English: A look at the translation process in students, bilinguals, and professional translators. Unpublished Ed.D. dissertation. Cambridge, Mass.: Harvard University.

Gernsbacher, M.A. and M. Shlesinger. 1997. The proposed role of suppression in simultaneous interpretation. Interpreting 2 (1/2): 119–140.

Harris, B. 1978. The difference between natural and professional translation. Canadian Modern Language Review 34: 417–427.

Hoffmann, C. 1991. An Introduction to Bilingualism. United Kingdom: Longman Linguistics Library.

Holmes, J.S. 1988. Translated! Papers on Literary Translation and Translation Studies. Amsterdam: Rodsopi.

Joly, J-F. 1995. Introduction. In J. Delisle and J. Woodsworth (eds.), Translators through History (xiii–xvi). Amsterdam/Philadelphia: John Benjamins and UNESCO.

Keeley, E. 2000. On Translation: Reflections and Conversations. Amsterdam: Harwood Academic Publishers.

Klaudy, K. 1998. Explicitation. In: M. Baker (ed.), Routledge Encyclopedia of Translation Studies (pp. 80–84). London/New York: Routledge.

——————— . 2003. Languages in Translation: Lectures on the Theory, Teaching and Practice of Translation. Budapest: Scholastica.

Krakauer, J. 1996. Into the Wild. New York: Villard Books.

Kraszewski, C.S. 1998. Four Translation Strategies Determined by the Particular Needs of the Receptor. New York/Ontario/Wales: The Edwin Mellen Press.

Levy, J. 1967. Translation as a decision process. In To Honor Roman Jakobson II (pp. 1171-1182). The Hague: Mouton.

Malmkjær, K. 2004. Translation as an academic discipline. In: K. Malmkjær (ed.), Translation in Undergraduate Degree Programmes (pp. 1–7). Amsterdam/Philadelphia: John Benjamins.

Mossop, B. 2001. *Revising and Editing for Translators*. Manchester, United Kingdom/Northampton, Mass.: St. Jerome.

Newman, A. 1987. Translation universals: Perspectives and explorations. In M. Gaddis Rose (ed.), *Translation Perspectives III: Selected Papers, 1985–86* (pp. 69–83). Binghamton: SUNY-Binghamton.

Olohan, M. 2003. How frequent are the contractions? A study of contracted forms in the translational English corpus. *Target* 15 (1): 59–89.

Piotrowska, M. 1997. *Learning Translation—Learning the Impossible?: A Course of Translation from English into Polish*. Krakow: 1997.

Presas, M. 2000. Bilingual competence and translation competence. In C. Schäffner and B. Adab (eds.), *Developing Translation Competence* (pp. 19–31). Amsterdam/Philadelphia: John Benjamins.

Rabadán, R. 1991. The unit of translation revisited. In M.L. Larson (ed.), *Translation: Theory and Practice, Tension and Independence* (pp. 38–48). U.S.A.: State University of New York at Binghamton.

Schjoldager, A. 2004. Are L2 learners more prone to err when they translate? In K. Malmkjær (ed.), *Translation in Undergraduate Degree Programmes* (pp. 127–149). Amsterdam/Philadelphia: John Benjamins.

Shlesinger, M. 1991. Interpreter latitude vs. due process: Simultaneous and consecutive interpretation in multilingual trials. In S. Tirkkonen-Conjit (ed.), *Empirical Research in Translation and Intercultural Studies* (pp. 147–155). Tübingen: Narr.

——————— . 1992. Lexicalization in translation: An empirical study of students' progress. In C. Dollerup and A. Loddegaard (eds.), *Teaching Translation and Interpreting: Training, Talent and Experience* (pp. 123–127). Amsterdam/Philadelphia: John Benjamins.

——————— . 2000. Strategic allocation of working memory and other attentional resources in simultaneous interpreting. Unpublished Ph.D. dissertation. Israel: Bar-Ilan University.

Simon, S. 1996. *Gender in Translation: Cultural Identity and the Politics of Transmission*. London/New York: Routledge.

Stratford, P. 1995. Translating Antonine Maillet's fiction. In: S. Simon (ed.) *Culture in Transit: Translating the Culture of Quebec* (pp. 93–100). Montreal: Véhicule Press.

Toury, G. 1979. Interlanguage and its manifestations in translation. *Meta* XXIV (2): 223–231.

Venuti, L. (ed.). 2000. *The Translation Studies Reader*. London/New York: Routledge.

Weinreich, U. 1953. *Languages in Contact: Findings and Problems*. New York: Linguistic Circle of New York.

Weissbrod, R. 1996. 'Curiouser and curiouser': Hebrew translations of wordplay in Alice's Adventures in Wonderland. *The Translator* 2(2): 219–234.

Whorf, B.L. 1956. *Language, Thought and Reality: Selected Writings of Benjamin Lee Whorf*, ed. J.B. Carroll. Cambridge, Mass.: MIT Press.

זְלוֹ שֶׁל הַגַּל קוֹרֵ׃
תּוֹ – שֶׁאָבוֹא אֲנִי

ON READING HEBREW POETRY
QUESTIONS AND ANSWERS

זְ בְּרֹאשׁוֹ, וְהִכִּינוּ זְ
וֹת, אָמֵן אָמֵן סֶלָה״

Edna Amir Coffin
University of Michigan

"WHERE LITERATURE IS TAUGHT there is an expectation that something unique will occur…but first and foremost, that some pleasure will be derived—the kind of pleasure that comes with discovery. And those who experience such occurrences will thrive, and those who miss them will be lessened in some way," wrote S. Yizhar (1990). Yizhar summed up his philosophy of education by stating that teachers have to "stop teaching literature" (1972). What Yizhar offered was an alternative way for introducing young people to literature. Some twenty years later, with the general acceptance of readers' reception theory and its introduction into the mainstream of the world of literary criticism, Yizhar's words seem not only to be taken for granted, but also to be well anchored in contemporary methodologies for teaching literature. In the same way that Yizhar's words apply to native readers of Hebrew literature, they also apply to those who study Hebrew literature in the programs of Hebrew studies within the American academic scene.

The introduction of students to Hebrew fiction, poetry, and drama presents a challenge to instructors and students alike. It is an increasingly difficult undertaking in today's reality of the global culture of digital technology, where reading of source language literature has almost become an esoteric task. This is even more true of literature that is either remote in time or is part of a different linguistic and literary legacy. Students in this rapidly changing culture tend to engage a great deal in text messaging, blogging, and using their bookish skills for daily communication and for professional purposes rather than engaging in the reading of fine literature. Viewing films and listening to popular music often replace the act of reading fiction and reading or listening to poetry. The readers' experience of literary works is frequently limited to the realms of the academic curriculum; this is particularly true of poetry. Leaving works of poetry out of a Hebrew literature curriculum is not an option, since this would diminish the essence of the literary tradition. Poetry constitutes the heart and soul of the cultural legacy and is part of the liturgical, as well as the secular heritage.

That task of introducing new readers to Hebrew poetry falls on the shoulders of the teachers of literature. There are several important requisites for teachers that can enhance their effectiveness when directing others in the process of reading. These include an awareness of the complexities and fine nuances of the source language of the poems, an understanding of the use of language registers and styles, knowledge of pragmatics and grammaticality, and acquaintance with the variety of genres of poetry and their conventions. Because of the intertextual nature of so many poems and other literary works, teachers ought to have access to a large body of poetry, be aware of the historical dimensions and poetic traditions tied to particular historical periods, and be familiar with the unique styles of individual poets.

Language components that make up a poem need to be addressed to begin with in order to enable a successful reading of a literary text; they are the building blocks from which a poem is constructed. Meanings assigned to vocabulary items and their distribution in the source language do not, for the most part, translate into exact equivalences. The same holds true when examining other forms of art. If we look at the world of music, it is clear that the foundations and traditions of western music differ from those in non-western countries. Each has its own musical traditions. In addition to differences in structure, there are also different musical instruments, styles of composition, and types of ensembles. The same is true of musical compositions that belong to the same culture but were written and performed in different historical periods. The act of listening to and appreciating other cultures' music requires knowledge and experience; it is often a matter of an acquired taste as a consequence of frequent exposure. Yizhar uses a similar analogy taken from the world of music when he compares the initial task of reading literature, and in particular poetry, to that of a musician becoming acquainted with the musical notes that make up a musical composition about to be performed. This is the same way readers need to see and distinguish each of the building blocks that make up a poem, while putting them together as a comprehensive text. The shifting nature of individual semantic units has to be taken into account, as meanings of words do not stay stable in the changing contexts within time and space dimensions. Like musical compositions, poems make up closed and discrete discourse units, yet they can also relate to other works, outside their closed entity, be they of another time or contemporary.

Ludwig Wittgenstein is quoted as saying that if we spoke a different language, we would perceive a somewhat different world. A somewhat similar position is held by Benjamin Whorf, an American linguist, who is noted for the basic assumptions underlying the nature of the relation of language to thinking and cognition. He writes, "Language shapes the way we think, and determines what we can think about" (in J. Carroll, 1956). Whorf's basic hypothesis postulates that the nature of a particular language influences the thoughts of its speakers and readers. His theory, often referred to as Linguistic Determinism, has been challenged in the light of some recent experimental studies. However, it posits a very useful concept to consider when examining the challenges facing readers who confront a literary text in a language different from their own native tongue. They encounter not only a different writing system and a different vocabulary inventory, but also cultural traditions and frames of reference that are different from their own. They are faced with the problem of how to treat the cultural aspects implicit in texts transmitted in another language and assimilating them into their own linguistic and cultural framework. The differences may range from the lexical content and syntax of the target text to ideologies and ways of life of the culture from which it emanates.

The Context of Reading

The context in which works of literature are read constitutes a significant factor in considering the reading process. Reading is thought of as a personal, individual experience, an act of choice rather than an obligatory one. Yet in the academic environment, reading literature is an assigned task for the readers and the selection of texts is, for the most part, a result of a planned curriculum rather than that of the readers' choice. And while much of the preparatory work may take place in individual settings, many of the interpretive activities take place in a structured environment, within a group encounter, usually led by an instructor. The instructor serves as the "experienced reader" who leads the discussion and decides the direction it takes. Individual instructors vary in the styles and ways in which they activate the discussion, depending on their methodological approach but also determined by their personality and temperament. A discussion can be anything, from a one-way directed lecture, offering the "right" reading of a given text, to one shaped by strategies promoting readers' responses based on their own experience and additional information provided by a variety of sources. However, often, it is a mixture of both directive and investigative experience. In addition, some instructors frame works of art within the boundaries of contemporary theories of literary criticism or socio-political contexts or a culturally bound one constrained by linguistic practices. At times the discussion is overwhelmed by the desire to fit the work of art into a theoretical framework, thus facing the danger of diminishing its status as an object brought as an example to prove a theoretical point. Robert Alter, in his book on reading (1989), warned that ideological discussion can outweigh the reading of the literary works themselves, and can turn students away from reading and, in extreme cases, even instill in them disdain for literature. He argued, "Without a sense of deep pleasure in the experience of reading, the whole enterprise of teaching and writing about literature quickly becomes pointless."

It is important to remember that the classroom constitutes a community of readers. In that community the readers assume a growing role in the discovery process as the role of the instructor becomes to a degree "equal among equals." Emphasis on the role of the readers, a transfer of authority for the interpretive process from the instructor to them, keeps the readers and the text as the focal points of the learning experience. Awareness of the nature of the text as being in a language other than that of the readers highlights the importance of the cultural and linguistic codes and their appreciation beyond the particular designated text. There has to be constant attention to the fact that the author and his intended readers are different from the audience of the actual readers in the learning environment we are considering. Umberto Eco (1984), whose focus is on the communicability aspect of a text, observed that "to organize a text, its author has to rely upon a series of codes that assign given contents to the expressions he uses. To make his text communicative, the author has to assume that the ensemble of codes he relies on is the same as that shared by his possible reader." In a sense, he creates a Model Reader, who has the ability to interpret the expressions in the text in a way close to that of the author. Operating within several cultural and linguistic environments, Eco is particularly aware of the fact that the Model Reader and the actual reader differ in many essential ways and calls attention to the need to close the gap. Wolfgang Iser, a noted literary critic, addressed himself particularly to the role of the reader in the reception of the text. Coming out of the phenomenological school of thought, he saw the act of reading as a dialogue between the text and the reader, and provided a valuable theoretical model for such interaction (1978). In the reading community of the classroom, the responsibility falls on the literature instructor to ensure that the conditions are met in order for the type of text-reader dialogue Iser and Eco talk about actually takes place.

Robert Alter, in *The Pleasures of Reading* (1989), pointed to the special properties of language when it is used in literary works and particularly in poetry. He contends that language of literature is different from other every-day common uses of language, and that it differs from them in its concentration and subtlety. It is distinguished by its density, its internal cross-references and resonances, and its emphasis on the purely esthetic pleasures of pattern and style. He took issue that the new directions in literary criticism tend to consider literary texts not so much as works of art, with their own distinct language and style, but rather as part and parcel of all written works. The written works can include daily newspapers, articles in magazines, comic strips, popular fiction, personal journals, research reports, etc. They all constitute artifacts that belong to the same type of written materials. The attempt to classify works that constitute the literary legacy is seen by some literary critics as stemming from an ideological stance that serves as an instrument of repression. Alter takes a strong stand that recognizes the emotional depth and the element of pleasure associated with reading and reflects on the danger of an emotional alienation that can result from such efforts to ignore the uniqueness of the imaginative life of a text under discussion.

Another interesting work that addresses the study of poetry and the search for meaning is that of Michael Rifaterre. Having had a great deal of experience in teaching French poetry at American universities, Rifaterre was very aware of what difficulties face the non-native readers. His study concentrated on the complex meanings that arise within poetic discourse, claiming that all "poetry expresses concepts and things by indirection…a poem says one things and means another." He further stated "poetry is peculiarly inseparable from the concept of text: if we do not regard the poem as a closed entity, we cannot always differentiate poetic discourse from literary language."

While the initial aim in the literature classroom is mostly to find ways to have the learners acquire skills and strategies for reading specific works of poetry, the ultimate goal and hope is that the readers will continue to pursue such activities beyond the classroom. For this end the readers need to find not only the differences of the target work of art but also the shared features and commonalities of human experience that are expressed in the text. At the same time they need to be aware of the unique qualities of particular poet and the style and central themes that inhabit his or her world.

Most readers need some assistance in developing the skills and strategies necessary for a successful outcome with the guidance of an experienced reader who can fill in the gaps that are left unspoken and unwritten, and who can point out the voice heard in the poem and its tone. Intentionality in speech acts (verbal or written) is as important as the text itself. All the above will give the readers the advantage available to native speakers and enable them to become critical readers, empowering them to do a meaningful analysis of poetry. Following Yizhar's observations, the role of teachers in a literature class is to serve as mediators between the text and its context and to understand that, rather than providing the answers to key questions, they need to lead readers to their own understanding of the meaning of the poem under discussion. The instructor is then to be viewed as the facilitator of the literary text and faces a special class of readers that we can label under the general rubric of "deficient readers," a term used here for readers who have deficiencies in several categories crucial to full comprehension and appreciation of a literary text. Their main deficiencies are not only in the purely linguistic level—in areas such as vocabulary and syntax—but also within the entire semiotic system.

Reading and Analysis

There are many published works that can be helpful to teachers, such as "How Does a Poem Mean" by John Ciardi, or "How and Why to Read" by Harold Bloom, or John Lye's useful guide "Critical Reading: A Guide," which is available online. Ciardi emphasized "analysis is never in any sense a substitute for a poem. The best any analysis can do is to prepare the reader to enter the poem more perceptively." Lye stated that "An analysis explains what a work of literature means, and how it means it; it is essentially an articulation of and a defense of an interpretation that shows how the resources of literature are used to create the meaningfulness of the text." Both authors resist the charge that analysis destroys a poem or in any way interferes with the direct esthetic experience of a work of art. Since a poem is an artifice, that is, it is made by someone, by appreciating the way in which it was constructed the reader can gain further understanding of its meaning.

Lye summarized the process of analysis:

> Analysis should also teach us to be aware of the cultural delineations of a work, its ideological aspects. Art is not eternal and timeless but is situated historically, socially, intellectually, written and read at particular times, with particular intents, under particular historical conditions, with particular cultural, personal, gender, racial, class and other perspectives... Through close reading and through reflection, analysis of a literary work can help in the understanding of the way ideas and feelings are talked about in a particular culture or in other times and cultures—to have a sense both of communities of meaning,

and of the different kinds of understanding there can be about matters of importance to human life. Art can give us access to the symbolic worlds of communities: not only to the kinds of ideas they have about life, but also to the way they feel about them, to the ways they imagine them, to the ways they relate them to other aspects of their lives.

Questions and Answers

We offer an example of an interpretive approach to a poem within the context of the classroom, encompassing both individual and communal experience. The poem is by the leading contemporary Israeli poet, Yehuda Amichai (1980). The poem is appropriately titled "Great Tranquility: Questions and Answers" [שלוה גדולה: שאלות ותשובות]. The choice of this poem as an example is not a random choice. The phrase in the title of the poem "Questions and Answers" sums up the direction and method by which a poem is to be approached. It typifies the nature of the dialogue between students and instructors. In the dialectic process of arriving at a meaning or meanings of this or any other particular poem, possible answers can be provided by all participants, rather than using an "instructor-centric" approach. When students learn how to pose meaningful and relevant questions, the learning process becomes more meaningful and not limited to answering the instructor's questions.

This short poem consists of ten lines, divided into two stanzas of four and six lines. It uses everyday language and contemporary imagery, yet its images, allusions, and metaphors reveal several layers of meaning, triggering different emotional and intellectual responses. They enhance readers' experience and make it possible for them to relate to the form and content of this poem.

שַׁלְוָה גְדוֹלָה: שְׁאֵלוֹת וּתְשׁוּבוֹת

אֲנָשִׁים בָּאוּלָם הַמּוּאָר עַד כְּאֵב
דִּבְּרוּ עַל הַדָּת
בְּחַיֵּי הָאָדָם בֶּן זְמַנֵּנוּ
וְעַל מְקוֹמוֹ שֶׁל הָאֱלֹהִים.

אֲנָשִׁים דִּבְּרוּ בְּקוֹלוֹת נִרְגָּשִׁים
כְּמוֹ בִּנְמָלֵי תְעוּפָה.
עֲזַבְתִּי אוֹתָם:
פָּתַחְתִּי דֶלֶת בַּרְזֶל שֶׁכָּתוּב עָלֶיהָ
"חֵרוּם" וְנִכְנַסְתִּי לְתוֹךְ
שַׁלְוָה גְדוֹלָה: שְׁאֵלוֹת וּתְשׁוּבוֹת.

A Great Serenity: Questions and Answers

People in the hall lighted so it hurts / spoke about Religion / in the life of contemporary Man /, and about God's place in it.

People spoke in excited voices / as at airports. / I left them: / I opened an iron door with the sign "Emergency" and entered / a great serenity: Questions and Answers.

Pre-Reading Preparation and Repeated Readings

There are a number of ways in which the poem can be introduced to the readers. One of them is to have the readers themselves do the preparatory work to close part of the information gap. There is a great deal of information available through various search tools, many of them on the Internet. One of the suggested steps is for the reader to look up a short biography of authors in order to situate them in time and place and learn details about their works. Because Amichai is recognized internationally as a leading, if not the leading, Israeli poet and because his poetry has been translated into many languages, there are many versions of his biography available to students online, both in English and in Hebrew. In addition, many of his poems are available on several web sites, such as http://famouspoetsandpoems.com/poets/yehuda_amichai /poems. In preparation for the class meeting, readers can also look up words and phrases to enable them to read the literal sense of the poem. The online multilingual Babylon dictionary is recommended, since it quotes from many sources and includes many synonyms, thus providing the reader with various nuances of meaning.

The second option for preparatory activities is for the instructor to go through this process during class time, when the poem is first presented. The advantage here would be that students can first be introduced to the poem through its sound. They can hear it read by the instructor, and they themselves can participate in some of the readings. Reading the poem aloud can be followed by discussions of the various elements of the language, with emphasis on very basic meanings of various vocabulary items, combinations of words, and their possible translations. Repeated readings of the poem acquaint students not only with the sounds of the poem but also with the sequence of the text. The more frequently it is read by different readers the more familiar it becomes, and the experience becomes shared by the community of readers. With repetitious readings, the poem sheds its status as an unfamiliar object.

Despite its seemingly linear order, the text is not as linear as it seems. It is a formal structure that is composed of various layers that are multidimensional in nature. Many texts, especially poems, are also circular in nature, as they suggest and even demand a second, third, and more readings to complete the process of appropriating them as one's own. The repeated readings can even result in memorizing part or the entirety of a poem. This leads to the intensification and appreciation of the work's esthetic qualities. Familiarity with the poem leads to a more informed analysis of its meaning. The teacher, who leads the group activities, initiates and directs the discussion. As students develop a closer acquaintance with a given poem they can assume a growing role in the discovery process and the direction of the discussion.

The Title and Last Line of the Poem

The title of a poem often points to the direction in which the author wants the reader to go. In this poem by Amichai, the last line of the poem also serves as is title. It therefore calls attention to its significance in the syntactic structure of the poem. It serves as the final destination to which the author guides his readers; therefore, each word and words connections are to be considered both separately and together. The choice of the word שלוה ("tranquility"), as indicated by the various suggested translations, is a world onto itself. Synonyms for שלוה are numerous: the Babylon dictionary suggests the following equivalents: ישיבה לבטח, שאננות, חוסר דאגה, שקיטה, רגיעה, רוגע, מנוחה, שקט, היות בניחותא, יישוב הדעת. The English translations supplied for the word שלוה by the Babylon dictionary include: tranquility, calmness, complacency, serenity, peace, quiescence, quiet, ease, equanimity, impassiveness, impassivity, imperturbability, limpidity, limpidness, peacefulness, placidity, placidness. The reader is therefore given a wealth of meanings from which to choose, which together create the various connotations of the word, both in the native tongue and in the target language. The adjective גדולה ("great") suggests the intensity and the all–encompassing nature that qualify the noun. The phrase שאלות ותשובות ("questions and answers") is probably the most relevant combination of words that lead to the heart of the poem; it is a phrase that consists of a pair of complementary nouns from spoken contemporary medium and that also evokes a rich historical reference to the traditional Responsa literature, in which rabbis respond to questions raised on a variety of subjects in Jewish life. Amichai manages to suggest both worlds at the same time and to provide a sense of ongoing existential questions raised through the ages for which answers are never easily or fully available. The title therefore needs to be addressed at the initial step of reading the poem, as well as when it appears in the closing line of the poem. The poem opens and closes with the same line, thus enveloping the structure as a world onto itself. At the same time, it provides an opportunity to relate the various intertextual connections to the poem. This line should be addressed first in its literary meaning on the level of everyday communication and later by introducing the students to the world of response literature, and by letting them gather whatever information they want to in this rich world of traditional existential epistemology. In second and third readings, students may want to consider the static nature of the first part of the title שלוה גדולה, which contrasts with the dynamic ongoing process of שאלות ותשובות. This is a great opportunity to introduce the students to both the simplicity of the text and how it manages to evoke a complex, rich world of associations. We have already noted that the final line of the poem is the same as its title, signifying a closed circle, a repetitive process that can recur an infinite number of times. While the ending of the poem does lead the reader to a place of tranquility, it also points to the constant recurrence of the process of questions and answers and the need to find a place of solitude away from the teeming crowd, where one can consider such matters outside of the public discourse domain.

Considering the Structure of the Poem

There are two basic kinds of structure: formal and thematic.

1. *Formal structure* is the way the poem goes together in terms of its component parts: if there are parts—stanzas, paragraphs or such—then there will be a relationship between the parts (for instance, the first stanza may give the past, the second the present, the third the future).

The poet organizes this poem into two distinct parts on the printed page. The division is marked by the space of an empty line between the two stanzas. However, the text itself demands that an additional division be examined, one that is determined by voice consideration, by the dynamics suggested, and by a turning point that changes the entire direction of the poem.

The first six lines have אנשים ("people," "someone") as the grammatical subject:

אֲנָשִׁים בָּאוּלָם הַמּוּאָר עַד כְּאֵב

דִּבְּרוּ עַל הַדָּת

בְּחַיֵּי הָאָדָם בֶּן זְמַנֵּנוּ

וְעַל מְקוֹמוֹ שֶׁל הָאֱלֹהִים.

אֲנָשִׁים דִּבְּרוּ בְּקוֹלוֹת נִרְגָּשִׁים

כְּמוֹ בִּנְמָלֵי תְעוּפָה.

The last four lines have *ani* ("I") as the grammatical subject:

עֲזַבְתִּי אוֹתָם:
פָּתַחְתִּי דֶלֶת בַּרְזֶל שֶׁכָּתוּב עָלֶיהָ
"חֵרוּם" וְנִכְנַסְתִּי לְתוֹךְ
שַׁלְוָה גְדוֹלָה: שְׁאֵלוֹת וּתְשׁוּבוֹת.

We can see that the organization of the poem has at least two possibilities, and that the principles of this organization consist not only of the two sets of different grammatical subjects, but also of the opposition between the types of verbs included. The first verbs engage in acts of speech (raising issues about their relevance and meaningfulness), whereas the second verbs are all verbs of action: "I left...I opened...I entered...," all of which set a new dynamic for the poem.

Sets of oppositions, especially in terms of imagery, can have further relevance to the organization of the poem. They will be discussed later in the article.

2. Thematic structure is the way the argument or presentation of the material of the poem is developed. In this case, the formal and thematic structures have a close relationship. The poem states the problem in the first six lines, and gives the poetic narrator's answer to the problem in the next four. When looking at the thematic structure, we see that the tensions in the poem are created by the meaningless chatter and discussion of God and religion. However, both topics give clear guidance for the direction of meanings in the poem, and the poem's "intensions." The escape from the chatter and noise leads the narrator into a dark and enclosed space, a place to raise questions and find answers. It also points out that the surface meaning may not be the deep meaning within the poem, that escaping from the very lit places to darkness may be an escape from light that may uncover some hidden truths, though the process may be painful.

The Use of Imagery as an Indicator of Meaning

When we look at the setting in terms of the physical world described in this poem, there are a number of evocations of specific moods and associations. We start with the background of a hall so brightly lit that it causes pain to those in it: אולם המואר עד כאב—the light is seen as a source of pain. This image of the lit hall is contrary to the expectations that light will bring comfort, instead of sitting in the dark. In retroactive reading, this image will take on a different meaning, shedding light into places of darkness where the person may not want to go can be very painful, like an overly lit place that causes discomfort. The reader is immediately faced with a seemingly positive image contrasted with the idea that excess causes discomfort and pain. This creates ambivalence and mixed feelings for the entire reading of the poem. The lit hall may be described in a concrete manner, an experience shared by people who find themselves in public places, or it might be used in a more tonal way, to create mood or associations, with the feeling of overexposure and anonymity in a public place. Another indicator of place is conveyed by the simile "like in airports." This figure of speech comes to evoke the associations of places like waiting rooms, which are places of anonymity. By the use of a simile, it refers more to a state of mind than to the actual experience of being at the airport awaiting a trip, or waiting to meet those who arrive.

The third image that sets the scene is the shelter to which the speaker seeks to flee. As in a monumental disaster, he searches for a safe place behind an iron door marked with the sign "emergency." This image suggests the depth of some dark place, such as a bunker. The word used for "emergency" is also multi-faceted, in the sense that *ḥeirum* in Hebrew also connotes stress, and has several synonyms that expand its meaning: צורך דחוף, מידיות, דחיפות, דחק, לחץ, מצוקה, צרה, פגע, אסון/פרענות, בהילות.

In addition to "emergency" as a semiotic sign, it also suggests the feeling of immediate and urgent danger, disaster, distress, trouble, calamity, anxiety, and pressure. From a simple descriptive phrase of an iron door bearing the sign חרום, this image evokes a set of emotional responses that go beyond this descriptive phrase. It should also be noted that the image of the bunker behind the iron door evokes an association with a prison cell behind an iron door. Thus, Amichai raises two different options for understanding the space: one is that of a shelter from disaster, but at the same time it is also that of a dungeon. The danger of fleeing to a safe place may hide within it another danger, that of loss of freedom. This double sword image puts forth the complexity of the existential situation from the point of view of the speaker in the poem. Amichai makes great use of simple descriptive settings that evoke places and objects of a concrete nature, and then sets a mood of anxiety, discomfort, and the fear of an impending calamity, which indirectly brings the reader into these surroundings.

Topic Aspects

As mentioned earlier, the topics of discussion raised in the first part of the poem are "religion" [הדת] and "God" [האלוהים]. They are raised by the anonymous figures אנשים ("people") in a public place that does not constitute the appropriate setting for profound philosophical discussions. Since the topics do not seem to fit the situation, the reader then has to change the situation to consider

circumstances that invoke a discussion of religion or a call for God. Moving
in that direction, the reader can identify with a common experience, such as
a situation of impending disaster, when even non-believers resort to God and
religion to save them from some unknown, unbearable stress. The use of the
definite article הדת and האלוהים brings the topics to a generic level rather than
to a specific religion or a specific realization of God. Hebrew uses the definite
article for such generic nouns in the way that English uses capitalization. The
expansion of the topics from nouns to phrases also elevates their meaning so
that they can be included in the philosophical realm and not only in the realm
of emotional response: הדת בחיי האדם בן זמננו ("religion in the life of contemporary man," i.e., the significance of religion in our times) and מקומו של
האלוהים ("about the place of God"). Both phrases can be further expanded and
extended by the readers with specifics that describe such disasters as wars,
natural disasters, or amazing happenings. The questions raised about how
religion or God can have a place in such events are left for the readers to determine. The poem's greatness stems from the readers' ability to read into the
meaning according to their own experiences. Readers may read the same
poem differently each time, or choose to mix the positive and negative implications. The tensions and ambiguities and relationship of man to God and
religion become as general or specific as the readers allow.

Voice

Identifying the voice in this poem contributes greatly to understanding it. The
poem begins with the voice of what seems to be an implied narrator, who
describes the subject of the narrative, "people," who speak about the topics
of God and religion. That narrator moves on to the second stanza, which
describes the manner in which the "people" speak—in emotional and excited
voices. In response to those voices there is a switch to a subjective voice "I,"
and "people" becomes the object: "I left them." Amichai chooses to make
the switch in voice in the third line of the second stanza. The sudden switch
in voice implies that the talking in excited voices creates noise and irritation
rather than helping to shed light on the situation. The implied narrator
switches from his descriptive state to a subjective voice of an involved first
pronoun "I," no longer neutral in reporting the happenings. The change of
voice, done seemingly with no warning or expressed emotion, actually says
more than words could express. A new perspective of the speaker is introduced. The subjective "I" has a response that expresses a strong attitude to
the useless discussion by taking action and escaping the speech or noise: "I left
them," "I opened a door," and "I entered."

Input from the readers can illuminate this aspect of the poem as perceived and thus made relevant to them as contemporary readers. The perspective can include political, intellectual, and religious perspectives that may lead to interesting discussions beyond the limits of this close unit of discourse.

Intertextual Connections

Seemingly closed units of discourse, such as this poem by Amichai, are often illuminated by other texts. The connections can be of various sorts, including references to historical texts, evocation of older texts by the use of language (unique words and phrases) or contemporary events, or comparison to other poems that use similar imagery and motifs. A good example is the first image Amichai employs in this poem, which sets the mood: מוּאָר עַד כְּאֵב. The notion of light here, used in the participial verb, is seemingly simple and straightforward, but in reality it is more complex when considering the major role it plays in setting the tone of this poem. Its wonderfully complex nature can be highlighted by relating it to another poem of Amichai's from the same collection, where light plays a similarly multifaceted role; the various oppositions of light and darkness are tied to the notions of remembering and forgetting, where opposites actually complete the full meaning of the idea:

לִשְׁכֹּחַ אָדָם הוּא כְּמוֹ
לִשְׁכֹּחַ לְכַבּוֹת אֶת הָאוֹר בֶּחָצֵר:
וְנִשְׁאָר דּוֹלֵק גַּם בַּיּוֹם
גַּם לִזְכֹּר אֲבָל זֶה
עַל יְדֵי הָאוֹר.

Forgetting Someone

Forgetting someone is like forgetting to turn off the light
in the backyard so it stays lit all the next day
But then it is the light that makes you remember.

Revisiting the Poem through Translations

While a literal translation of the poem is offered above by the author of this article, two other translations are available as well. The existence of several versions of this poem in translation indicates the intricate nature of the text, even though it misleadingly appears as simple and straightforward. The several translations in English depend mainly on the translators' perceptions of the poem, their efforts to render it as an esthetic artifact, and their preference in choosing near-equivalents for the various groups of words and phrases. No one translation is more "correct" than the other.

A translation is offered by Chana Bloch and Stephen Mitchell:

A Great Tranquility: Questions and Answers

The people in the painfully bright auditorium
spoke about religion
in the life of contemporary man and about God's place in it.
People spoke in excited voices
as they do at airports.
I walked away from them:
I opened an iron door marked "Emergency"
and entered into a great tranquility: Questions and Answers.

Another translation if offered by Benjamin and Barbara Harshav:

Great Calm: Questions and Answers

People in the hall lighted so it hurts
Spoke about religion
In the life of contemporary people
And about the places of God.
People spoke in excited voices
As at airports.
I left them:
I opened an iron door with the sign
"Emergency" and entered
A great calm: questions and answers

Students can offer their own translations of the poem as well, and thus have a fruitful discussion of their own perceptions as well as those available in published translations.

Additional Information

Once the poem has been fully discussed, additional information can be supplied in the form of relevant articles on formal analysis and critical reading of poetry, articles on this specific poem and others by Amichai, and personal informal notes. The latter can enhance the reading experience as well, emphasizing the more personal aspect of the connection between the text and the author. Included here are remarks made in an interview with Amichai's daughter, Emmanuella. They highlight the personal meaning that this poem has for her and her relationship with her father. The following informal comments on the poem appeared in the Israeli daily newspaper *Maariv* (2001). The interview was conducted by Sara Fuchs in the תרבות ("culture") section of the paper:

> "Emmanuella, what poem best expresses your father in your recollection?"
>
> "There is one poem that truly represents him as I see him. How I feel about him. A simple and fascinating poem: '*People in the hall lighted so it hurts / spoke about Religion / in the life of contemporary Man /, and about God's place in it. People spoke in excited voices / as at airports. / I left them: / I opened an iron door with the sign / "Emergency" and entered / a great serenity: Questions and Answers.*' When I read it I actually see him saying this. I actually see his face and his eyes. He was like that—a man of great tranquility with many questions and many answers. His 'emergency' was serenity. And this is, of course, a great irony, since it is precisely that particular door that we all see at all times, on which there is a sign 'emergency'; it is precisely that door that he uses in order to arrive at a state of tranquility, at those questions and answers. This is how it takes place during the process of creation: in emergency situations you arrive at some kind of serenity when questions and answers originate in you."[5]

Conclusion

The beauty of this poem lies in its simplicity and complexity. The mixture of abstract and concrete concepts builds the images and ideas the poem evokes. Through a series of oppositions, from the spacious noisy open place of the public domain to the confined space to which the subject flees, to the tranquility of contemplation about religion and God, the complex issue of questions and answers renders the poem both as open ended and as a closed signature to the poem.

It is important to keep in mind that the main objective is for the student to attain the skills and motivation to continue to read Hebrew poetry, to discover not only the rich Hebrew poetry of the ages but also to discover an aspect of themselves. "Reading well is one of the great pleasures that solitude can afford you, because it is, in my experience, the most healing of pleasures," writes Harold Bloom in his book "How to Read and Why." He adds that "reading well is pursued as an implicit discipline; finally there is no method but yourself."

REFERENCES

Alter, R. 1989. *The Pleasures of Reading in an Ideological Age*. New York: Touchstone.

Amichai, Y. (980. *Great Tranquility: Questions and Answers*. Jerusalem and Tel Aviv: Shoken.

Bloch, C. & Mitchell, S. (translators) (1992). *The Selected Poetry of Yehuda Amichai*. Berkeley: University of California Press.

Bloom, H. 2000. *How to Read and Why*. New York: Scribner.

Ciardi, J. 1959. *How Does a Poem Mean?* Boston: Houghton Mifflin.

Eco, U. 1984. *The Role of the Reader*. Bloomington: Indiana University Press.

Fuchs, S. (2001). Interview with Amichai's daughter Emmanuella on 26 January. *Maariv* Culture section [*tarbut*].

Harshav, B. and B. Harshav (translators). 1995. *Yehuda Amichai: A Life of Poetry 1948–1994*. New York: HarperCollins.

Iser, W. 1978. *The Act of Reading*. Baltimore: Johns Hopkins University Press.

Lye, J. 1996. Critical reading: A guide. Brock University. Retrieved 22 February, 2008 from [http://www.brocku.ca/english/jlye/criticalreading.html].

Rifaterre, M. 1984. *The Semantics of Poetry*. Bloomington: Indiana University Press.

Whorf, B. 1956. In J.B. Carroll (Ed.), *Language, Thought and Reality: Selected Writings of Benjamin Lee Whorf*. Boston: MIT Press.

Yizhar, S. 1990. The polemic of education. In Yizhar, S. *Two Polemics* [*shnei pulmusim*]. Tel Aviv: Zmora Bitan.

Yizhar, S. 1972. Stop teaching literature. *Education* [*haḥinukh*].

Appendix A
Hebrew translation of interview with Amichai's daughter Emmanuella.

עמנואלה, איזה שיר מבטא בזיכרון שלך את אבא שלך? "יש שיר שבאמת מייצג אותו כמו
שאני רואה אותו. איך שהרגשתי אותו. שיר פשוט ומקסים:'אנשים באולם המואר עד כאב/
דיברו על הדת/ בחיי האדם בן זמננו/ ועל מקומו של האלוהים. / אנשים דיברו בקולות
נרגשים / כמו בנמלי תעופה./ עזבתי אותם: / פתחתי דלת ברזל שכתוב עליה / "חירום"
ונכנסתי לתוך / שלווה גדולה: שאלות ותשובות'. "כשאני קוראת את זה אני פשוט רואה
אותו מספר את זה. אני ממש רואה את הפנים עם העיניים. הוא היה כזה. הוא היה איש
של שלווה גדולה עם המון שאלות והמון תשובות. החירום שלו היה השלווה. וזאת אירוניה
כמובן. דווקא אותה דלת שכולנו רואים כל החיים, שכתוב עליה 'חירום', דווקא בה השתמש
כדי להגיע אל אותה שלווה גדולה, אל אותן שאלות ותשובות. כך קורה בתהליך יצירה:
במצבי חירום אתה מגיע לאיזושהי שלווה כשעולות בך שאלות ותשובות".

Technology and Language Teaching in Higher Education

Some Thoughts about the State of the Field

לֹו שֶׁל הַגֵּל קוֹרֵ׳
תוֹ – שֶׁאָבוֹא אֲנִי

מ

ז בְּרֹאשׁוֹ, וְהֵכִינוּ ז
וֹת, אָמֵן אָמֵן סֶלָה״

Vered Shemtov

Stanford University

INTERFACES AND WEB PAGES resemble Talmud folios in interesting ways. Moreover, hot (linear) pages and cool (interactive) pages represent competing notions of communication: the Hellenistic model, in which the world is an information vacuum to be filled by the communicator, and the talmudic model, in which the world is an information plenum, absolutely full of knowledge and requiring guides and navigators (Weiss, 1998).

It is quite common nowadays to compare Web pages and pages of the Talmud. Some, such as Weiss, even argue that the Web reflects a Jewish way of thinking about information and about learning. Jonathan Rosen (2000) devotes an entire book to the Talmud and the Internet, stating that despite the many differences between the two,

> when I look at a page of Talmud and see all those texts tucked intimately and intrusively onto the same page, like immigrant children sharing a single bed, I do think of the Internet. For hundreds of years, responsa, questions on virtually every aspect of Jewish life, winged back and forth between scattered Jews and various centers of Talmudic learning. The Internet is also a world of unbounded curiosity, of argument and information, where anyone with a modem can wander out of the wilderness for a while, ask a question and receive an answer. I take comfort in thinking that a modern technology medium echoes an ancient one.

But beyond pointing out these similarities, how can Jewish perspectives of organizing and studying texts influence technology? How can new, emerging technologies impact Jewish Studies?

Since joining the Stanford Center for Innovation in Learning four years ago, I have been involved in studying the use of technology in Hebrew classrooms. Hebrew was taught for many years with no high-tech support. As much as we were interested in being up to date with the world around us, it was also important for us not to lose sight of the advantages of traditional teaching methods. We did not want the use of technology to result in a loss of what seemed to us an important connection among language, identity, and education. What and how we teach, what and how we learn, and what we become as a result of what and how we learn or teach—all these issues cannot be easily distinguished or dismissed. Moreover, they cannot be seriously addressed if methods used for Spanish, German, or English teaching are adopted for the Hebrew class without considering their effect on the relationship among the three aspects mentioned above.[1]

Recreating our courses to adapt them to the technology-enhanced environment that Stanford offered us was an opportunity to rethink our goals and revisit our teaching philosophies. In the process, the Web changed dramatically. In the last few years, we witnessed a major increase in online social networks, including blogs, wikis, trackback, podcasting, and videoblogs. This "explosion of new Web services, such as 'blogs' and 'wikis,' has led many to believe that the Internet is now entering a second phase. It's finally beginning to resemble a truly interactive learning tool" (O'Hear, 2005). Students can collaborate with peers, as well as with people from other places, to create new information. The question, as Janise Paulsen writes (2001), is no longer "*whether* to take advantage of these electronic technologies in foreign language education, but *how* to harness them and guide our students in their use...authentic, meaningful, interactive, student centered, Web-based learning activities can improve student performance in much the same manner as learning a language while studying abroad."[2] With Web 2.0, technology became not just a means or a tool for teaching Hebrew but also one of our goals. Feeling comfortable not only with searching for information but becoming immersed in the Hebrew Web, being part of online communities, expressing opinions, and contributing and being exposed to the Web

---

1. This is the case, for example, in the Rosetta Stone Beginning Hebrew software.

2. See also: Uschi Felix (2002). The web as a vehicle for constructivist approaches in language teaching. *ReCALL 14*: 2–15. Felix's study leads him to conclude that the Web has the "potential to engage students in creating information gap activities and real experiential learning in the form of meaningfully, process-oriented projects in authentic settings."

in Hebrew is now part of functioning in the language. Technology is essential not only as a tool for obtaining knowledge and conducting research, but, as Robert Godwin-Jones argued, it also offers less immediately evident benefits, such as identity creation and collaborative learning (2005).

Technology was often regarded as a way to make current methods of teaching Hebrew more efficient. As technology developed, the workbook drills were placed first on CDs and then online to enable immediate responses and self-corrections. Audio tapes used in the language lab were also placed online for easier distribution. Students uploaded files instead of submitting work in class, and the dialogues and photos in the textbook turned into video clips and images online. All these major steps were directed at managing the material and at using technology for improving the existing systems by making them more efficient, and at increasing exposure to material. But technology is no longer merely a tool; it is the way we communicate, interact, and function in the world. The success of Facebook or YouTube, especially with high school and college students, is now unquestionable. The interest of individuals not only is to search the Web but to actively be part of it, to contribute material, to manage relationships, and to join and create communities calls for reevaluating what language teachers define as functioning and communicating in the language. The Internet, especially the user content-generated Web sites, changed basic concepts in learning, communication, and communities. The Internet enables us not only to cross geographical boundaries but to immerse ourselves in cultures and languages. Joining these communities can be as intimidating as finding oneself in a room full of Israelis with no knowledge of the language and the culture. It requires skills that can be practiced, much like any other major communicative function.

On one level, the application can include small but important changes in the curriculum, such as teaching how to use the keyboard as soon as students are introduced to the alphabet; teaching students to check if their syntax is commonly used in Hebrew by searching how many sites appear in a search that includes a specific combination (for example: "I go in" versus "I go to"); asking them to follow up on a topic studied in class by searching for new information on the issue and sharing it in class; and asking students to find how Hebrew speakers in different blogs feel about a certain event in the news, rather than having the teacher be the main source of information about the culture and the different communities. All these activities create in the class the expectation of learning not only from the instructor but also from the diverse Hebrew communities on the Web.

On another level, these new concepts question the philosophy of teaching and the ideologies reflected by the textbook, institutions, and specific teachers, whether religious or secular, Zionist or other. To bring the Internet into the classroom not as a tool controlled by the instructor but gradually as one open for the learners' navigation is to accept the existence of multiple communities with different perspectives and different uses of the Hebrew language (including common non-grammatical uses) and with different ideologies. This marks for some a return to the text as home. Consider, for example, the following passage from Rosen's book (2000):

> The Talmud offered a virtual home for an uprooted culture and grew out of a Jewish need to pack civilization into words and wander out into the world...Jews became the people of the book and not the people of the temple or the land...the Internet, which we are continually told binds us all together, nevertheless engenders in me a similar sense of Diaspora, a feeling of being everywhere and nowhere. Where else but in the middle of Diaspora do you *need* a home page? (14)

The Internet can potentially promote the "text" over geographical space. This perspective stands in opposition to the many textbooks and practices of teaching Hebrew in universities. The ideology that associated the revival of Hebrew with the return to the land and Zionism, and the identity formed in the process of learning Hebrew with that of Israelis, is still extremely popular. Any use of the Hebrew Internet will place Israel in the center as the major location in which these sites are created. The sites themselves reflect Israeli life and culture. Where else would you find an ad for a guitar teacher in Hebrew, an original sitcom in Hebrew or Hebrew daily newspapers? But these materials reflect the ideology, collective history, and language of users and of the online community, and not of the teacher, the textbook, or the institution.

Recent research shows that students in Canada learn Hebrew not necessarily because they are planning to visit Israel or to identify with the culture and people. Avital Feuer (2007) argued, while

> educators assume that students' motivations to learn the language relate to an integrative or utilitarian desire to associate with the target community, a semester-long, ethnographic, qualitative study of an advanced undergraduate modern Hebrew language course at a large, urban Canadian university determined these Hebrew heritage language learners with diverse backgrounds held complex notions of the community whose language the professor and I assumed they wished to acquire, maintain or emulate. When initially asked about students' motivations to study advanced Hebrew, Aviva, the profes-

sor, expressed a vague opinion that students would use Hebrew in future travel to Israel. In fact, the study found that most students enrolled in the course not to improve their linguistic skills to use in future communication in Israel, but rather to strengthen social ties in Jewish community sub-groups in Canada.

In seven years of teaching at Stanford, I can count on two hands the number of beginning Hebrew students who ended up in Israel for more than a short trip. Students join our classes to find a space here, for Hebrew within their Jewish and other communities.

Hebrew found on Web sites from different geographic locations opens the door to different levels or kinds of affiliations with the target language and culture. Although instructors are not expected to adopt a specific ideology because of technological advances, I believe they should be aware of these conceptual changes, which can be used for evaluating the relationship between the content of the lesson and the process of learning.

With the rapid decline in the number of students traveling to Israel, the Web has become the main space for interactions with Hebrew speakers and for exposure to Jewish and/or Israeli life in Hebrew. Unlike course books (often created in Israel for *ulpan* students) or conversation with a Hebrew (and in many cases, Israeli) teacher, the Web enables the student to easily switch between identities and languages. The Web serves as a hybrid space not bound to an actual physical location, reflecting a wider understanding of what it means to be part of different Jewish/Hebrew-speaking communities than is usually present in a classroom. One can still find sites that follow the model of the book or the traditional class, presenting a step-by-step introduction to the language and the culture from a specific perspective.[3] But the Web as a whole allows for exposure to a wide range of connections among language, text, space, and time. Students can explore ancient and contemporary religious texts, cooking classes, news, videos, and blogs by Israelis in and outside Israel, by Jews, and even by non-Jewish Hebrew speakers.

This leads us to another major shift technology created in our teaching: the transformation from teaching to learning. Through online resources, the student is able to take a much more active role in the process of learning. Although the teacher is still instrumental, his or her role changes as the student

---

3. See, for example, the wonderful BBC online language programs for Hebrew, "Hevenu Shalom Aleikhem," developed by the Pedagogic Center of the Jewish Agency for Israel, the Department for Jewish and Zionist Education, and prepared for the Web by Hebrew classes at Stanford University.

also has the opportunity to be easily directed to new information by links, to move in an associative manner between topics, and to converse with partners online. In class, the structure of the new technologically enhanced spaces affords students more control over the boards and the electronic texts, and encourages collaboration in groups or between partners. This, too, marked for us to some extent a return to some of the more traditional Jewish methods of learning in groups.

The two changes described above—the shift from technology as a means to technology as a goal and from teaching to learning—are the focus of the second part of this chapter. From the many different uses of educational technology I will limit the discussion to two major examples: Course Management Systems (CMS) and the classroom. I will also discuss interactions between the two.

Web Technology and Course Management Systems

The vast number of Web sites available for Hebrew students and instructors can be divided into three categories: (1) material designed specifically for language students; (2) Course Management Systems; and (3) Web sites for Hebrew speakers. In many cases, the three categories intersect through links. While the amount of material for Hebrew students is still scarce compared to the sites available for students of English, Spanish, or French, in the last few years individual instructors and institutions have posted drills, video and audio clips, flash cards, images, texts, and grammar lessons online. Most of the materials are aids that support but do not replace the teacher or the book. The Hebrew program at the University of Texas, for example, provides free access to video clips, drills for different levels of Hebrew, and much more. The Israeli Ministry of Education sponsored several sites, including one with reading tools for levels one to four in the *ulpan*. And these are just a few of the many examples of the material available to Hebrew students today. There are also a number of comprehensive online programs that focus on distance learning, such as "Milingua," or programs that enable students to communicate live with teachers, usually from Israel, such as the program "Hebrew Online."[4]

Course Management Systems, or Learning Management Systems (CMS/ LMS), became extremely popular in schools and universities in recent years and currently enable instructors not only to administer the course online (with

---

4. On distance learning and Jewish education, see Dov Teni and Baruch Ofir (2003), Learning through teleprocessing. Retrieved March 2003 from [http://www.daat.ac.il/tikshuv/lemida-2.htm].

grades, attendance, syllabi, email announcements, course material, etc.) but also to create and manage assignments and tests in the four major skills: reading, writing, listening, and speaking. The assignments can include fill-in-the-blank, matching, and multiple-choice questions, and submitting essays and short answers. In some CMSs, such as those developed recently by the SAKAI project, students can record answers at home. These and similar tools aided in the development of the SOPI, a simulated oral-proficiency interview based on the guidelines of the American Council for the Teaching of Foreign Languages (Stanford Report, 2003):[5]

> Students log on to the course site for their SOPI, run through the questions that appear in a timed sequence on their screen and speak their answers directly into their computer's microphone. The answer is recorded to the server, where the instructor can access and review it without having to schedule an office appointment.

One of the advantages of CMSs is that they can help integrate online material for language students with links to "original" material created for the Hebrew-speaking/reading community. When learning about apartments, for example, students can practice gender agreement in nouns and adjectives through matching drills, read an ad or a text (even a scene from a novel or short story) on the subject, and work on multiple-choice questions developed in the assignment tool. They can view short clips created for language speakers of people renting apartments, and write a memo or a rental agreement using the main details in the clip. Other options include recording an audio message showing interest in an ad for a roommate, or creating and uploading a video describing one's own room/house. All this can be done either with material developed for learners or with links to authentic online sites related to housing. Students can go, for example, to the Hebrew University Web site to search for rooms or apartments near the university. They can choose furniture from online stores and read an article in the news or a blog about the real estate situation in Israel or in other places. The activities can be monitored and graded by the instructor, who can comment online on the students' achievements. The CMS also allows for discussions between students. In short, they provide ample opportunities to immerse in the culture and to work both on accuracy as well as on communicating and functioning in different situations.

---

5. On the advantages of SOPI, see Elizabeth B.Bernhardt, Raymond J.Rivera, and Michael L. Kamil (2004), The practicality and efficiency of Web-based placement testing for college-level language programs. *Foreign Language Annals* *37.3*: 356–366.

Image 1. Stanford Hebrew Program Web-site

Center: Placing sites with material for Hebrew students within a CMS. On the right navigation bar: Links to managing information about the course, grades, homework, and texts and the bottom of the bar including links to the Hebrew Web Center: Using an online dictionary with a search engine in CMS. The online dictionaries do not allow easy translation of words without a comprehensive knowledge of the verb system or morphology; they also let the students read or hear the word in different contexts, as in the example shown above.

The major advantage of CMSs is that teachers can place all electronic material and data (both administrative and academic) for a course in one Web location and subject for grading. The initial work in creating assignments, gathering links, etc., enables the teachers to break away from the strict linear program of the textbook and tailor the curricula to the needs of their institutions and students. But the challenge of all CMSs is that this process requires a major investment of time and a major commitment. It also requires better coordination between those who work on developing the systems and the instructors and students. The shift from defining these systems as Course Management Systems to Learning Management Systems and finally to Collaboration and Learning Environments presents new attitudes that are not yet reflected in the systems; collaborative learning and creating spaces and tools for students to generate material and share it with the class are still not easily achieved in many of the systems. Moreover, many instructors ignore the shifts in the management systems and still limit their use to information distribution, grading, and other administrative functions. According to a 2004 study by Robert Woods, Jason D. Baker, and Dave Hopper, despite frequent use of a CMS for course-administration purposes, the faculty does not appear to be harnessing the full pedagogical potential of Web-based augmentation via LMSs such as blackboard.[6] Similar conclusions were found in a 2006 study by Steven R. Malikowski, Merton E. Thompson, and John G. Theis: "CMSs are primarily used to transmit information to students." The same results were reported in a recent European study by Ramon Garrote and Tomas Pettersson (2007). While these systems were modeled after the traditional course structure and objectives (announcements, homework, grading, syllabus, etc.)— and in some cases even their names (Inclass, Coursework, Blackboard) try to preserve the connection to the classroom—they also open a door to changing these models and expanding the ways and spaces in which learning takes place. By adding discussion tools, links, etc., teachers can set expectations and provide tools for navigating in the world of the Hebrew Web. CMSs can introduce students to sites and direct them to online dictionaries, search engines, and portals, and provide them with a safe, closed environment (much like the role of the class for face-to-face communication) for online discussions in Hebrew using blogs, shared videos, and wikis. Students learn to

---

6. See also Morgan, G. (2003). Faculty use of Course Management Systems 2. Retrieved 27 November 2005 (2003) from [http://www.educause.edu/ir/library/pdf/erso302/rs/erso302w.pdf].

immerse themselves and gain confidence in being part of online Hebrew communities.

Bryan Alexander, Director of Research at the National Institute for Technology and Liberal Education (NITLE), writes:

> Amid this flurry of Web services, what are the pedagogical possibilities? Like many computer-mediated techniques for teaching and learning, some of these possibilities start from pre-Web practices. For example, we have long taught and learned from news articles...Since blogs, most social bookmarking tools and other services are organized in reverse chronological order, their very architecture orients them, or at least their front pages, toward the present moment. (2006)

Similarly, Uziel Fox (2008) demonstrates in his article on the Internet, talmudic literature, and the teaching of Gmara how to apply to the Internet the pre-Web idea that the Talmud can be taught by starting at any page (and how the Internet metaphor can be used for understanding the Talmud). It does not matter which text or topic is taught first since one is always "in the middle of things" when studying the Talmud, and it is only by continuing to read texts and by finding connections between the texts that understanding and learning gradually takes place. CMSs can lead students to "the middle of things" from the very first lessons by directing students to sites they may return to when they need help.

Technology in the Classrooms[7]

Wallenberg Hall at Stanford is "a working laboratory where the learning tools and methods of the future are being forged" (Wallenberg Web site, 2008). Teaching in this space provided us with the opportunity to test and study the classes' configurations and technologies. We sifted through the many options available for technology that work well and, at the same time, defined activities that add variety but do not improve students' proficiencies.

Unlike the traditional language lab, which promotes individual work (mostly practicing, training, and testing next to a tape or a computer screen), the space in Wallenberg Hall enabled us, and even encouraged us, to use technology while following both the communicative language approach to

---

7. I would like to thank Dan Gilbert, Academic Technology Specialist at the Stanford Center for Innovations in Learning, for his support in designing, executing and evaluating innovative learning activities.

teaching and preserving the traditional *ḥevrutah* model of Jewish learning.[8] The rooms were designed to promote communication and to afford constant and smooth transitions between an environment controlled by the teacher to a class that follows the interests and directions of the learner.

While some of these technologically enhanced classrooms make room for endless possibilities of new and engaging ways of learning Hebrew, they do not necessarily help students advance in the language. Using the SIMS computer game to build a house and furnish it in Hebrew and having students use virtual tours of houses to play the role of real estate agents trying to describe and sell these houses was fun but less effective and more time-consuming than having two students simply design their dream house on whiteboards. In the same way, trying to organize video conferences with Israelis was more complex than simply inviting local Israelis to join us in class and converse with students. In general, working too much next to the screen reduced the time of instruction and communication.

The new attitude toward the idea of "the board" presented in these rooms was one of the most useful and successful tools. From the students' very first steps in Hebrew they work with a partner on the many whiteboards in class and on the huddleboards, lightweight portable whiteboards that can be used for small-group collaboration or presentations. The huddleboards enable the students' work to be seen by other students and by the instructor at all times. At certain points in the lesson the students switch boards, move freely in the class from one board to another, correcting, adding, editing, commenting, and conversing with other students about their work. The teacher can also have at every moment a clear picture of the students' progress. The language and ideas generated on huddleboards can be converted into digital images using the Copy Cam. Images from the copy camera can be retrieved from the classroom Web site. At the end of the lesson, students can use these images to continue projects at home, during the next class, or to present the work to the class. The online images could be viewed and instruction could be limited to concepts requiring the teachers' help. This method leaves most of the responsibility for studying to the students and promotes maximum creativity, independence, and collaboration.

Using this method for teaching reading and writing, for example, decreased the time spent on acquiring these skills by more than fifty percent. After five or ten minutes of general, basic instruction and with the help of a

---

8. *ḥevrutah* is a model of group study.

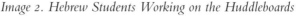

Image 2. Hebrew Students Working on the Huddleboards

simple handout with all the letters and their sounds, the students start writing. They can check if the word they wrote exists by googling it; they can check what their friends are doing and learn from them; they can listen and watch the instructions the teacher gives other individuals or groups; and, most importantly, they can think together—in Hebrew—about ways to find the spelling of specific words. The teacher can follow all the stages of the learning process, from the hand motions used while the students write to their repeated spelling mistakes. He or she can then provide guidance and instruction without having to place the student in the center of the classroom in front of a board.

Much like in the "top-down" approach to language teaching, the method described here helped us to skip many directions and rules that students could figure out by themselves (such as how to write each letter and the sound of each letter). Students learned by experience and were responsible for their own and their partners' learning. In less than two weeks, the students mastered the new alphabet and could read familiar words, and in the following weeks they wrote short essays on the boards (on which they commented in the same manner). They gained confidence in sharing their work and being part of a community of speakers. We slowly moved from the huddleboards to Hebrew wikis, with the aim of making the students comfortable enough to add their comments online to blogs or articles, to post their work, or to be part of a conference meeting with Hebrew speakers in other locations.

The Hebrew classroom at Wallenberg also includes twenty laptop computers, each with software that enables users to move files from one computer to another and to take control of the Webster. This experimental, open-source software helps students to collaborate with each other and with faculty during class. The Webster boards work as computer screens and as whiteboards where the teachers and students can display digital information but also write on the digital documents or Web sites. Students can add information and raise questions by taking over the boards and either directing the class to the relevant Web site, video, file, etc., or pointing to certain information that is already displayed. The ability to share control over the boards, together with the fact that the board can display Web pages, completely changes the dynamic of the class. Students can take an active role not only in group projects but also in class discussions and during instruction. The multiple boards (two in one classroom, three in another) allow for displaying material that supports more than one opinion, enabling comparisons between cultures, texts, text and media, etc.

The idea of the class as more than one space supports an understanding of learning as an activity that is less linear, central, and unified than reflected in the old classroom model. Having several spaces but being able to connect to each of them through a Webcam or by moving from one space to another opened a wide variety of possibilities for the language classes. We were able to create a divide between a Hebrew space and an English space, between a direction space and immersive and experiencing spaces (such as using one space as a theatre, a cooking area, and a shop), between a warm-up space and a course space, and between group work and all-class work spaces. We divided the class into different spaces in a way that enabled students to choose among activities according to interests or learning styles.

Technology moves fast, innovations are made daily, and the examples provided in this paper might be common practice in classrooms by the time this book reaches the shelves. What might continue to be relevant, though, is the way we think about technology. The process suggested here goes against a "blind" application of the latest audio recording tool or the most innovative "touch board," and instead promotes questioning if and how each type of technology can be used to serve the specific goals of the Hebrew learner, how it can help immerse the student in today's Hebrew-speaking communities, and finally, how each technology changes the relationship among language, education, and ideology.

References

Alexander, B. 2006. Web 2.0: A new wave of innovation for teaching and learning? *EDUCAUSE Review* 41.2: 32–44.

Bernhardt, E.B., R.J. Rivera, and M.L. Kamil. 2004. The practicality and efficiency of Web-based placement testing for college-level language programs. *Foreign Language Annals* 37: 356–366.

Felix, U. 2002. The Web as a vehicle for constructivist approaches in language teaching. *ReCALL* 14.1: 2–15.

Feuer, A. 2008. Speaking like an Israeli: A reconsideration of the target language group in today's Hebrew classes. Paper prepared for National Association of Professors of Hebrew conference and found in Feuer, A. (2008) *Who Does This Language Belong to? Personal Narratives of Language Claim and Identity*. Charlotte, N.C.: Information Age Publishing.

Fox, U. 2008. Internet, oral Torah, and Gmara instruction (in Hebrew). Retrieved from http://daat.ac.il/daat/toshba/horaat/fux-2.htm.

Garrote, R. and T. Pettersson. 2007. Lecturers' attitudes about the use of Learning Management Systems in engineering education: A Swedish case study. *Australasian Journal of Educational Technology* 23.3: 327–349.

Godwin-Jones, R. 2005. Emerging technologies: Messaging, gaming, peer-to-peer sharing language learning strategies and tools for the millennial generation. *Language, Learning and Technology* 9.

Malikowski, S.R., M.E. Thompson, and J.G. Theis. 2006. External factors associated with adopting a CMS in resident college courses. *The Internet and Higher Education* 9.3: 167–174.

Morgan, G. 2003. Faculty use of Course Management Systems 2. Retrieved 27 November 2005 from [http://www.educause.edu/ir/library/pdf/ers0302/rs/ers0302w.pdf].

O'Hear, S. 2005. Seconds out, round two. *The Guardian* 15. Retrieved from [http://education.guardian.co.uk/elearning/stroy/0,10577,1642281, 00.html].

Paulsen, J.B. 2001. New era trends and technologies in foreign language learning: An annotated bibliography. *Interactive Multimedia Electronic Journal of Computer-Enhanced Learning*.

Rosen, J. 2000. *The Talmud and the Internet: A Journey Between Worlds*. New York: Farrar, Straus and Giroux.

Stanford Report. 2003. Course work's online drills and tests help foreign language instruction by focusing on oral skills, saving test time. *Stanford Report 23*. Retrieved 23 April 2003 from [http://news-service.stanford.edu/news/2003/april23/courseworkside-49.html].

Teni, D. and B. Ofir. 2003. Learning through teleprocessing. *Da'at*. Retrieved in March 2003 from [http://www.daat.ac.il/tikshuv/lemida-2.htm].

Wallenberg Hall Website. 2008. Retrieved 13 February 2008 from [http://wallenberg.stanford.edu].

Weiss, E.H. 1998. From Talmud folios to Web sites: HOT pages, COOL pages, and the information plenum. *IEEE Transactions on Professional Communication* 41.2.

Woods, R., J.D. Baker, and D. Hopper. 2004. Hybrid structures: Faculty use and perception of Web-based courseware as a supplement to face-to-face instruction. *The Internet and Higher Education* 7.4: 281–297.

יִלוֹ שֶׁל הַגֵּל קוֹרֵ:
תּוֹ – שֶׁאָבוֹא אֲנִי

ז בְּרָאשׁוֹ, וְהֲכִינוּ זִ
וֹת, אָמֵן אָמֵן סֶלָה״

HEBREW-YIDDISH BILINGUALISM AMONG ISRAELI HASIDIC CHILDREN

Miriam Isaacs
University of Maryland

YIDDISH-HEBREW BILINGUALISM has been an integral part of the Jewish tradition for centuries. That being so, one might anticipate that the perpetuation of this pattern should not cause a stir, but in the context of today's Israel, the presence of Jewish children growing up with Yiddish as a mother tongue runs counter to the central ideology of the country. Indeed, it was the force of ideology that propelled the revival of Hebrew, with the attendant rejection of Yiddish, and it is again ideology that prompts the maintenance and revival of Yiddish on the part of "recalcitrant" segments of the Haredi[1] Jewish community.

This discussion is from the perspective of language preservation, the reversal of language shift. The various Haredi and, within that larger category, certain Hasidic (dynastic rabbinic) sects provide an instance of a network of communities in which children are schooled and generally live their lives in at least two languages, Hebrew and Yiddish. Even the most reclusive of Hasidic enclaves demonstrate a continuum of ethnolinguistic vitality. The languages are in diglossic relationship in some domains (Poll 1980: 120–24) but in competition in others (Isaacs 1999b). In this article we will explore the ways in which such religious communities shape language policies.

Hebrew language acquisition, both for first and second languages, generally is connected directly to Jewish identity. Yet there are other Jewish languages in existence and some, as Weisser (1995) suggests, are still evolving.

---

1. Haredi is the Israeli term for ultra-orthodox. Hasidim are Haredim who are followers of traditional rabbinic dynastic sects.

139

Despite terrific declines, Yiddish still has a population for whom it is a primary language, and a portion of that is situated in Israel. Hebrew–Yiddish bilingualism (Isaacs 1999b) as it functions in the enclaves of certain Hasidic sects reveals a variable pattern with respect to which language is used as a vernacular, but also permits Yiddish to serve as both vernacular and as a medium of instruction. Yiddish is an optional language, Hebrew a necessary one; uses of both are directly tied to religiosity (Isaacs 1999a).

Language maintenance is evidenced by schools and attendant school materials, as well as by new musical and verbal tape recordings. Yiddish is mainly oral, an insider language. Bilingualism between Yiddish and Hebrew, interwoven since the nascence of Yiddish a thousand years ago, is now resulting in a new range of interlinguistic phenomena.

Traditional and Present Hebrew-Yiddish Bilingualism

Bilingualism is, as it was historically for Hasidim in Europe, a natural outgrowth of language function and religious tradition. Historically, traditional Jewish multilingualism has been the normative state for religious Jews. Languages had a variety of religious and practical functions, and multilingualism was part of the general apparatus of a transnational population that continually was migrating and disbursing. The legacy of this history is an awareness that the use of languages can be essential, that traditional languages function as the glue of a people.

Much of the standard terminology of bilingualism does not fit the societal bilingualism in Israel; neither Hebrew nor Yiddish is clearly a first or second language, neither is native or foreign, classical or modern. The two languages are acquired simultaneously, because they are rooted in the functions of the community. The old pattern had traditionally been Yiddish, the insider vernacular Hebrew, and at least one co-territorial language, such as Polish, Hungarian, or Latvian (Fishman 1981). In contrast to the traditional Eastern European pattern, in Israeli Haredi life today, Hebrew is not one entity but two, each with distinct functions and forms, each subject to radically different attitudes. Still revered and protected is Hebrew-Aramaic, *Loshn Koydesh* (LK), used for special purposes. This sanctity contrasts with the role of modern Hebrew, Ivrit, the transformed Hebrew that is the national language of Israel. Because Ivrit is a profane vernacular to Haredim, it must, in psychological terms, be viewed as a different entity from prior versions of Hebrew, biblical and rabbinic, in phonological and morphological terms.

Still, despite lingering qualms, Ivrit is used widely by all stripes of Hasidim out of sheer necessity.[2] LK is assiduously taught and is the focus of instruction, whereas Yiddish is present mainly in a variety of oral and a few written uses. What is new is that Yiddish-speaking Hasidim are set in a larger context of non-Yiddish-speaking Haredim, that is, other ultra-Orthodox Jews outside the Hasidic tradition, so Yiddish is now almost exclusively theirs.

Ben Rafael (1995: 181) describes new kinds of bilingualism generated by the establishment of Hebrew in the State of Israel. The population is segmented with respect to language use and language attitudes. This is true even within the Jewish population, disregarding the Arab and other populations. Di-ethnia within Israeli Haredi life results in variability with respect to whether Yiddish is used and how it is valued. Across Haredi society in all its many forms, use of Yiddish ranges from minimal, as a mere marker of ingroup identity, to extensive use in many domains of daily life.

The most active use of Yiddish is isolated to some sects of Hasidim and Yerushalmim (who are descendants of *misnagdim*) in highly concentrated Hasidic enclaves. In the largest of these, Mea Shearim in Jerusalem, many Hasidim use only Ivrit. But, especially in the small, back streets, one can also hear Yiddish. Walking down one of the inner streets, I heard a Hasid in a striped caftan shouting above the local din in Yiddish into his cellular phone. For this Hasid, his wife and children would use Yiddish pervasively as the language of home, elementary education, and in their religious establishment. Emerging from the home into the streets and shops of the Israeli neighborhood, the children need to use Ivrit, but, in a new twist, for children, Ivrit is also an insider language because there may be relatives or friends who speak only Ivrit.[3]

Ivrit is at once the dominant national language of the secular (*khiloni*) Israeli outsider, but also the language of some insiders. Unlike Polish in the European past, Ivrit is learned easily because it is a version of LK, sharing the same orthography, lexicon, syntax, and morphology, though not the same phonology as Yiddish (see Table below).

The Table below displays the interrelationships among the languages. The pronunciation of Ivrit follows the Sephardic traditional pronunciation of Hebrew, adopted for Ivrit. Usually LK and Yiddish pronounce LK words the

---

2. Poll, 1980: 120–24. He calls it by the Haredi pronunciation, "Ivris."

3. Weinreich, Max (1980) *History of the Yiddish Language* translated from the Yiddish *Geshichte fun di Yidishe Shprakh*. Chicago.

TABLE: INTERRELATIONSHIPS AMONG LINGUISTIC COMPONENTS
The chart below indicates the ways in which components of the three systems interconnect.

Language System	IVRIT	LOSHN KOYDESH	YIDDISH
Phonology	Sephardic pronunciation	Ashkenazi pronunciation	
Role	national official language	insider languages traditional	
Morphology/ Syntax/ Lexicon	Semitic: some Yiddish influence		Indo-European
Orthography	fixed and important		varied
Curriculum	used for practical reasons	necessary, often taught by rote	mainly vernacular, means of instruction

same way and basically share the same phonological system. However, morphologically and syntactically, as well as lexically, Ivrit and LK are basically the same.

Contrasting bilingualism for Hasidim in present Israel to traditional Eastern European patterns, there is a significant difference of context. Yiddish, once a common link to most Jews across all strata of society, now differentiates Hasidim from the general Jewish population. At the same time, having Ivrit as the national and official language creates a new situation, one in which the national language is automatically familiar and yet also a means of communication with undesirable outsider influences.

Impact of Language Attitudes on Patterns of Language Use

The continuity of traditional bilingualism is rooted in reverence for forefathers. Yiddish is a powerful link to tradition and sanctity. Yiddish helps maintain tradition and a sense of collective identity.[4] Because the most immediate and strongest connection between language and identity is with LK (Fishman 1981: 13), the Jewish tradition has been permissive with respect to accompanying languages, be they Polish, Hungarian, or now English. In writing about American Haredim, Chayim Weisser (1995),[5] in describing the importance of traditional languages such as Yiddish, observes on the simultaneous openness to other languages, such as English.

Only when the sacred language is perceived as profaned do Hasidim express a sense of violation. For instance, when the Soviet Jews spelled Yiddish words of LK origin phonetically or eliminated word final consonants in the orthography, there was a feeling of violation, even by less religious Jews.

Tradition is upheld at a cost. Hanging onto tradition under difficult circumstances is nothing new to Hasidim. Yiddish can be a tool to separate Hasidim from the rest of the dominant culture in the closed contexts of home, school, or *kloyz*. Such use of Yiddish means flying in the face of Israeli policy, where pressures against continuity of Yiddish are great. Hebrew, as the national, official Jewish language, is a powerful integrating force that has pervaded the innermost chambers within the Hasidic world. Many Ivrit-speaking Haredim do not know much or any Yiddish, coming from Sephardic, Mizrachi, or other backgrounds.

How do ideological forces influence the language-acquisition processes of the Hasidic children? By using Yiddish in outside encounters, children become aware that they are members of a group that differs from general Israeli society. Language is keyed to identity. The Ivrit-speaking shopkeeper down the street, the guard who admits them to the compound that houses the school, the Russian immigrant shoe-repair man, and even the school maintenance man do not respond to Yiddish. Thus, children have their own additional language, unknown to these "outsiders." Yiddish marks them as outsiders because it is never evident in official places or on road signs. Official writing is usually in Hebrew, often with Arabic (the official language of Israeli Arabs) and English (seen as an international language and the language of the former colonial ruler)—but never Yiddish. The medium is the message, that Yiddish is marginal and unwelcome.

---

4. Isaacs (1999a).

5. Introductory remarks expand on attitudes to languages.

Official Israel's attitude to Yiddish also has an impact on perceptions. Romaine (1989: 25) points out that the same language may function in a number of different ways in different countries, and the awareness of language through such official channels as census statistics may be clouded by attitudes toward certain languages that have lower status. Such is the case with Yiddish, which is very much "clouded" as a result of attitudes that have their roots in the very founding of the country. Thus, official estimates of Yiddish are suspect and language attitudes become mutual means of dismissal of the other.

Hasidic Language Policies

To use Yiddish in public in Israel is not an easy task, but Hasidim believe in following (in Yiddish, *folgn* means both "follow" and "obey") rabbinic leaders. Linguistic behavior has institutional sanction and is governed by rabbinic leadership. When an authority figure expresses a desire, individuals and families work assiduously to achieve those goals. Although there are many official rabbinic pronouncements with respect to the basics of life, food, and dress, language has been left relatively open to individual and sect discretion resulting in variable rabbinic policies. At times rabbis will take a pragmatic course over an ideological one. They will bend to difficulties inherent in using Yiddish when there are many Hasidim coming into the group who have not been raised in Yiddish by accommodating them in various ways or by teaching the children of non-Yiddish speakers Yiddish.

Hasidim with a Zionist orientation—many are non- or anti-Zionist—will be less likely to have pervasive use of Yiddish. The Lubavitch Hasidim are a case in point, for although they are Hasidim and the head *rebbe* gave all his addresses in Yiddish, Habad (Lubavich) schools in Israel teach mainly in Ivrit.

In Yiddish language schooling, control over curricular decisions is up to the schools and communities. Bogoch (1999) states that three-quarters of the twenty-seven schools that teach in Yiddish are receiving partial government subsidies. Others shun government connections. She estimates that some 10,000 boys study in Yiddish at the elementary school level in partially subsidized Yiddish-language schooling. Yet, of the whole Haredi[6] population, only a small proportion of children are studying in Yiddish.

---

6. I will be using the term Haredi when I wish to speak of the whole ultra-Orthodox population.

Language, Territory, and Social Networks

The Satmar, Reb Aarele, Stolin-Karlin, Belz, and Viznitz Hasidic sects are among those that use Yiddish as a primary language. They usually elect to live in close quarters, creating linguistic networks that are embedded in a larger Ivrit-dominant linguistic network. These enclaves are expanding into a variety of Israeli cities, including newer parts within Jerusalem, B'nai Brak, and Safed, and to new enclaves in Ashdod and Beit Aaron.

Yiddish maintenance is made possible by both physical and social boundaries. The physical boundary is symbolized by the *eruv*, which limits movement on the Sabbath and holy days and thereby requires congregants to live within walking distance of where they pray. There are less formal boundaries beyond which children are not expected to roam. The social barriers consist of sanctions that reinforce community coherence and keep outside influences to a minimum. Children are watched closely to make sure they do not go beyond "safe" boundaries and are not subject to "undesirable" influences. To this end, the mass media are forbidden, so that television, radio, and movies have little influence. Linguistic networks are varied because children are often in contact with non-Yiddish speaking relatives or with children from different (Haredi) backgrounds.

As Heilman (1992) notes, Hasidic society is full of children; they are everywhere, he claims, and, therefore, they are exposed to all the linguistic networks of the society. By the time the children are mature enough to expand their range of movement, they have internalized sanctions. They slowly progress to partake, selectively, in their own closed society and then, more gradually, in general society. Children occasionally range outside their tight circles, usually with parents or in groups. Hasidic children often can be seen in Jerusalem peering into shop windows. I once observed a large group of teen-age Haredi boys in a shopping center near the central bus station of Jerusalem, near a religious area that houses many yeshivas. From a safe distance, the boys were intently watching a basketball game on a television suspended over a bar.

Demographics and economics play their part in determining whether a Hasidic family will use Yiddish. There needs to be a critical mass of eligible families to make it viable to have a school in Yiddish. If such a school is not available, then the parents may have to settle for the closest approximation. Haredi enclaves need a critical mass in order to support the necessary kosher food shops, yeshivas, and also a host of associated specialty shops. Economic factors are also significant when it comes to Yiddish retention, for Haredi life considerably limits how one makes a living.

Early Hebrew-Yiddish Acquisition

The pattern of childhood language acquisition involves simultaneous, although not balanced, acquisition of Yiddish and Hebrew in its various forms. As mentioned earlier, the concept of first- and second-language acquisition does not apply in this kind of societal bilingualism, since Yiddish, Ivrit, and LK form parts of a whole. In a typical household, a mother may wake a child by speaking in Yiddish. That same child may then recite a blessing in LK, then answer the mother in Yiddish, and go out and play speaking Yiddish or Ivrit. One addresses the deity in one language, one's family in another, and people outside and some also inside the family in yet a third language (Fishman 1981: 13).

Family and early schooling shape early language. Considerable language learning takes place from siblings and family networks. Families tend to have many children, so that siblings figure prominently in language acquisition. Because most households have many children, they need to be funneled quickly into kindergartens, which influence the linguistic environment of a toddler. Social life centers on family events, such as holidays or marriages, and extended-family visits occur frequently, so that family influences and peer influences are often one and the same.

An indicator of the dominance of Yiddish in the earlier years is the fact that some health care workers in Jerusalem need enough Yiddish to give small children basic instructions, for example, to open their mouths for the dentist. A teacher of blind Haredi children first had to teach some of her children Ivrit in order to work with them.

Bilingual skills are enhanced by the fact that children have constant linguistic input in a highly verbal society. Intensity of learning is augmented by zeal, the sheer volume of singing and chanting. For instance, during a holiday I once observed a mini-drama in which the narrator told a story and the children were to shout at the top of their lungs, punctuating each segment of the story with the Yiddish expression, *"shrayt gevald!"* ("shout help"). Storytelling is a common form of instruction (Heilman 1992) in Hasidic circles, where inspirational, didactic stories, and parables are integral to transmission of culture. Yiddish in Jerusalem Hasidic circles is the language in which the culture is transmitted, in which the conceptualization of the secular world occurs (Poll 1980). Socialization also takes place in Ivrit, whereas idealization is still principally in LK.

Learning and Acquisition for Schoolchildren

Formal instruction that uses Yiddish as a medium of instruction begins in the pre-school years and continues through elementary school and beyond. The schools play a large role in the development of societal bilingualism, though the schools do not view what they are doing in terms of bilingualism *per se*. In fact, nowhere does any equivalent of the term occur.

Study is intensive and extensive. Schooling begins at age two or three for boys and in kindergarten for some girls. School runs for six days a week, eleven months a year. The schools teach languages informally and indirectly, through storytelling, having students learn texts by rote, singing, and dramatization. Thus, even when children do not know much Yiddish to begin with, they acquire it in the process of early schooling. Grammar and language *per se* are not subjects.

In schools, language mixing is common. Indeed, it is needed, given the variability in the language patterns of the population, for some comprehend better in one language and some in another. Schools vary with respect to in-class language policies. Instruction may be in Yiddish, Ivrit, or a combination of the two. Each school seems to have its own system. Yiddish-language schools strive to maximize Yiddish and minimize Ivrit. In one girls' school, Ivrit was used in the teachers' room but not the classroom or hallways. All the teachers came from Ivrit (Beis Yaakev) training institutions but were expected to use Yiddish exclusively in the classroom. This meant constant shifting back and forth for them, and Ivrit often intruded into classroom explanations, albeit briefly. But in the domain of the classroom, Yiddish predominated, with Ivrit serving as a default language. If there was a possibility that a word or phrase would be unclear, Ivrit often was added to ensure comprehension.

Outside the school there is less control over language choice than is exercised in school, and the degree to which children mix languages mirrors language mixing societally. Thus, children playing in the streets or schoolyards often mix Ivrit and Yiddish. Even within the family unit, interactions may be either in Yiddish or Ivrit. In some families the grandparents speak Yiddish whereas the parents are more comfortable in Ivrit. Siblings may not be dominant in the same vernaculars, for boys often engage in more Yiddish-medium studies than do girls. Sometimes, in the same family, different children study in different languages. For example, a Hasidic family in Ashdod, adhering to the Pittsburgh Hasidim, because they immigrated from America and first lived in an Ivrit dominant section of Haredi Jerusalem, have their six children in a variety of schools, some of which are in Yiddish and some in Ivrit.

In the several classes I observed (Isaacs 1999b and c) in Jerusalem elementary schools for girls (the Satmar, Stolin-Karlin and Belz, Viznitz, and Boyan Hasidic schools), Yiddish conversational ability on the part of the child is required for admission and is presumed to be the child's household language. As children move up through the grades, the expectations of family and schools is that they will function multilingually, but it is not expected that skills in the different languages will be the same.

Gender

Gender greatly influences linguistic patterns at all levels and ages. It is a common pattern in multilingual communities that women are the first members of the minority group to accommodate to the dominant language of a place (Gal 1997: 376). This pattern is certainly borne out in Haredi society, where women are often the breadwinners, the ones to intersect with Israeli society at the shop, post office, or bank. At the same time, women are not required or expected to function in LK more than minimally. Indeed, female language patterns differ markedly from male patterns; perhaps so much that they may constitute yet another layer of societal diglossia.

Gender differences by language manifest themselves in the schools where, from kindergarten on, boys and girls are separated—the schools are separate and not at all equal. Objectives and linguistic practices and methods vary considerably, as does the content of education. Boys study much more LK and girls are given comparatively more secular knowledge. Yeshiva Yiddish is very specialized, usually not comprehensible to the female counterparts.

For girls, knowing Yiddish will augment their marriageability and possibly enable them to teach in Yiddish-language schools (Bogoch 1999). The education of girls in Yiddish usually ends with the elementary years and a couple of years of "seminary." College or university is off limits to both males and females but males often can continue higher studies in *kolels*.

There is a kind of complementary distribution of status across gender in which Yiddish is a home-spun vernacular, not used for "high language" functions by females. But in the male world of the yeshiva, it is the oldest, most high-level *rebbes* who give their talks in Yiddish. Therefore, Yiddish is low function for females and high level for males.

Because it is not traditional for girls to learn certain texts in LK, less is expected of girls in the study of sacred texts. Girls are merely supposed to know what the texts are about, and this instruction can be done in Yiddish.

Thus, as is explained in the preface to a copy of the Megilla, the story of Queen Esther, the girls are given this to read in Yiddish translation.[7]

Oral and Written Languages and Bilingual Function

Yiddish was mainly an oral language in traditional Europe until segments of the Jewish population, moving away from what they saw as "religious fanaticism," began to develop a worldly Yiddish literature. But for the Hasidim, this literature was out of bounds. Yiddish only was spoken and used for writing letters at times—but little beyond that. Now, however, there is a body of written Yiddish for Hasidim, including some Yiddish-language books and newspapers, largely produced in America.

School reinforces the role of Yiddish as an oral language, though writing and reading are taught, whereas Ivrit is dominant as the written language. Efforts are made to prepare school materials in Yiddish. For example, in the library of the Stolin-Karlin school for girls in Jerusalem, there is a growing Yiddish collection, but the headings are all in Ivrit and the library is called a *sifriya* (Hebrew), not a *bibliotek* (Yiddish).

The strong oral tradition uses music extensively. Rote memorization, recitation, and oral translation are common tools. Children are expected not only to read the texts, but to be able to retell, discuss, and demonstrate understanding of the material as well. With adults, too, Yiddish is predominately oral in many domains. When I mentioned an absence of cookbooks in Yiddish at any of the shops in Mea Shearim, where there were many cookbooks in Hebrew, my Hasidic listener simply looked at me and asked me what it was I wanted to make. She would tell me how to make it and a book was not needed.

Though Hebrew dominates as the written language, Yiddish textbooks and workbooks for subjects taught in Yiddish are being produced in both Israel and the United States and are shared internationally to meet the demand for such materials (Bogoch 1999). Books are distributed through clearinghouses specializing in Haredi books and cassettes. Textbooks for the school are in LK, Yiddish, or some combination of the two. Increasingly, Yiddish

---

7. *Megilas Ester, Nes Purim* (Union City, N.J.: Bais Rokhl Publishing Co., 1983). This book was brought to Israel for a particular school, not an uncommon phenomenon. It is a Yiddish account, intended for girls, of the Book of Esther, to be used in schools where girls may not be taught the original Hebrew text. The preface explains to the reader that all subjects should be taught in the Yiddish language and, therefore, this book has been published in Yiddish.

texts for general subjects are being written, as the schools grope for technical modern vocabulary in Yiddish.

There is variability with respect to orthographic conventions. Some Hasidim use pointing for vowels, others do not. There is a semi-relaxed attitude toward standardization of spelling, especially for words not from LK, though, by and large, Hasidim tend to adhere to normative rather than prescriptive standards.

A common complaint of bilingual educators anywhere is the lack of availability of the right books in the right languages. In these schools, teachers and administrators engage in finding or creating their own books and mimeos (Bogoch 1999; Isaacs 1999b). Parents, too, occasionally complain about a shortage of storybooks and cassettes, since television is off bounds. The *Yiddishe Likht*, a publication of stories, mainly for women, provides some, but not enough, for this growing population that is creating a new market. Materials evidently are growing in availability and being produced on both sides of the Atlantic (Bogoch 1999).

A twenty-something Viznitz Hasidic woman expressed a demand for more stories and cassettes for her children in Yiddish. She especially likes what she calls the *amulige* ("old time") stories. Presently her source is old copies of the *Yiddishe Likht*, which could be purchased in used condition at a place called Glupnick's, in Mea Shearim. Perhaps driving this young woman's quest for reading material is her upbringing in Ivrit, for which reading material was plentiful. Now, she wants to restrict herself to Yiddish, but will not read the material that comes through "non-kosher" sources. She also knows there is more in Yiddish than is available to her locally. Just as food is carefully watched and controlled in its production, so too are written materials guarded. A child's textbook often contains a preface that assures parents that everyone involved in the production of the book, from typesetters to writers to illustrators, is from within the community.

Methodologically, Hasidim have children functioning in the various languages using oral translation, explication of difficult terms or words, and question-answer format. Children use languages with relatively little worry about how they are speaking, little concern about lexical borrowings, dialects, grammatical variability, or orthographic conventions. There is also flexibility in uses of grammatical gender, case, and pronunciation. Classroom focus is on the content rather than on the form of the language. In contrast, LK is invariable, a fixed form. Yiddish and Ivrit are presented as means for achieving specified ends.

In terms of bilingual function, there is much to be learned from the ability that Hasidim have to switch from one language in writing to another for discussion. Functions across languages do not need to be parallel for skills to cross over. Abstract terms and concepts are presented to children in LK, and then they are explained and discussed in Yiddish. Some texts will be learned by rote in LK, but then the discussion of these texts will be in Yiddish. This system creates a duality in language proficiency—students formally acquire reading skills in one language and oral, discourse skills in another.

The ability to shift is especially remarkable, since Yiddish and Hebrew are not cognates, the former being Indo-European and the latter Semitic. No formal grammar is taught in any language, so language skills are learned through use and language awareness is built up through translation. Expectations of oral and written proficiency vary greatly among schools. By the end of the first year, following pre-schooling, which is universal, the children usually can read both Yiddish and LK. At the Belz elementary school, whole classes could read LK texts silently but articulate the concepts in Yiddish, decoding one language and encoding the other.

Conclusions

The life-style of Hasidim often seems extreme and exclusionary. Yet, there is something to be learned with respect to the use of traditional and current languages.

Theirs is a system that presumes multilingual function. Hasidic schools and homes provide a model for how a group can retain a traditional language and still function in the economic sphere. Bilingualism is not seen by Hasidim as problematic. Schools and parents are in agreement as to which languages their children should learn. Furthermore, the children understand that these languages will be used in their lives, and so bilingualism flows naturally. Relationships among individual, community, and school mutually reinforce the traditional home language. Children grow up with both Yiddish and Hebrew as native languages as a product of the alliance of school, religious institutions, and family.

Yet this tradition has its costs. Adherence to language has promoted community survival, but this survival must be reinforced by a degree of separation from mainstream society. There is a myth that bilingualism opens doors across peoples, that if we could but speak the same language, we would communicate and transcend barriers. Bilingualism, in this instance, achieves the opposite effect; language is a bond for the subgroup and marks those excluded as different.

This arrangement shows signs of instability and shift as Ivrit gains political and social value in permitting Hasidim to enter the political fray and to take part in social programs. Other ways of separation from the mainstream are in place. What does this model for bilingualism imply in terms of the ethno-linguistic vitality of Yiddish? Will social and political forces ultimately push Yiddish out, thereby eradicating the last bastions of living Yiddish? These bilingual schools must grapple with basic decisions with respect to language: the grouping of students, what to teach in what language, staffing, balancing competence in the language of instruction with knowledge of content, availability and appropriateness of materials, teacher training, and sources of funding.

Schooling and child-rearing practices are central to the continuity of bilingualism. The lessons for those interested in systems that maintain minority languages is that there needs to be consistency between the home/community and the school; the children need to understand that the languages they are working to master are relevant. Effective language instruction depends on motivational, affective factors, appreciation of the languages and culture of the students, a built-in homogeneity of purpose and background, and honoring the languages as essential and culture-internal. Clearly, the dynamics are highly complex and undergoing change.

Within Jewish Studies, if one can put politics and rivalries aside, one might realize that this very traditionalist camp is a potential source of important cultural and linguistic information. As the last of the non-Hasidic Yiddish speakers are no longer available, a vast amount of knowledge, written and oral, in Yiddish will disappear unless we acknowledge its existence and cultural importance.

REFERENCES

Ben Rafael, E. 1994. A sociological paradigm of bilingualism: English, Yiddish and Arabic in Israel. *Israel Social Science Research*, vol. 9: 181–206.

Berman et al. 1987. *Prophets: Daniel, Ezra, Yonah.* Israel: Mahadura Mekhudeshet Press.

Bogoch, B. 1999. Gender, literacy and religiosity: Dimensions of Yiddish education in Israeli government-supported schools. In M. Isaacs and L. Glinert (eds.), *Pious Voices: Languages among Ultra-Orthodox Jews.* International Journal of the Sociology of Language 138. Mouton.

El Or, T. 1994. *Educated and Ignorant: Ultra-Orthodox Women and Their World.* Boulder, Co.: Lynne Rienner.

Fishman, J.A. 1967. Bilingualism with and without diglossia: Diglossia with and without bilingualism. *Journal of Social Issues* 23, 29–38.

——————— . 1980. Bilingualism and biculturalism as individual and societal phenomena. *Journal of Multilingual and Multicultural Development*, 3–17.

——————— . 1981. Sociology of Jewish languages from the perspective of a general sociology of Jewish languages. *International Journal of Social Languages* 30. The Hague: Mouton.

Fishman, J.A. and D. Fishman. 1977. Yiddish in Israel: A case study of efforts to revise a monocentric language policy. In Joshua A. Fishman (ed.), *Advances in the Study of Societal Multilingualism.* The Hague: Mouton.

Friedman. M. 1986. Life tradition and book tradition in the development of Ultra-Orthodox Judaism. In H. E. Goldberg (ed.), *Judaism Viewed from Within and Without: Anthropological Studies* (pp. 127–48). New York: SUNY Press.

Gal, S. 1997. Language, change and sex roles in a bilingual community. In Nikolas Coupland and Adam Jaworski (eds.), *Sociolinguistics: A Reader* (pp. 376–90). New York: St. Martins Press.

Giles, H. 1977. Toward a theory of language in ethnic group relations." In R. Cooper *et al.* (eds.) *Language, Ethnicity and Intergroup Relations.* New York: Academic Press.

Glinert, L. and Y. Shilhav. 1991. Holy land, holy language: A study of Ultra-Orthodox Jewish ideology. *Language and Society* 20, 59-86.

Gold, D. 1989. A sketch of the linguistic situation in Israel today. *Language and Society* 18, 361–88.

Hakuta, K. 1985. *Mirror of Language: The Debate on Bilingualism.* New York: Basic Books, Harper Collins.

Heilman, S. 1992. *Defenders of the Faith: Inside Ultra-Orthodoxy.* New York: Schocken.

Isaacs, M. 1999a. Haredi, Haymish and Frim: Yiddish vitality and language choice in a multicultural community." In M. Isaacs and L. Glinert (eds.) *Pious Voices: Languages among Ultra-Orthodox Jews.* International Journal of the Sociology of Language 138. Mouton.

—————— . 1999b. Contentious partners: Hebrew and Yiddish in Haredi Israel." In M. Isaacs and L. Glinert (eds.) *Pious Voices: Languages among Ultra-Orthodox Jews.*

—————— . 1998. Yiddish in the Orthodox communities of Jerusalem. In Dov Ber Kerler, ed., *Politics of Yiddish* (pp. 85–96). Altamira Press.

Isaacs, M. and L. Glinert. 1999. *Pious Voices: Languages among Ultra-Orthodox Jews.* International Journal of the Sociology of Language 138. Mouton.

Landry, R. and R. Allard. 1993. Acadians of New Brunswick: International demolinguistic realities and the vitality of the French language. *International Journal of the Sociology of Language* 106, 181–215.

Romaine, S. 1989. *Bilingualism Language in Society* 13. Blackwell.

Spolsky, B. 1983. Triglossia and literacy in Jewish Palestine of the First Century. *International Journal of the Sociology of Language* 42, 95–109.

—————— . 1988. Bridging the gap: A general theory of second language learning. *TESOL Quarterly.*

Weinreich, M. 1980. *History of the Yiddish Language.* Chicago: Chicago University Press.

Weisser, C. 1995. *M. Frumspeak: The First Dictionary of Yeshivish.* New York: Jason Aronson.

ְלוֹ שֶׁל הַגַּל קוֹרֵ׃
תוֹ – שֶׁאָבוֹא אֲנִי

רִא

ז בָּרָאשׁוֹ, וְהַכִּינוּ ז
ֹות, אָמֵן אָמֵן סֶלָה״

Language Policy and the Teaching of Hebrew

Bernard Spolsky
Bar-Ilan University

1. *The State of Hebrew Language Teaching*

The recent end of the millennium is a fitting time to check, a century after its revitalization, the current state of the teaching of Hebrew. Five hundred years after the Gentile world rediscovered the language, and a hundred years after Jews started again to make sufficient commitment to its learning as to lead to a major revolution and produce one of the rare cases of a language re-establishing natural intergenerational transmission, it is appropriate to take the pulse of the language again, as it were. What chance does Hebrew have to avoid the fate of most of the 6000 languages spoken in the world today (Dorian 1981; Hale 1991; Krauss 1991) so as not to slowly die out? Is Modern Hebrew going to follow the large number of Jewish languages, such as Ladino, Judeo-Tat, Judeo-Venetian, Judeo-Sicilian, Judeo-Greek, Judeo-Persian, and Judeo-Arabic and become just a curiosity for language scholars? Or will it, as many members of the Hebrew Language Academy fear, become a "kitchen language," serving the vernacular functions for people who conduct all their important and high linguistic functions in English?

This paper was read at the conference on the Acquisition of Hebrew as a First or Second Language, held under the sponsorship of the Meyerhoff Center for Jewish Studies at the University of Maryland on March 1, 1998. The paper was written while I was on sabbatical leave from Bar-Ilan University as Senior Research Fellow at the National Foreign Language Center of the Johns Hopkins University.

Whatever the answer to these questions may be, is there anything we can do about it? Can a carefully designed and implemented language policy be more successful in changing the course of language shift and loss than King Canute was in holding back the waves, or than the Weather Bureau is in modifying the effects of El Niño?

Before answering these questions, we need to clarify a few things. Although linguists tend to speak about languages and their speakers, and define a language community as all the people who speak that language (the English-speaking world, the Hebrew-speaking world, etc.), sociolinguists and students of language policy find it more useful to start with the notion of a speech community with a complex repertoire of languages and varieties. True, my knowing Hebrew makes it possible for me to relate to speakers of the language wherever they are, but, so too, my knowing English and French enables me to relate to quite different groups. It is better to start with a speech community that is locally defined. Thus, I might ask about the role of Hebrew in the Israeli speech community (where I might be interested in how Hebrew fits in with other languages, such as Russian, Arabic, English, Yiddish, and French) or in the American Jewish speech community.

The two speech communities are obviously quite different. In the one case, Hebrew is the official and dominant language, supported by ideology, education, and public use, all the while working against the interests of minority languages, such as Arabic, and immigrant languages, such as Russian. In the other, it is one of a number of community and heritage languages struggling for survival in the face of an as-yet-unwritten English-only policy (Judd 1987; Ricento 1996). Once this is realized, it is easy to see why the teacher of Hebrew in the United States faces many of the same problems as does the teacher of Arabic in Israel. There are many sound, logical rhetorical arguments that can be made for Hebrew's usefulness or even necessity, but somehow they do not seem to cross the barrier to lead to active and successful language learning.

I shall deal with this issue after I have explained language policy.

2. *What is Language Policy?*

The term "language policy" is comparatively new—the first books to include the words in the title appeared in 1945[1]—although it now has developed into

---

1. In the Library of Congress catalogue, the earliest recorded are Nesiah 1954 and Cebollero 1945.

an area of major concern for scholars in a number of fields.[2] Known also as "language planning,"[3] it grew as a sub-field of sociolinguistics (a scholarly specialty that identified itself in the 1960s), but was soon recognized to overlap with political science (especially policy studies) and education (especially educational linguistics).

We might start by asking what a language policy looks like. The easiest to recognize are those that exist in the form of explicitly labeled statements in official documents. These might be national constitutions, language laws, cabinet documents, or administrative regulations.

France, a country with one of the most highly developed national language policies in existence, records its policy in several places, ranging from the 1539 Article 111 of the *Ordonnance de Villers-Cotterêt* requiring that French be used in law courts, through the 1794 decrees requiring French as the language of instruction in all schools, reaffirmed in the 1881 Ministerial decree, extended in a 1975 law, enshrined in a 1992 constitutional amendment, and most recently augmented by the 1994 Toubon Act requiring French in the domains of consumer protection (including advertising, employment, education, audio-visual communication, and international scientific congresses held in France).[4] Somewhat harder to locate and interpret are cases in which, as in Australia,[5] language policies are cabinet documents setting out priorities for funding of school language teaching. Additional complication is produced when there is tension, as in India,[6] between federal and local policies. The most difficult to deal with are, no doubt, cases in which there is no single explicit policy and in which, as in England (Thompson, Fleming, and Byram 1996) or the United States (Lambert 1994), one must search for the implicit lines of language policy in a maze of practices, laws, regulations, and court decisions.

---

2. A Library of Congress catalogue search found 903 books, some 66 with "language policy" in the title.

3. A less popular term producing 255 items (some 63 with "language planning" in the title) in a Library of Congress search, the first of which is the classic Haugen 1966.

4. For details, see Ager 1996. The last of these provisions was held unconstitutional by a French court.

5. See, e.g., Eggington 1994; Herriman 1996; Lo Bianco 1987.

6. See, e.g., Chaklader 1990.

Language policies tend to grow without much official intervention. Those writing constitutions for newly independent states are often forced to define the role of the competing languages. In such cases, the policy-making process may have been obvious and is then easily studied. More often, any existing national or local language policy has evolved piecemeal, with a combination of law, regulation, and custom. From time to time, a concerted political effort is made to proclaim a new policy (such as the French Language Law of 1975, the English Only movement in the United States, or the various forms of the Australian National Language Policy), or a ministry of education sets out to redefine the school-related aspect of policy, as in the Dutch National Foreign Language Action program or in the new Israeli language education policy. But for the rest, the task of deciding what policy a country follows often first is taken on by a scholar of language planning and policy.[7]

One useful way of answering the question is to ask another: *Who* does *what* to *whom how* and *why*? Who makes a policy? What is a policy? Who is supposed to follow the policy? How is a policy made? Why is a policy made?

First, it is clear that we need to define level. An individual might have his own policy (I will speak only English with my grandchildren and only Hebrew with my students). A family will have its own policy (we speak Hebrew at the table on Shabbat; we speak Yiddish so the children won't understand). A school has its policy (Hebrew is taught in Hebrew; Arabic is taught in Hebrew; Spanish may not be used on the telephone in the teachers' room; anyone speaking Welsh will be punished). And policies can be made by official bodies, whether national or local.

What exactly is the scope of making language policy, or selecting among alternatives a course of action to guide and determine present and future decisions about language choice and use? From the sociolinguist's or language planner's point of view, there are two main kinds of language policy and planning, one concerned with the nature of the language itself ("corpus planning") and the other concerned with the decision on language use and choice ("status planning"). From the policy student's perspective, there is a set chain of processes ideally involved in any policy-making, ranging from initiation to evaluation. And the educational linguist adds to this package the issue of what Cooper (1989) identified as "acquisition planning or policy," the decision as to what language should be learned and taught.

---

7. Thanks to the interests of the General Editor and to his policy of devoting individual issues of the journal to issues, regions, and countries, the *International Journal of the Sociology of Language* provides the best collection of such studies.

The four perspectives are intimately connected. It is, perhaps, easiest to start with status policy, the principles, regulations, and practices that determine which language variety should be used for what purposes.

Essentially, status planning or policy are decisions on desirable or required functional allocations of languages, decisions as to which language is appropriate or should be used for which domain or function. We mentioned earlier the case of French language policy, a series of laws and regulations laying down the use of French in an increasing number of domains. Similarly, Québec language law was a clear specification of a requirement for the use of French, where, previously, the use of English and/or French had been optional. Often, the statement is negative and categorical: the 1794 ban on the use of German in Alsace; the Turkish ban on the use of Kurdish; the punishment inflicted on students who used Welsh in school; and the imprisonment of Hebrew teachers in late Soviet Russia.

Language revival is essentially a change in functional use. It may take a classical language, such as Hebrew, and attempt to revitalize and "revernacularize" it by turning it into the language of everyday speech, or it may take a vernacular language, such as Yiddish, and try to standardize it and use it for literary and educational functions. Status policy, then, essentially involves assigning, rather than assessing, status; it determines which languages should be used by which people in which situations and for which functions. In many immigrant communities, there is a clear distinction between home language use (the immigrant language) and work language use (the new language). Of course, any individual functions in more than one domain and has many roles—a father in the home can be a colleague at work. This model allows for normal switching as roles change. A friend of mine spoke French at home to her son, but then switched to Hebrew as they crossed the road from their home into the school grounds, where she was a teacher and he was a student.

Status planning, from this point of view, might be seen as determining which languages are appropriate in which domain. The 1994 Toubon Act in France used this term specifically, requiring that French be used in sales and advertising, employment, education, audio-visual communication, and colloquia congresses, but leaving home language use untouched (Ager 1996). The 1977 Charter of the French Language (Bill 101) in Québec required the use of French, especially on all public and commercial signs (Daoust 1990). The founders of the city of Tel Aviv included status planning in their prospectus for the new city:

> We must urgently acquire a considerable chunk of land, on which we shall build our houses. Its place must be near Jaffa, and it will

form the first Hebrew city, its inhabitants will be Hebrews a hundred percent; Hebrew will be spoken in this city, purity and cleanliness will be kept, and we shall not go in the ways of the goyim.[8]

These are questions of status planning.

A second area of major importance, "corpus planning," attempts to fix or modify the structure of a language. An obvious instance is the need to establish a writing system for an unwritten language, an extremely common task historically, as only a handful of languages developed their own writing systems. A second instance is the need to supply new words for a language that must address new functions and concepts. A third case is the need to agree upon a set of conventions concerning appropriateness of form, especially when a language's texts are sacred or when it is used in school.

Issues of normativism and corpus are particularly sensitive in the case of Hebrew. The fact that Hebrew is a revived language, but one that has naturally changed in the process, and that so many of its speakers are non-native speakers or the children of non-native speakers produces many problems concerning normativism.

I have already mentioned one important aspect of acquisition policy, namely, the decision as to the language of instruction. Although this may be subordinated to educational concerns (as when there are simple arguments concerning the value of using the target language as the language of instruction in the foreign-language classroom, or even in the concept that immersion teaching is the most efficient way of teaching another language (Baetens, Beardsmore, and Swain 1985; Genesee 1987; Johnson and Swain 1998; Ritchie 1994; Tedick and Walker 1996) it is a decision that generally calls for more than educational motivation. An acquisition policy takes the form of a statement as to what segment of the population (such as all or part of the school population, or of a specific occupational group) should spend a defined amount of time acquiring defined levels of competence in specific languages.

The number of languages depends, in part, on the national language policy. If there is more than one national or official language, there are likely to be more languages included in the policy. Officially bilingual countries start with the requirement of adding the second official language after the first mother tongue (e.g., French or Dutch in Belgium, Finnish or Swedish in Finland, Hebrew or Arabic in Israel, English or French in Canada). Coun-

---

8. Cited and translated in *Harshav* 1993: 143 from the 1906 Prospectus for Tel Aviv.

tries with official regional languages produce a similar requirement in the regions, as Catalan and Spanish in the Catalan Autonomous Region. More complex requirements are added when there are several official languages, as in India, South Africa, and Eritrea.

The fourth kind, "diffusion policy," involves active efforts by a governmental or semi-governmental body to encourage the acquisition of a national or official language outside the political boundaries of the state. It might be seen as a continuation of imperialist or colonialist language policy over areas no longer or never under the political domination of the state. Ammon (1992) provides a full account of the development of German diffusion policy at the end of the nineteenth century. This policy had interesting effects in Palestine.

Whom are policies for? We might start from a general assumption that language policies are intended for all who are subject to the control of the policy-making institution or person. This essentially sets their relevance to power in a social situation. By limiting access to certain information (such as education) or certain institutions (e.g., voting, law courts) to people who speak Xish, boundaries are set that effectively exclude non-Xish speakers from power and even protection. The most controversial language policy issues, then, are those that affect the status of minorities or other powerless groups. Change in the official language—addressed in the next section—is one of the most effective ways to change access to power in a society.

Educational linguists see students as the first target of any language policy, but add to that a concern for the language use of teachers. As many studies have shown (e.g., Amara 1988), often teachers themselves do not use or master the target language they are supposed to be teaching.

Finally, we ask about the "why," the reasons and rationales behind a language policy. Policy analysts who see policy-making as the rational balancing of a number of equally plausible options and pressures tend to see the ends as responding to pressures and re-establishing equilibrium. Underlying this, of course, is the assumption that a pressure group has a reason to influence language policy, and that various decisions are likely to favor different groups. One reason is power. Whereas some linguists have recognized the inevitability of the growth and stature of prestige languages (Kahane 1986), others see their role as siding with the weak languages, in an effort to resist the pressure of the dominant. It is, of course, important to note that this implies accepting the relevance of language to power. To better understand the issue of rationales and motivations for language policy, one should try to differentiate between instrumental (or functional or objective) rationales and motivations and integrative (or symbolic or subjective) rationales and motivations.

Like most attempts at dichotomies, this fails because of blurring at the boundaries. Nonetheless, attempting to distinguish rationales along these lines is a useful heuristic.

Knowledge of a sacred language, for all its symbolic importance, may also be seen as a method of providing access to other knowledge or information. The teaching of Hebrew for Jews, of Sanskrit for Hindus, of Greek, Latin, Old Church Slavonic, Geez, or other languages of scripture translation for Christians, of Arabic for Moslems, all have a simple first rationale of enabling access to the knowledge included in sacred texts. Perhaps out of this arose the Western tradition of providing access, through a foreign language, to the culture and literature of prestige Western languages (Kahane 1986). Of course, in these cases, too, the rationale is value laden, depending on the assignment of a high value to the religion or culture, and carrying with it a lower regard for the local or vernacular culture. Typical of this view is the member of the English Advisory Committee of the Israeli Ministry of Education who in the 1950s was still willing to say that Israelis must learn English to have access to English literature, because there is no worthwhile literature in Hebrew. Perhaps because of the prestige of high cultures and the elitism implied, foreign language education in many parts of the world has come under the authority of literature scholars and teaching, leading to a gap with those who are concerned with more practical goals.

It is symbolic power that is more important in arguing for religion and for identity purposes. This was the classic argument between the German and American Reform movements and the orthodox establishment over the proposal to use the local vernacular in synagogue prayers. The maintenance of Arabic for the Qur'an has been key to holding together Moslems wherever they are. On the other hand, the decision of Vatican II to drop Latin produced major identity problems for the Roman Catholic Church.

National identity—even more than religious identity—is closely tied to language choice. The debates in the Jewish world at the turn of the nineteenth century pitted two movements, each with its identifying language, against each other: territorial Zionism with Hebrew against cultural nationalism with Yiddish. Thus, group, ethnic, and national identities are key elements in status debates.

Economic motivation is clearly a major rationale for language policy. In the market-place phenomenon, sellers learn the buyers' language in order to be able to compete. A body of interesting work has shown the additional economic value to those immigrants who gain control of the language of their new country (Arcand 1996; Chiswick and Miller 1994, 1995a, 1995b, 1995c;

Cooper and Seckbach 1977; Coulmas 1991; Sproull 1996). There are beginning attempts to show the economic value for workers in knowing another language (Grin 1996a, 1996b). This added-value rationale underlies the argument for the importance of national-language capacity as a driving force for language education (Brecht, Caemmerer, and Walton 1995; Brecht and Walton 1998).

An instrumental rationale also underlies the commercial programs for language for travelers or business, the definition of instrumental practical goals for language programs for government workers (Sollenberger 1978), and for the so-called threshold level of the Council of Europe language programs (van Ek 1975; van Ek and Trim 1984). It is also the focus of the language for special purpose movements. It is important to stress that the objectivity of these approaches is in selection of languages and language goals, but all assume the value of the purpose and language selected.

We can now ask our questions about where Hebrew fits in more precisely. We will look first at Israel, then at the United States.

3. *Hebrew in Language Policy in Israel*

From a national point of view, Israel shows evidence of an ideological monolingualism, in part a continuation of the force of Hebrew language revitalization that was a defining feature of modern Zionism, and in part a normal effect of a dominating national language on minority groups and immigrants. This extraordinary ideological pressure was enough to persuade the early Hebraists, most of them fully capable of speaking to each other in Yiddish or Russian, to make the effort required for themselves and their children to become speakers of Hebrew. The struggle was difficult and the effort great, but by the time the British Mandatory government took over in the 1920s, it was easily convinced to leave the Jewish Yishuv to conduct its own affairs in the newly revitalized language, which was firmly declared the language for all public functions within the Yishuv. New immigrants were encouraged, or later forced, to accept this new reality, and give up other languages, except perhaps for home use or for restricted functions. There was resistance, especially in home language use and in literacy functions, but the general pressure for everyone to speak Hebrew continued to mount.

The first clear language policy probably was the acceptance of the concept of *ivrit b'ivrit* adopted by Hebrew teachers in the 1890s. Haramati (1972) traces the independent way that a number of contemporary Hebraists developed this idea as the basis for a teaching methodology. In the second stage, this was taken outside the classroom, in a general approach represented by the slogan "*Ivri, daber ivrit*," which became a socially supported call for public use of the new language. Within the Yishuv it was a powerful movement, with enforcement provided by youth groups, a period well described and analyzed by Harshav (1993). There was external recognition when the British Mandatory Government and the League of Nations Mandate proclaimed the official status of Hebrew, alongside English and Arabic. One of the most important decisions was to allow the two communities to run their own educational systems. Thus, the Yishuv was able to continue a policy supporting Hebrew and to take formal steps to weaken competing languages.

The new State formalized this situation, keeping Hebrew as an official language. Arabic, also, was officially recognized, but the *de facto* application of this policy was, apart from symbolic use of Arabic on coins and stamps, limited to the minority sector and its schools. Over the next three decades, as Ben-Rafael (1994) has documented, there was constant pressure toward a new Hebrew monolingualism, or rather a modified bilingualism, with a new Hebrew-English combination replacing the multilingualism of the earlier generations. The new policy (1) accepted English *de facto* as needed, despite seeing it as a threat; (2) paid lip service to Arabic, generally restricting its use to the minority and to a tiny elite of Arabists needed by the army and the academy; and (3) discouraged other languages, especially the large number of heritage languages brought by the immigrants.

The result is that Hebrew now dominates language use and teaching. But there have been cracks in this edifice. The very place of English, the existence of a sizable group of English-speaking immigrants, and the fact that English is the language of the largest Diaspora community have had a major impact (Spolsky 1996). Another factor is the continued resistance of some other languages, e.g., the minority use of Arabic and the Haredi use of Yiddish. A third factor is the enormous change produced by the recent immigration of 750,000 Russian speakers with high language loyalty, and the isolated 75,000 speakers of Ethiopian languages. A fourth could be the huge number of foreign workers. All these factors have resulted in a weakening of the hegemony of Hebrew and burgeoning support for multilingualism (Shohamy 1995; Shohamy and Spolsky 1998; Spolsky and Shohamy 1997, 1999).

There have been non-material changes to accompany this, a slow but visible trend toward pluralism, noted especially among the more liberally minded members of the population. This group provides intellectual and moral support for the interest expressed in other languages, which was clearly revealed in the new language policy adopted by the Ministry of Education

(1995, 1996). It also provided support for the recent grassroots-level program to revive the teaching of Arabic in elementary schools in Tel Aviv.

The hegemony of Hebrew is being weakened, then, by these attacks from within, and there are those who see it as an endangered language. In fact, as early as Kodesh (1972), there were calls for the *Knesset* to pass a Hebrew-only law. The Hebrew Language Academy sees itself on the defensive. Part of this weakening of resolve, no doubt, has influenced the situation of Hebrew in the United States, to which we now turn.

4. *Hebrew in Language Policy in the United States*

Although there is a strong movement to defend English from the threat of other languages—especially Spanish—the absence of any reference to language in the Constitution and the fact that education policy is a state, rather than a federal, concern means that the United States lacks a clear language policy (Lambert 1994). This initially tolerant position, one that allowed for a good deal of multilingual education up until about 1919, was more or less frozen into a *de facto* English-only policy, with subsequent damaging effects, even to language education. In fact, apart from the unrelated bursts of post-Sputnik language-teaching efforts and the bilingual-education movement of the 1970s, any attempts at serious language teaching tended to be restricted to the army or State Department. A modicum of this initiative supports some teaching of less commonly taught languages, but, in essence, the educational language-teaching establishment supports the literary interests of a decreasing band of traditional scholars. In national or state policies, then, we find little that could count as support for the teaching of Hebrew.

Hebrew teaching has been forced to depend on the Jewish community for resources. There was one potential "golden age," during which there was a movement that led to the publication of *Hatoren* and the development of the *Histadrut Ivrit*. Mintz (1993a) deals with this phenomenon, a secular Hebraist movement that paralleled the Yiddish secular movement that had started a bit earlier. The journal reached a maximum circulation of 13,000, and was distributed through agents in 38 cities. In a letter in March 1915, David Persky set out a key belief:

> For such an ordinary Jew [like myself who does not believe in religion], nationalism is incorporated by the language, which fills his entire being and to which he will devote his entire life.[9]

---

9. Mintz 1993b: 43.

Similarly, the public statement of nine Hebraists who founded the *Histadrut Ivrit* in 1917 explained how centrally they viewed Hebrew:

> All have begun to acknowledge that Hebrew nationalism and Hebrew culture are one and inseparable, for without the Hebrew language there is no possibility of a national existence for our people anywhere.[10]

Had it been continued and sustained, this commitment to Hebrew might well have provided a second Hebrew-speaking community in the United States, capable of interacting with that in Israel to form an even tighter bond. But the movement was caught between stronger forces. Its secularism was not able to stand up either to the radicalism of one sector of the Jewish community or to the orthodoxy of another. It could not provide the spark needed by the large mass whose apathy for Judaism in any form made assimilation an obvious choice.

The lack of orthodox religious support is paradoxical in some ways but obvious in others. The new secular language that was the result of the revitalization process (a language in which *musaf* is neither a temple sacrifice nor a synagogue service, but a weekly supplement to the newspaper) had no appeal for those concerned for teaching *lashon kodesh*, and even less with those who accepted that the teaching of sacred ideas could be conducted in any language. If Yiddish was good enough for the East European yeshiva as it is for its Haredi successors, why shouldn't English be good enough for the burgeoning *hozrei b'tshuva* movement?

How, then, can one argue for the need to teach Hebrew? If I am Orthodox, I can read even highly technical books of very esoteric matters of Halakhah in English. And if I am interested in Israel, I can now read *Ha'aretz* in an English Internet edition (or in a version tacked onto the *International Herald Tribune*).

It is not surprising that the American Jewish community has taken a minimalist position regarding its Hebrew language policy. What are still ironically called "Hebrew schools" are, at best, places where initial literacy is a goal. Where once there were ten teacher colleges using Hebrew as a language of instruction and several Hebrew-speaking camps (Ackerman 1993), now it is considered appropriate to conduct Hebrew teachers' conferences in the co-territorial vernacular, which Weinreich 1980 dubbed "goyish." Clearly, in the United States Hebrew is now an endangered language.

---

10. Ibid., p. 58.

REFERENCES

Ackerman, W. 1993. A world apart: Hebrew teachers colleges and Hebrew-speaking camps. In Mintz 1993a (pp. 105–28).

Ager, D. 1996. *Language Policy in Britain and France: The Processes of Policy.* Open Linguistics Series. Robin F. Fawcett (ed.). London and New York: Cassell.

Amara, M.H. 1988. Arabic diglossia: Conditions for learning the standard variety. [Arabic]. *Aljadid* 12, 14–23.

Ammon, U. 1992. The Federal Republic of Germany's policy of spreading German. *International Journal of the Sociology of Language* 95, 33–50.

Arcand, J-L. 1996. Developmental economics and language: The earnest search for a mirage" *International Journal of the Sociology of Language* 121, 119–58.

Baetens Beardsmore, H. and M. Swain. 1985. Designing bilingual education: Aspects of immersion and 'European schools' models. *Journal of Multilingual and Multicultural Development* 6, 1–15.

Ben-Rafael, E. 1994. *Language, Identity and Social Division: The Case of Israel.* Oxford Studies in Language Contact. Peter Mülhäusler and Suzanne Romaine (eds.). Oxford: Clarendon Press.

Brecht, R.D., J. Caemmerer, and A. R Walton. 1995. *Russian in the United States: A Case Study of America's Language Needs and Capacities.* NFLC Monograph Series. Washington D.C.: National Foreign Language Center.

Brecht, R.D. and A.R. Walton. 1998. System III: The future of language learning in the United States. In Richard D. Lambert and Xueying Wang (eds.), *Walton Memorial Volume.* Washington, D.C.: National Foreign Language Center.

Cebollero, P.A. 1945. *A School Language Policy for Puerto Rico.* San Juan de Puerto Rico: Impr. Baldrich.

Chaklader, S. 1990. Language policy and reformation of India's federal structure: The case of West Bengal. In Weinstein 1990 (pp. 87–107).

Chiswick, B.R. and P.W. Miller. 1995a. Language and labor supply: The role of gender among immigrants in Australia. *Research in Economic Equality* 5, 153–89.

———. 1994. Language choice among immigrants in a multilingual destination. *Journal of Population Economics* 7/2, 119–31.

———. 1995b. The endogeneity between language and earnings: International analyses. *Journal of Labor Economics* 13/2, 246–88.

———. 1995c. Ethnic networks and language proficiency among immigrants. *Journal of Population Economics.*

Cooper, R.L. 1989. *Language Planning and Social Change.* Cambridge: Cambridge University Press.

Cooper, R.L. and Fern Seckbach. 1977. Economic incentives for the learning of a language of wider communication: A case study. In Joshua A. Fishman, Robert L. Cooper, and Andrew W. Conrad, (eds.), *The Spread of English.* (pp. 212–19). Rowley, Mass.: Newbury House Publishers.

Coulmas, F. 1991. *Language and Economics*.

Daoust, D. 1990. A decade of language planning in Québec: A sociopolitical overview. In Weinstein 1990 (pp. 108–30).

Dorian, N. 1981. *Language Death: The Life Cycle of a Scottish Gaelic Dialect*. Philadelphia: University of Pennsylvania Press.

Eggington, W. 1994. Language policy and planning in Australia. *Annual Review of Applied Linguistics* 14, 137–55.

Genesee, Fr. 1987. *Learning through Two Languages: Studies of Bilingual and Immersion Education*. Cambridge, Mass.: Newbury House Publishers.

Grin, F. 1996a. Economic approaches to language and language planning: An introduction. *International Journal of the Sociology of Language* 121, 1–16.

———. 1996b. The economics of language: survey, assessment and prospects. *International Journal of the Sociology of Language* 121, 17–44.

Hale, K. 1991. On endangered languages and the safeguarding of diversity. *Language* 68/1: 1–3.

Haramati, S. 1972. *Shitat ha-ulpan* (The Ulpan Method). Benzion Fischler (ed.). From the Workshop. Jerusalem: Council for the Teaching of Hebrew.

Harshav, B. 1993. *Language in Time of Revolution*. Berkeley: University of California Press.

Haugen, E. 1966. *Language Conflict and Language Planning: The Case of Modern Norwegian*. Cambridge, Mass.: Harvard University Press.

Herriman, M. 1996. Language policy in Australia. In Herriman and Burnaby 1996. (pp. 35–61).

Herriman, M., and B. Burnaby, eds. 1996. *Language Policies in English-dominant Countries: Six Case Studies*. Clevedon, Philadelphia and Adelaide: Multilingual Matters Ltd.

Johnson, K. and M. Swain, eds. 1998. *Immersion Education: International Perspectives*. Cambridge: Cambridge University Press.

Judd, E.L. 1987. The English language amendment: A case study on language and politics. *TESOL Quarterly* 21: 113–36.

Kahane, H. 1986. A typology of the prestige language. *Language* 62/3, 495–517.

Kodesh, S. 1972. *Me-'inyan le-'inyan ba-ulpan* (Issues in the Ulpan). Tel Aviv: Hamatmid.

Krauss, M. 1991. The world's languages in crisis. *Language* 68/1, 4–10.

Lambert, R.D. 1994. Problems and processes in U.S. foreign language planning. *The Annals of the American Academy of Political and Social Sciences* 532, 47–58.

Lo Bianco, J. 1987. *National Policy on Languages*. Canberra: Australian Government Publishing Service.

Ministry of Education, Culture and Sport. 1995. *Policy for Language Education in Israel*. [Hebrew]. Office of the Director General.

———. 1996. *Policy for Language Education in Israel* [Hebrew]. Office of the Director-General.

Mintz, A., ed. 1993a. *Hebrew in America: Perspectives and Prospects*. American Jewish Civilization Series. Detroit: Wayne State University Press.

Mintz, A. 1993b. A sanctuary in the wilderness: The beginnings of the Hebrew movement in America in Hatoren. [Hebrew]. In Mintz 1993a.

Nesiah, K. 1954. *The Mother Tongue in Education and a Language Policy for Ceylon.* Colombo: Ola Book.

Ricento, T. 1996. Language policy in the United States. In Herriman and Burnaby 1996. (pp. 122–58).

Ritchie, J. 1994. Development of Maori immersion early childhood education. In *International Language in Conference.* University of Hong Kong.

Shohamy, E. 1995. Problems in Israeli language policy: Language and ideology. In David Chen (ed.), *Education in the Twenty-first Century.* (pp. 249–56) Ramat-Aviv: Ramot Publishing, Tel Aviv University.

Shohamy, E. and B. Spolsky. 1998. An emerging language policy for Israel: From monolingualism to multilingualism. *Plurilingua.*

Sollenberger, H.E. 1978. Development and current use of the FSI oral interview test. In John L.D. Clark (ed.), *Direct Testing of Speaking Proficiency: Theory and Application.* (pp. 3–12). Princeton, N.J.: Educational Testing Service.

Spolsky, B. 1996. English in Israel after independence. In Joshua A. Fishman, Alma Rubal-Lopez, and Andrew W. Conrad (eds.), *Post-Imperial English.* Berlin: Mouton.

Spolsky, B. and E. Shohamy. 1997. Planning foreign language education: An Israeli perspective. In Kees de Bot and Theo Bongaerts (eds.), *Perspectives on Foreign Language Policy: Studies in Honour of Theo van Els.* (pp. 99–111). Amsterdam and Philadelphia: John Benjamins Publishing Company.

————. 1999. Language in Israeli society and education. *International Journal of the Sociology of Language* 137.

Sproull, A. 1996. Regional economic development and minority language use: The case of Gaelic Scotland. *International Journal of the Sociology of Language* 121, 93–118.

Tedick, D.J. and C.L. Walker. 1996. *Immersion Language Teaching Bibliography.* Minneapolis: Center for Advanced Research on Language Acquisition.

Thompson, L., M. Fleming, and M. Byram. 1996. Languages and language policy in Britain. In Herriman and Burnaby (pp. 99–121).

van Ek, J.A. 1975. *The Threshold Level.* Strassbourg: Council of Europe.

van Ek, J.A. and J.L.M. Trim, eds. 1984. *Across the Threshold—Readings from the Modern Languages Project of the Council of Europe.* Oxford: Pergamon Press.

Weinreich, M. 1980. *History of the Yiddish Language.* Translated by Joshua A. Fishman and Shlomo Noble. Chicago: University of Chicago Press.

Weinstein, B., ed. 1990. *Language Policy and Political Development.* Norwood N.J.: Ablex Publishing Company.

CONTRIBUTOR BIOGRAPHIES

Sharon Armon-Lotem finished her Ph.D. in Linguistics (syntax and language acquisition) at Tel-Aviv University in 1997. After three years as a visiting researcher at the University of Maryland, College Park, she moved to Bar-Ilan University, where she holds a position as a senior lecturer. She studies the language of English-Hebrew and Russian-Hebrew that typically develops among bilingual preschool children and bilingual children with Specific Language Impairments (SLI). Her focus is on syntax and morpho-syntax.

Shmuel Bolozky (Ph.D., U. of Illinois Urbana in Linguistics, 1972) is a Professor of Hebrew at (and former Chair of) the Department of Judaic and Near Eastern Studies of the U. of Massachusetts Amherst, specializing in Israeli Hebrew phonology and morphology. He has also been teaching Hebrew Linguistics as a Visiting Professor at various universities in Israel, is Past President of the National Association of Professors of Hebrew, and has been serving as member of the Program Committee of the NAPH's annual International Conference on Hebrew Language and Literature. He also serves as Associate Director at the National Middle East Language Resource Center.

Edna Amir Coffin is the Arthur H. Thurnau Professor Emerita of Hebrew Language and Literature at University of Michigan's Department of Near Eastern Studies. She holds a Ph.D. from the University of Michigan and an honorary doctorate from Hebrew Union College at Los Angeles. She is a founding member of NAPH Modern Hebrew Language and Literature Conference and the author of numerous articles on Hebrew language and literature, translation theory and practice, pedagogical applications and instructional multimedia software. Her books include *Reference Grammar of Modern Hebrew* (2005, co-author Shmuel Bolozky), *Encounters in Modern Hebrew* Levels I, II and III, and *Lessons in Modern Hebrew* Levels I and II.

Avital Feuer is Visiting Assistant Professor specializing in language education at the University of Maryland. She researches second/heritage language learning and socialization in formal and informal learning settings and teaches courses in language pedagogy and Hebrew. She is the author of *Who Does This Language Belong To? Personal Narratives of Language Claim and Identity* (2008). Recent journal articles include "School's Out for the Summer: A Cross-Cultural Comparison of Second Language Learning in Informal Settings" in *International Journal of Bilingual Education and Bilingualism* (2009) and "Nation and ethnic identity self-definitions in a Canadian language class" in *Diaspora, Indigenous and Minority Education* (2008).

Lewis Glinert is Professor of Hebraic Studies and Linguistics at Dartmouth College. He is the author of *The Grammar of Modern Hebrew* (Cambridge), *Modern Hebrew: An Essential Grammar* (Routledge), *Hebrew in Ashkenaz: A Language in Exile* (Oxford), *and The Joys of Hebrew* (Oxford). His 1992 BBC documentary on the rebirth of Hebrew, *Tongue of Tongues*, was nominated by the BBC for a SONY award.

Einat Gonen is a Visiting Assistant Professor at the Joseph and Rebecca Meyerhoff Center for Jewish Studies at the University of Maryland where she has been teaching since 2001. She received her Ph.D. in 2007 from the Department of Hebrew Language at the Hebrew University of Jerusalem. Before coming to the U.S., she taught at the Hebrew University, both as an instructor in the Hebrew linguistics department and as a teacher of Hebrew language in their summer language ulpan. She also worked as a scientific researcher at Academy of the Hebrew Language. Einat Gonen's current research focuses on the morphology of spoken Hebrew.

Miriam Isaacs is a linguist who specializes in language and culture. She has been teaching and writing in Yiddish Studies for the past fifteen years. Dr. Isaacs has also published essays in English and Yiddish in numerous volumes and journals. Recent articles include "Yiddish in the Aftermath: Speech Community and Cultural Continuity in the Displaced Person's Camps" in *Jewish Cultural Studies: Expression, Identity, and Representation*. Another recent article is on Yiddish theater: "Language and Genre in Peretz Hirshbein" in *Jewish Literature and History: An Interdisciplinary Conversation*. Her most important work has been on the question of language loyalty in the context of the Displaced Persons Camps and for contemporary Hasidim. She has been teaching at the University of Maryland since 1995.

Brenda Malkiel spent six years directing the Hebrew-English Translation Program at Beit Berl College and currently teaches in the Department of Translation and Interpreting Studies at Bar-Ilan University. Her research interests range from corpus linguistics ["Identifying Universals of Text Translation" – *Journal of Quantitative Linguistics*] to translator training ["What Can Grades Teach Us?" –*Perspectives*] to the translation of cognates [Translation as a Decision Process: Evidence from Cognates – *Babel*].

Vered Shemtov is the Co-Director of the Taube Center for Jewish Studies at Stanford University and the coordinator of Hebrew Language and Literature. Her current book project on Prosody and Ideology will be published this year by Bar Ilan University Pres. Some of her recent publications include a co-edited volume on Jewish Conceptions and Practices of Space, "Between a Jewish and an Israeli Perspective of Space: A Reading in Yehuda Amichai's 'Jewish Travel' and 'Israeli Travel'" (JSS, Summer 2005), "The Bible in Contemporary Israeli Literature: Text and Place in Zeruya Shalev's Husband and Wife and Michal Govrin's Hevzekim," (*Hebrew Studies* 2006) and Attraversando I Confini: Dallo Spazio Letterario Alle Frontiere Geografico-Politiche Nei Romanzi la Sposa Liberata Opera Letteraria di Yehoshua. Einaudi (Venice, 2006). Professor Shemtov developed the Hebrew@ Stanford Multimedia program and workbook.

Bernard Spolsky was appointed professor emeritus at Bar-Ilan University, Israel on his retirement in 2000. He has continued to publish: his latest books are *Language Policy* (Cambridge UP 2004), *Handbook of Educational Linguistics* (Blackwell 2008) and *Language Management* (Cambridge UP 2009).

STUDIES AND TEXTS IN JEWISH HISTORY AND CULTURE

The Joseph and Rebecca Meyerhoff Center for Jewish Studies
University of Maryland

General Editor: Bernard D. Cooperman

Vol. 9.   *Rememberings: The World of a Russian-Jewish Woman in the Nineteenth Century*
Pauline Wengeroff; translated by Henny Wenkart, edited with afterword by Bernard D. Cooperman
ISBN: 1883053-587 (hard.), ISBN: 1883053617 (soft.); xvi + 306 pp.; 2000.

Vol. 10.   *Biblical Translation in Context*
edited by Frederick W. Knobloch
ISBN: 1883053404; xiii + 221 pp.; 2002.

Vol. 11.   *Argentina, Israel, and the Jews: Peron, The Eichmann Capture and After*
Raanan Rein
ISBN: 1883053722; xxii + 275 pp.; 2003.

Vol. 12.   *Jews, Antiquity, and the Nineteenth-Century Imagination*
edited by Hayim Lapin
ISBN: 1883053781; viii + 157 pp.; 2003.

Vol. 13.   *Early Judaism: Religious Worlds of the First Judaic Millennium*
Martin S. Jaffee. ISBN: 9781883053932; x + 277 pp.; 2006.

Vol. 14.   *Hebrew, Gender, and Modernity: Critical Responses to Dvora Baron's Fiction*
edited by Sheila E. Jelen and Shachar Pinsker
ISBN: 9781883053956; x + 291 pp.; 2007.

Vol. 15.   *Jewish Literature and History: An Interdisciplinary Conversation*
edited by Eliyana R. Adler and Sheila E. Jelen
ISBN: 9781934309131; x + 248 pp.; 2008.

Vol. 16.   *Manual of Judeo-Spanish: Language and Culture*
Marie-Christine Varol
ISBN: 9781934309193; 331 pp.; 2008.

Vol. 17.   *Philosophers and the Jewish Bible*
edited by Charles H. Manekin and Robert Eisen
ISBN: 9781934309209; 256 pp.; 2008.

Vol. 18.   *Issues in the Acquisition and Teaching of Hebrew*
edited by Avital Feuer, Sharon Armon-Lotem, and Bernard Dov Coopermman
ISBN: 9781934309216; 184 pp.; 2009.